VERDI

Verdi

THE MAN REVEALED

John Suchet

PEGASUS BOOKS
NEW YORK LONDON

Verdi:
The Man Revealed

Pegasus Books Ltd
148 West 37th Street, 13th Floor
New York, NY 10018

ISBN: 978-1-68177-768-9

10   9   8   7   6   5   4   3   2   1

Printed in the United States of America
Distributed by W. W. Norton & Company, Inc.

For my darling wife Nula, whose love
for Verdi the man, as much as his music,
was a constant inspiration.

CONTENTS

1

CONFUSED BEGINNINGS

Giuseppe Verdi, the greatest of all Italian operatic composers and a patriotic advocate of Italian independence, was born a Frenchman. The village of Le Roncole, in the Po valley, where he was born, had been annexed by Napoleon a matter of months before his birth.

If his nationality at birth comes as a surprise, we might be no more certain of the date on which Verdi was born, nor of the house in which he was born. We might consider these facts to be beyond doubt – but Verdi himself disagrees with us.

The entry in the register of births, dated 12 October 1813, records Carlo Verdi reporting the birth of a son at eight o'clock in the evening of 10 October. The baptismal certificate is dated 11 October, and records that the baby was 'born yesterday'.

Both official documents seem to agree, therefore, that the baby was born on 10 October 1813. Verdi himself, though, stated later in life that his mother always told him he was born at nine in the evening of 9 October 1814. Clearly exasperated at repeated requests for more information once he had achieved fame, he wrote to a local official, 'Which of the dates is correct, I do not know, nor do I care to know.' He appears to have accepted later that the year was indeed 1813, but he stuck to the 9th as the date of his birth.

The confusion might have arisen because in old Italy (during the early nineteenth century before the country was unified) it was customary to count a new day as beginning at sunset. What was the evening of the 9th to Verdi's mother could well be the start of the 10th to the authorities. Verdi himself was in no doubt. He took his mother's word for it and throughout his life he celebrated his birthday on 9 October.

History has trusted the evidence of multiple official documents, rather than Verdi's personal belief. International celebrations marked the bicentenary of his birth on 10 October 2013, with productions of his operas in the great opera houses of the world.

When it comes to identifying the house in which Verdi was born, there is similar confusion. His grandparents leased a grocery store and inn in the centre of Le Roncole. They traded in a wide range of goods – from coffee, cured meats and spices to wine and possibly brandy and liqueur as well. The entry in the birth register describes Verdi's father as an innkeeper and his mother as a seamstress.

In time Carlo took over the business and the family retained the lease until 1830, when Verdi turned seventeen. The Church authorities, who owned the building, stipulated that the lessees were to occupy the house; it could not be sub-let. When the lease expired the family moved into the house that has come to be regarded as the composer's birthplace and was destined to become a national monument. However, there is no documentary evidence that the Verdi family lived there any earlier than 1833.

Later in life, Verdi told family members that the house that even in his lifetime was preserved as his birthplace was not actually where he was born. He apparently added that the actual dwelling in which he was born had been burned down by Russians.

But the house his grandfather had leased had not been destroyed by fire; in fact parts of it are still standing to this day. And when foreign armies did march through Le Roncole, demolishing buildings as they went, there is no evidence that Russian soldiers were among them. The Verdi biographer Mary Jane Phillips-Matz, however, reports that it was a local legend in Le Roncole that several Russian soldiers had been killed by local people and buried at night at the roadside. As late as the 1960s, she writes, when a tree was weighed down with fruit, local farmers would say, 'There's a Russian buried there.'

Considerable uncertainty, then, about both the date on which Verdi was born and the house he was born in. I suspect that is what Verdi himself would have wanted.

I feel I have come to know Verdi well during the writing of this book. He was a man who rejected adulation, had a certain contempt for formality and officialdom, and was truly happy only when he was pursuing one of his two passions: agriculture and music. Even with music, it was only when he was in the process of composition that he was really at peace with himself. Whenever he had to deal with all the layers of authority involved in the staging of an opera, he reverted to his curmudgeonly self.

It seems to me entirely in character that he should take delight in casting doubt on apparently established facts or legends, particularly when people purported to know more about his early life than he himself did.*

Above

The house recognised today as the birthplace of Giuseppe Verdi in Le Roncole.

---

* Quite extraordinarily, as we shall see, in later life he misremembered the dates – wilfully or otherwise – of the tragic events that were to befall him as a young man.

So lovers of Verdi's work can surely feel (almost) justified in celebrating his bicentenary on 10 October 2013, while visitors to the national monument that proclaims itself Verdi's birthplace can be in (almost) no doubt that they are in the right place.

In 1813, Le Roncole belonged to France. It was situated in the province of Parma, which was annexed to the First French Empire established by the newly crowned Emperor Napoleon. The man we know as Giuseppe Francesco Fortunino Verdi was born French and baptised Joseph Fortunin François.

A week later, Napoleon – still reeling from his disastrous invasion of Russia – suffered a devastating defeat at the Battle of Leipzig, fought over four days from 16 to 19 October 1813. Russia, Prussia, Austria and Sweden joined forces on the battlefield and outnumbered the French emperor.

Following this defeat, Napoleon was forced to abdicate and was exiled to the island of Elba. There followed an almost farcical exchange of territory as the victorious alliance sought to divest the French empire of land it had seized.

Not so farcical, though, for the people living in the area that matters most to our story. The province of Parma was overrun by troops of the anti-French alliance. On 11 February 1814 the French prefect who had been put in control of the city of Parma handed it over to the Austrians. Three days later French soldiers retook the city. Two weeks after that they lost it again. Not until after the Battle of Waterloo in June 1815 would the people of the province be able to call themselves Italian.

The whole province, including Le Roncole, was overrun with soldiers of the anti-French alliance. Boots trampled through the village while Carlo Verdi attempted to run his grocery store and tavern, and his wife Luigia nursed their newborn son.

Late in life, when Verdi was seventy years old, he gave an interview to a German writer, who described him pointing up at the old bell tower of the Church of San Michele Arcangelo (where he was baptised and played the organ as a boy), and telling his interviewer that his mother had hidden there, with him as a five-month-old babe in her arms, as soldiers brought terror to the village:

> *During this whole time, she hid herself up in the middle of the tower, which was reached by one single ladder, terrified that I with my cries could betray our hiding place. Luckily, though, I slept almost all the time, and when I awakened I smiled contentedly.*[2]

We have only Verdi's word for the story, recounted a lifetime later. It is certainly true that soldiers rampaged through Le Roncole, and perhaps it is not too fanciful to imagine Luigia scurrying the short distance to the church and taking refuge there.

I particularly like the last sentence. It is easy to imagine Verdi, an old man, famous throughout Europe, his eyes twinkling as he persuaded a German interviewer that his placid nature as a baby saved both him and his mother from certain death.

Let us not forget, though, that Verdi was not averse to gilding the lily. In old age he was more than ready to stress his humble and poverty-stricken childhood. He described himself as a simple peasant from Le Roncole, rough-hewn and ignorant, shoes slung round his shoulders to save wear on the leather.

In reality both sets of his grandparents were relatively well-off as grocers and innkeepers, and his father carried on the family tradition. Carlo Verdi leased just over forty acres of land around Le Roncole, and was frequently absent from home tending the land or buying provisions. They might not have been wealthy, but the family was certainly not as poor as Verdi later made out. Furthermore, both godparents to the new arrival owned property and land. Carlo's younger brother Marco also ran a grocery store in Le Roncole. Between them, Verdi's father and uncle had substantial holdings in and around the village.

Giuseppe was born to Carlo and Luigia Verdi after almost nine years of marriage. His birth fell just a day or two – depending on whether he was born on the 9th or 10th! – before the wedding of his uncle Marco.

There was thus a double celebration in Le Roncole with the two brothers throwing a lavish party to celebrate, attended by locals, friends and the clergy who had officiated at the wedding and the baptism.

It is said that one of Verdi's godfathers hired a band of local musicians to play as the infant was taken back to the family home after he was baptised. We have no reason to doubt it. The future composer thus heard music for the first time at one (or two!) days old.

A second baby, a girl, was born to Carlo and Luigia Verdi on 20 March 1816, though you would be hard put to it to find much reference to her in biographies of her brother. He rarely spoke about her in later life, except to family members, and the earliest mention of her is in the first biographical sketch of Verdi, written by a boyhood friend of his by the name of Giuseppe Demaldè.

Demaldè uses the most general language, describing her as a 'handsome girl, with excellent manners and beautiful hopes for the future', and writes that there was a strong bond between brother and sister.[3]

Bizarrely the baptismal certificate refers to the baby as a 'child of male sex', given the names Giuseppe Francesco. This was corrected only on her death. She grew up as Giuseppa Francesca (Giuseppe and its female equivalent being traditional Verdi family names).

A later biographer, Carlo Gatti, suggests that Giuseppa was mentally disabled or incapacitated in some way, quoting his source as Verdi's niece, whom he interviewed. There have been suggestions she suffered brain damage as a result of meningitis.

Certainly her life was a short one, and we know almost nothing about it. Her death at the age of seventeen robbed Verdi of his only sibling, at a time in his young life when he needed as much support from family and friends as he could get.

But that lies in the future.

Giuseppe Verdi – 'Peppino' to his family – could hardly be said to have been born either in the right place or at the right time for a future career in music. Or, indeed, into the right family.

There is no suggestion of any musical talent in the Verdi family in immediate or preceding generations. An ancestor of Verdi's mother married a niece of the composer Alessandro Scarlatti, but there is no direct line to Verdi. If the boy were to develop a gift for music, it would not be down to genetic inheritance.

As to time and place, neither were particularly propitious to a burgeoning musical talent. Music was largely the preserve of the aristocracy. Composers relied on patronage and commission. That was how Mozart made a living, and if Beethoven was breaking away from that tradition, he was still prepared to compose for money when the opportunity arose.

It was largely thanks to great musical names such as Mozart and Beethoven, Haydn and Bach, that the geographical focus of musical excellence lay primarily north of the Alps. Vienna was indisputably the musical capital of Europe. Salzburg, the birthplace of Mozart; Bonn, the birthplace of Beethoven; Munich, Augsburg, Mannheim, Leipzig,

Dresden, and numerous other cities, mainly in German principalities, were the places where music flourished, with resident orchestras and a wealth of players.

In one musical genre, though, Italy outshone them all. Opera. No other country could match names such as Bellini, Donizetti, Cherubini, Rossini. Just as so many German towns and cities had their resident orchestra, so any Italian city worth its salt had an opera house, or at least a theatre where opera was regularly performed.

It was no accident that when Leopold Mozart wanted his son Wolfgang to win commissions to compose opera, he brought him to Italy. Together father and son toured the country no fewer than three times, performing from Milan in the north to Naples in the south, and sundry points in between.

This was the one point that would seem to be very much to Verdi's advantage – a future composer of opera born in the country that was the home of opera. In addition, the Po valley lay conveniently between two cities that could boast a fine operatic tradition.

Milan, around seventy miles to the north-west of Le Roncole, had had an opera house since 1778. La Scala remains to this day the most prestigious opera house in Italy. Just twenty or so miles to the south-east, Parma – known as the Athens of Italy – had its own theatre dating back more than a hundred years, which would be rebuilt as an opera house in the mid-nineteenth century.

Though both opera houses would go on to play a large part in Verdi's life, neither was of much concern to the residents of Le Roncole. Milan was a full day's coach ride away, Parma a journey of several hours. Neither company felt the need to send its singers out to perform in remote towns and villages. It is safe to say the residents of Le Roncole had never heard the work of Italy's great operatic composers.

Music existed, though, as we saw with the local band accompanying the newly baptised infant back to the family tavern. And growing up in a tavern exposed the boy to all forms of local music, from folk songs to fiddlers.*

Describing his childhood, Verdi himself spoke of being in ecstasy when he heard an itinerant musician playing in Le Roncole. His

---

* A decade earlier, and to the north, another future musician, Johann Strauss the Elder, was hearing music in the same way in his father's tavern on the banks of the Danube Canal in Vienna.

mother told a friend that when her son heard the sound of a hand-organ, he pestered her until she let him go outside and stand near it. Demaldè recalled that his friend was hypnotised by the sound of any musical instrument.

In later years Verdi's relationship with his parents was not always good, and he would describe his childhood as difficult, spent in poverty and obscurity. But his parents in fact deserve more credit than that.

Carlo Verdi was determined his son should have a good education. He hired a local schoolmaster to teach Peppino Latin and Italian privately when the boy was just four – further evidence his parents were not as poor, nor his childhood as poverty-stricken, as Verdi was later to claim.

At the age of six, Peppino was enrolled in the village school, which was run by the same teacher who had taught him privately. By a fortunate coincidence, for which the world can be forever grateful, this schoolmaster, an aged gentleman by the name of Pietro Baistrocchi, was also the organist at the Church of San Michele.

In a further stroke of good fortune, Baistrocchi recognised Peppino as a clever and intelligent boy, and was keen to encourage him in whatever pursuit took his interest. It is therefore almost certainly thanks to Baistrocchi that when Peppino expressed a desire to play the church organ at San Michele, Baistrocchi allowed him to do so.

We have no direct evidence of it, but we can safely assume Baistrocchi was hugely impressed, and reported the fact to Peppino's parents, because they then did something quite remarkable.

They acquired a spinet, a small keyboard instrument, for their eight-year-old son. It is possible they bought it, or borrowed it on some sort of long-term loan, from Baistrocchi, who at an advanced age and in ill health no longer played it and wanted to see it put to good use.

It was a beautiful instrument. A keyboard of four octaves set in a wide wooden case. Now we have, for the first time, direct evidence of just what a skilful keyboard player young Peppino was. The spinet needed restoring. This was undertaken by one Stefano Cavaletti, who left an inscription inside stating that

> I, Stefano Cavaletti, have remade these keys and leather jacks and have adapted the pedals that I added as a gift; just as I have remade the keys free of charge, seeing the aptitude shown by the young Giuseppe Verdi for learning to play this instrument, which for me is payment enough. Anno Domini 1821.[4]

"Verdi spoke of being in ecstasy when he heard an itinerant musician playing in Le Roncole."

Verdi himself said later in life he did his first lessons on the spinet, that he appreciated the sacrifice his parents made to acquire it for him, and that having it made him 'happier than a king'.[5]

This spinet became Giuseppe Verdi's most treasured possession. It stayed with him for the rest of his life. It had pride of place in his home, and is today in the Verdi room of the La Scala museum.

Young Peppino was now clearly recognised in his own village as a boy of remarkable musical talent. It is no surprise that Baistrocchi allowed the boy to assist him in church services, playing the organ, singing in the choir and possibly even coaching the singers.[*] Soon he was playing alone for Sunday service in Baistrocchi's absence.

It was during this time that a notorious incident occurred, which has become part of Verdi legend. It is a riveting story and throws light on Verdi the man. Throughout his life Verdi was sceptical of religion. His wife described him as an atheist, and he had a lifelong and overt antipathy towards priests.

It is possible the seed for that was sown in the Church of San Michele, packed for Sunday Mass. Peppino, aged around seven, was not at the organ, but assisting the priest, one Don Giacomo Masini. At a crucial point in the service, listening intently to the music coming from the organ loft, he failed to hear Masini calling for the water and wine to be passed to him.

Masini, angry that the boy was not paying attention, gave him a swift kick. Peppino lost his balance and fell down the altar steps. Humiliated in front of the congregation, he gave back as good as he got.

'Dio t'manda na sajetta!' ('May God strike you with lightning!') he shouted at the priest.

God was clearly listening. Eight years later Peppino was due to sing in the choir at Le Roncole's other church, La Madonna dei Prati, at half-past three in the afternoon on the Sunday of the Feast of the Nativity of the Virgin.

On his way across the fields, he called in on friends, possibly for lunch. While he was there, a violent storm blew up, of the kind local people were used to on the open plain of the Po valley.

He arrived at the church to find his nemesis, Don Masini, sitting outside, his thumb pressed against his nose as if he was taking snuff.

---

[*] Echoes of the young Beethoven, who at the age of thirteen was appointed assistant court organist to his teacher Gottlob Neefe.

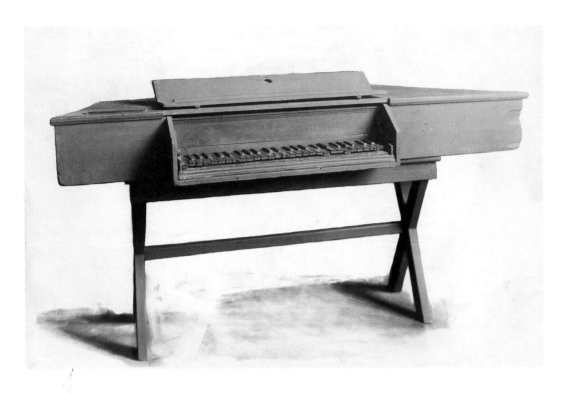

The spinet Giuseppe
Verdi played as a child.

But his face was blackened and terrifying. God had indeed struck him with lightning.

The event was a local tragedy. Lightning killed four priests, two members of the choir, a mare, a dog and a puppy, and there was widespread mourning, as well as prayers to the Holy Virgin imploring her protection from storms, hail, lightning and earthquakes.

The only source we have for the tale (apart from the deaths from lightning, which were documented) is Giuseppe Verdi himself. But the story of how he was humiliated in church and cursed the priest is one he would tell for the rest of his life.

One can imagine friends and relatives at Sant'Agata, the villa that was his refuge for half a century, settling back with fixed grins on their faces as the famous composer, in old age, would regale them once again with 'Have I told you about the time I cursed the priest . . .?', almost certainly ending the story with 'Just imagine if I had not stopped off to see friends. I would have been outside the church when the lightning struck.' In which case the history of music would have been rather different.

By the time Peppino reached the age of ten, he had outgrown the village in which he had been born. It was evident to all that in one area, at least, he had an ability that no one, trained musicians even, could match.

Credit is due to his father for recognising that his son needed further education, and for being prepared to lay out funds to pay for it. As Mary Jane Phillips-Matz has pointed out, Carlo could quite easily have put Peppino into one of the fields as a labourer, or used him as an extra pair of hands in the tavern. This was a time when very few children even attended school and most country people were illiterate. It once again suggests that when Verdi later described his childhood as being spent in 'poverty and obscurity' and his youth as 'very hard', he was guilty of a certain amount of exaggeration.

In 1823, at the age of ten, Giuseppe Verdi was sent away from home to be educated in the town of Busseto. It was, as things would turn out, the best possible development that could have happened to him.

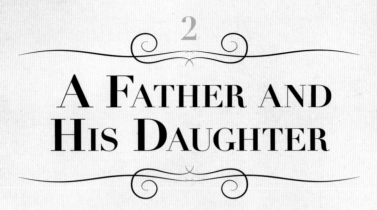

A FATHER AND HIS DAUGHTER

Giuseppe Verdi was a rather withdrawn, isolated boy, lost in his own world. We know this because many of his contemporaries were keen to offer their assessment of him once he achieved fame. Consider this description:

> [He was] quiet, all closed within himself, sober of face and gesture, a boy who kept apart from happy, loud gangs of companions, preferring to stay near his mother or alone in the house. There lingered about him an air of authority; and even when he was a boy, the other children pointed him out as someone different from the rest of them; and they admired him in a certain way.

This description came from boys who knew him as a schoolmate, offering their opinions many decades later, when the man they had known as a child was universally admired. Their opinions obviously benefited from hindsight. But such a vivid description offers a real insight into the character of this young musical prodigy.

We can clearly picture a boy who kept himself apart, who did not join in with other youths of his age in schoolboy pranks and games. While the others were letting off steam, Giuseppe no doubt preferred to go to San Michele and practise the organ. There was a separateness there, a seriousness that set him apart.

No doubt the boy was joshed by his schoolmates, until they attended Sunday Mass and witnessed for themselves what he was capable of
on the organ. Small wonder they 'admired' him. One can imagine them
giving him something of a wide berth. 'Different from us,' they might
well have said. Giuseppe must have been aware of this, and so the apartness would have grown still more marked.

We can imagine a shy, reticent boy, at the age of ten – at the time
his life was about to change – blessed with an extraordinary talent that
marked him out as different but that at the same time confined him to
his own world.

If Giuseppe felt any trepidation at being about to leave his family,
and the village he had been born in, perhaps he also felt some relief that
he could now indulge his 'differentness'. He knew he was unlike those
he had grown up with. Time to spread those musical wings.

The town of Busseto lies just three miles from Le Roncole but it
seems a world away, now as it did in Verdi's time. Situated between the
bustling cultural centres of Milan and Parma, it might easily have been
squashed into insignificance. But since the Middle Ages it has boasted a
tradition of art, music, literature, philosophy and architecture.

When Carlo Verdi decided his son needed to further his education
away from Le Roncole, no discussion was necessary as to where that
should be. Busseto was the obvious choice. Apart from its tradition of
culture and learning, it lies less than an hour's walk from Le Roncole.

Shortly before Giuseppe left Le Roncole, his early teacher and benefactor Baistrocchi had died. Giuseppe was his natural successor as organist
at San Michele. This necessitated playing at Sunday Mass, and he would
be able to make the journey home to Le Roncole easily each weekend
without the cost of transport.

Later in life Verdi would complain about this. Pleased though he
may have been to get away from the confines of Le Roncole, he nevertheless was having to study away from home, lonely enough in itself,
but added to this was the fact that when he should have been concentrating on his studies he had to make the arduous trek to Le Roncole
every weekend to perform his church duties.

He told an interviewer many years later that on one occasion, on a
winter's day in frost and snow, he fell into a deep ditch, 'where I would
probably have drowned if a peasant woman on the path had not heard
my cries and pulled me out'.[6] There could well be some truth in this,
though I suspect those twinkling eyes might have betrayed a certain
embellishment in the telling.

Left

The church of San
Michele Arcangelo.

Giuseppe moved into lodgings with a few worldly goods and his beloved spinet. He enrolled in the local school for boys, the *ginnasio*, and there encountered the first of three men in Busseto who were to have the most profound effect on him.

The school was run by Don Pietro Seletti, who ensured Giuseppe received instruction in Italian grammar, Latin, humanities and rhetoric. Seletti was something of a polymath. He had written academic works on Greek and Hebrew, was a historian and astronomer, ran the well-stocked local library, and would go on to found an academy of Greek language and literature.

But of more relevance is the fact that Don Seletti was an amateur musician who played the viola in the local church orchestra. His initial inclination was to steer Giuseppe towards the priesthood. It was not long, though, before the boy demonstrated where his talent lay, and Seletti had the good judgement to realise the nature of his true vocation.

Through Seletti, Giuseppe was brought to the attention of Ferdinando Provesi, organist at the Church of San Bartolomeo, and director of Busseto's music school. Provesi was a highly talented musician, a composer of operas, Masses, symphonies, songs and cantatas. Young Giuseppe Verdi could not have fallen more firmly on his feet.

It was not long before Giuseppe was actually teaching his fellow pupils. If there were any lingering doubt as to just how talented the boy was, it was dramatically dispelled when an elderly gentleman engaged to play at a special church service withdrew.

Seletti, clearly confident of the boy's abilities, asked Giuseppe to take his place. He played with such virtuosity that all those present were stunned. Afterwards Seletti asked Giuseppe whose music he had played. Giuseppe, blushing, replied, 'My own, Signor Maestro. I just played it as it came to me.'[7]

It was Giuseppe Verdi's first public performance in Busseto. He was no more than thirteen years of age.

He also began to compose around this time, and compose prolifically. In a letter written many decades later, he stated that:

> *From my thirteenth to my eighteenth year . . . I wrote a wide variety of music, marches by the hundred for the band, perhaps hundreds of little works to be played in church, in the theatre, and in private concerts; many serenades, cantatas (arias, duets, many trios), and several religious compositions, of which I remember only a Stabat Mater.*[8]

"*He was no longer Peppino; he was Verdi the musician, keyboard virtuoso and composer.*"

Given that few of these 'hundreds' of pieces have survived, we can assume a degree of exaggeration on Giuseppe's part. But the fact remains: in his teenage years he was not only performing music, he was writing it as well.

A year or so after that first public performance, he made his debut as a composer. He wrote an overture for Rossini's *Il barbiere di Siviglia*, which was performed by an opera company visiting Busseto. The audience was enraptured. Applause and ovations were 'long and extremely noisy'.[9]

Small wonder that before he reached the age of twenty, he was renowned in all quarters of the highly cultured and sophisticated town of Busseto as a young man of quite exceptional musical talent. He was no longer Peppino; he was Verdi the musician, keyboard virtuoso and composer.

Busseto boasted its own Philharmonic Society, in which Provesi was a leading light. Through Provesi, Giuseppe Verdi became involved with the Society. One of the venues in which the Society's orchestra performed was the salon of a handsome town house owned by one of the leading citizens of Busseto, Antonio Barezzi.

We do not know exactly when and how Verdi met Barezzi, though we can safely assume it was at a musical performance in Barezzi's house. The relationship he would develop with the older man would alter the course of his life.

A portrait of Antonio Barezzi painted ten years after his death shows a formally dressed man in old age, wearing a black bow-tie, a starched white dress shirt with studs, a low-cut waistcoat sporting a gold watch chain, and a black evening suit. He has immaculately combed grey hair, parted on the left, an elaborate and perfectly coiffed moustache, heavy eyebrows, dark eyes and a serious unsmiling expression.

Barezzi was a wholesale grocer and distiller, and had grown wealthy on the success of his business. Of the utmost significance to the young Verdi, he was also dedicated to music. He was competent on several instruments, among them the flute, clarinet and ophicleide (a forerunner of the tuba). Demaldè described him as a 'manic dilettante' of music.

Barezzi played in the orchestra of the Philharmonic Society, as well as making his salon available for rehearsals and performances. It was inevitable that he would sooner or later meet the young musician who was making such a name for himself in Busseto. Inevitable, too, that Verdi would meet Barezzi's eldest daughter, Margherita, a fine singer who was seven months younger than him. It was not long before he began to teach her, accompanying her on the piano.

Nor was it long before a mutual attraction developed. His friend Demaldè wrote later that such was Verdi's shyness in front of other people that no one realised he and Margherita had fallen in love. It would be some time, though, before the romance was allowed to flourish, and a number of setbacks would have to be overcome first.

Verdi's natural shyness was compounded by a fierce independence of spirit, something that would mark him out throughout his life. In Busseto he was the country boy, the outsider. Beyond his talent for music, there was little about him to attract attention. He moved in a very small circle of boys of his own age, and with the exception of Demaldè, who would be the first to write an (unfinished) biography, his 'apartness' prevented any really close friendships from developing.

One quality Verdi most certainly did not lack: confidence in his own musical ability. Perhaps to distance himself from the people of Busseto, perhaps to prove to them his worth, he applied for the post of organist at a church in a small town close to Le Roncole. He was sixteen years of age. He was turned down. It must have been a huge blow to his self-esteem, but it was nothing compared to what lay ahead.

Just a few months later he received the devastating news that his father, who had failed to keep up the rent on the family home and lands in Le Roncole, was to be forcibly evicted with his wife and daughter. Carlo Verdi had overstretched himself, and was already in arrears when he renewed the lease.

His petition to remain, and his promises to clear the debt, fell on deaf ears – the deaf ears of the local bishop to be precise, who prevailed on the court to issue an eviction order. On 11 November 1830 the Verdi family moved out of the house they had lived in for nearly forty years – the probable birthplace of their son – and took up a tenancy in the tavern that today claims that distinction.

At this point Antonio Barezzi became more than just an admirer of the young musician; he became Verdi's protector and benefactor. He took Giuseppe Verdi into his own house and gave him a room. This marked the beginning of a relationship that both individuals would treasure, Verdi expressing his gratitude to the older man until his dying day.

Barezzi gave Verdi a comfortable and spacious bedroom-cum-sitting room off the landing on the first floor of the house, with a bed at one end, and a sofa, two armchairs and several upright chairs at the other. The

Left

Antonio Barezzi.

window was hung with heavy curtains, and the walls covered with French paper. On the plaster over the door Verdi himself wrote, 'G. Verdi'.*

I have seen it written that neither Barezzi nor his wife were aware of the mutual attraction that had developed between their daughter and the young musician, but that is surely not credible. It is more likely that not only were they aware of it but that they did little to discourage the two young people. Barezzi, with his passion for music, might even then have been eyeing up Verdi as a potential son-in-law.

For the immediate future, though, Barezzi had other plans. He could see better than most that Verdi, now eighteen years of age, had outgrown Busseto. There was nothing in the town for the young man to aspire to. Barezzi knew that there was only one path for this remarkably

---

*The room was preserved in its original state well into the 1960s.

talented musician to take. He needed to go to the cultural capital of northern Italy, Milan, and study at the Milan Conservatory.

No doubt encouraged by Barezzi, Verdi's father applied to a charitable institution in Busseto for a four-year scholarship for his son to study music in Milan. When it seemed as if the application would fail, it was Barezzi's agreement to subsidise the first year that probably did the trick. Once again Verdi had reason to be grateful to his benefactor. All that lay between Verdi and the conservatory was the entrance exam; with his innate musical talent that would be a formality.

Giuseppe Verdi, approaching his nineteenth birthday, was about to leave the town where he had lived for almost ten years. The big city awaited him. This, surely, was where his extraordinary musical talent would be discovered, encouraged and nurtured; where he could attend opera at La Scala and meet those with influence in the world of music. He would fit into the milieu there with far more ease than he ever had done in Busseto.

But that was not how it was to be. Things were to go wrong for him from the start.

3

'HE IS A RUDE, UNCIVIL SCOUNDREL'

Milan in **1832** was still for the most part a medieval city. It was enclosed by a series of walls, with gates set into them, unchanged since the Middle Ages. Medieval houses stood alongside Roman ruins.

There was another side to the city, though. Austrian rule, which still continued in northern Italy, had left its mark. Ornate buildings bearing coats of arms, with wrought-iron balconies and inner courtyards with fountains, created enclaves for the wealthy. These mansions boasted salons. Newly wealthy Milanese, growing rich on the boom in trade that followed the collapse of the Napoleonic empire, patronised artists, writers, musicians, as the aristocracy in Vienna had done for decades past.

Fashion was as important to Milan two centuries ago as it is today. Wives of wealthy merchants competed to hold the best salons, dressed in the latest styles. Milan was emerging from years of war and occupation, and was beginning to rival Paris and even London.

Everywhere there was noise: street vendors shouting their wares, carriage wheels and horses' hooves clattering on cobbles, and the sound of bells. Churches, monasteries and convents stood on almost every street.

In one important respect Milan was unrivalled throughout Italy. It housed the opera house of La Scala, which had stood for more than half a century and was able to seat upwards of three thousand people. Such

was the natural love of Italian audiences for opera that La Scala had become Europe's pre-eminent operatic venue very soon after it was built.

Six tiers of boxes accommodated the aristocrats and the wealthy. But standing below them and seated above them were the true opera aficionados, ready to make their opinions known swiftly and decisively. From that time to this, reputations have been made and lost on the stage of La Scala.

It is easy to imagine Verdi standing and gazing at the building that would go on to play such a large part in his life. But there were plenty of hurdles ahead for an eighteen-year-old boy from the provinces who had yet to impress anyone in the big city.

In order to make the journey to Milan, Verdi had been issued with his first passport. It described him as having chestnut-brown hair, grey eyes, a high forehead, black eyebrows, an aquiline nose, a small mouth, a thick beard and pock-marks.* His profession is given as 'studente di musica'.

Lodgings had been found for him in the home of a Bussetan, Giuseppe Seletti, the nephew of Verdi's first schoolteacher in Busseto. It was

---

* It is not known at what age Verdi had contracted smallpox.

an unfortunate choice. Seletti took an instant dislike to the teenager. There was a rumour at the time that he might have lent Verdi's father money and the debt remained outstanding. He was known as a prickly character, and the likelihood is he simply resented having this young man foisted on him.

Verdi's first task was to apply for entry to the Milan Conservatory. Once he was established as a student, his time would be fully taken up with study – best for him, and best too for his landlord.

As soon as he could Verdi formally applied for a place at the conservatory. In his application he acknowledged that at eighteen he was four years over the age limit, but asked that his musical talent be judged sufficient to allow him a dispensation.

On a hot day in late June, Verdi appeared before a panel of four: the head of the conservatory, and professors of composition, violin and piano. He presented some of his own compositions, and performed a well-known piano piece by a Viennese composer. In the second part of the exam he composed a four-part fugue.

A week later he was told he had failed. In the first place he held his hands incorrectly over the keyboard, and at the age of nearly nineteen that would be difficult to correct. Although his compositions showed some merit, the professor of composition expressed the opinion that Verdi would turn out to be a 'mediocrity'. The word was underlined in the report.

It was the most devastating blow. Verdi's confidence in himself as a musician, specifically as a composer, was irreparably damaged. That is not an exaggeration, because Verdi never got over it. He kept the letter of rejection on his desk at Sant'Agata for the rest of his life. Across the envelope he had scrawled, 'In the year 1832 22 June Giuseppe Verdi's request to be admitted to the Milan Conservatory was rejected.'

Sixty-five years later he reacted with fury when it was proposed that the Milan Conservatory should be named after him.[†]

Perhaps the rejection was something of a blessing in disguise. Had Verdi been accepted, he would have had to wear a uniform, conform to rules and regulations, and spend all his time within the walls of the conservatory.

He might have emerged a thoroughly competent musician, but if he was to write opera – the creative seeds of which were soon to take

[†] Which it was, and remains so to this day.

root – then he needed to learn about more than just music. He needed to experience life.

That he was about to do with some gusto.

It was recommended by the conservatory that Verdi should take private music lessons, and this he began to do with a certain Vincenzo Lavigna, whose name they suggested. They at least got that right.

Lavigna was a composer of opera and had himself enjoyed recent success at La Scala. Now in his mid-fifties, he had decided to turn to teaching. Verdi could not have asked for a better teacher, nor Lavigna a better student.

Lavigna belonged to a vanishing world. He had been in the music business all his adult life, had seen musicians come and go, and knew the music scene in Milan. And he enjoyed passing on his knowledge to a younger man, a younger man with obvious musical talent.

The first thing Lavigna did was to ask to see some of his pupil's compositions. He professed himself impressed. Later he was to say he found it quite unbelievable that Verdi had been refused entry to the Milan Conservatory.

Within a short time Lavigna realised that Verdi was exceptionally gifted, and did all he could to encourage him. It was exactly what the young musician needed to restore his battered confidence.

Lavigna arranged for Verdi to have a subscription to La Scala, and enrolled him at a music library so that he could bring scores home. Together teacher and pupil would study them. Often Lavigna would invite luminaries from the musical world to come to his home, where the talk was of music and theatre.

Verdi was immersed in a world he wanted so much to become a part of, meeting a wide spectrum of personalities from musicians to singers, writers, agents and impresarios. No wonder that, to the end of his life, Verdi talked fondly of the older man whom he credited with giving him his first real introduction to the world of music.

As for his introduction to the world outside music, which as a young man on the brink of his twenties Verdi was more than ready for, he began to indulge himself in a way he would not have been able to had he been a student at the conservatory.

Artistic life revolved around La Scala, which itself was a stone's throw from the cathedral, the other main attraction in the centre of the city. Between the two a new *galleria* of fashionable shops had opened. Cafés, restaurants, bookshops abounded. Musicians who befriended Verdi at Lavigna's showed him the sights, took him out to eat and drink, accompanied him to the opera house and concerts.

The boy from the sticks, rejected by the conservatory, was being educated in big-city life, artistic and social. He was indulging himself, and loving it. In February 1834, in the *galleria* just a few paces from La Scala, a tumultuous masked ball was held. Six thousand people joined in, elaborately dressed and wearing masks. Thousands of lanterns lit the walkways. Men and women caroused and flirted. Venice had come to Milan. The festivities went on all night, ending at eight the next morning.

It is inconceivable that young Verdi and his musical friends did not partake of what was on offer – which was most certainly not to his landlord's liking. It was now that Seletti allowed his resentment of the young man he was housing to bubble over. On 22 June 1834, two years to the day since Verdi's rejection by the conservatory, Seletti sat down to write a letter to Antonio Barezzi, Verdi's benefactor back in Busseto.

It is a quite extraordinary letter, full of venom and bile. Could Verdi really have merited Seletti's character assassination, because that is what it is? It is worth quoting at length:

> *You, who live with the delusion that Verdi is another Rossini, will be mortified to hear me speak of him in these terms; but you must understand that being a good musician does not make him an honest man; and even if Verdi were to turn out a thousand times better than Rossini himself, I would still say that I found him rude, uncivil, proud, and acting like a scoundrel in my house. I write this to you because he is not yet your son-in-law; and when he becomes that, I will keep my mouth shut rather than lie to you about him . . . I cannot tell you how much damage he has done to my family, because it is [too indecent] to write about . . . Don't ever speak to me again about Verdi, nor ask me to do anything for him. Just his name alone is too disgusting to me. I pray to God that I may forget him for ever.*

Rude, uncivil, proud, a scoundrel and dishonest. Something had set Seletti off, and we can guess what it was. Seletti had a daughter, Dorina, with whom Verdi was deliberately and publicly flirting. He even went so far as to take Dorina back to Busseto with him and flaunt her, when everybody knew he was all but engaged to Margherita.

That one incident aside, there were mitigating circumstances for Verdi's behaviour. Still smarting from the conservatory's rejection, the

"I found him rude, uncivil, proud, and acting like a scoundrel in my house."

Giuseppe Seletti on Verdi.

following year he received dreadful news from home. His sister Giuseppa, about whom we know so little, had died at the age of just seventeen.

News also reached him from Busseto of the death of his old benefactor and teacher Provesi. He was Provesi's natural successor as organist and music director in Busseto, but still in the midst of his musical studies he was not ready. It was too early.

I suspect, though Verdi never actually said so, that he was not overly disappointed when the post of Provesi's successor went to someone else. He was in Milan, the cultural and musical capital of northern Italy, and just now, unexpectedly, he was about to make his mark.

Through Lavigna he learned that a local music society was planning to perform Haydn's late oratorio *The Creation*. Lavigna suggested he go along to rehearsals to gain experience.

As he recounted many years later to a French biographer, the keyboard accompanist was absent on a crucial day, and he offered to step in. So successful was he that he was asked to direct the chorus and accompany on the keyboard for the actual performance. The performance itself met with such an enthusiastic reception that it was repeated, this time in one of the grand salons of the aristocracy, in front of the cream of society.[10] Verdi's name was now known in extremely high places.

More importantly for the history of music, Verdi was commissioned to write an opera. But what should have been a fairy-tale beginning to the illustrious career that we know was soon to come in fact fizzled out. Verdi was dissatisfied with the libretto he was given, entitled *Rocester*. He toyed with it for some time, eventually abandoning it.

However, he was also commissioned to compose a cantata in honour of the Austrian emperor, which received a performance in the palace of a Milanese count. Verdi now most definitely had acquired a taste for life in Milan. He saw his future there, not in the provincial town of Busseto, which he had never liked anyway.

Unfortunately for him, that was not the way Busseto saw it, and in particular his supporter and benefactor Antonio Barezzi. Barezzi had been bankrolling Verdi all the time he was in Milan, and now he put his foot down.

Barezzi wanted Verdi to return to Busseto, where he and a number of musical colleagues were prepared to challenge the appointment of Provesi's successor, on the grounds that he had been selected without being examined, and without Verdi being allowed to compete for the post.

Verdi had no choice but to return to Busseto and do as he was told. He was nowhere near ready to support himself in Milan. He needed

"Verdi had acquired a taste for life in Milan. He saw his future there, not in the provincial town of Busseto."

gainful employment. That was more likely to come in Busseto than in Milan.

Once Barezzi and his colleagues launched their challenge, all hell broke loose in Busseto. That is no exaggeration. The town was split down the middle, with one half supporting Verdi, the other his rival Giovanni Ferrari. There were arguments, vitriol was flung, and so were fists. There were actual fights in the streets between the two factions. The people of Busseto took their music seriously.

Verdi went through the motions, but it has to be said that he did little to advance his own cause. He made it clear to anyone who would listen that he disliked the town, and had no wish to stay there any longer than was necessary.

He also formalised his relationship with Margherita Barezzi, telling her that he would marry her and they would move to Milan together as soon as the opportunity presented itself. She, taking her lead from him, left her father in no doubt that her future lay with Giuseppe Verdi in Milan.

Poor Barezzi must have wondered why he ever took on young Verdi in the first place. He had harboured two clear desires for the musical prodigy: that he should bring musical glory to Busseto, and that he should become his son-in-law. It now looked as if he could not have both. Which of the two he would have preferred, had he been given the choice of only one, we cannot know. What we do know, with the benefit of hindsight, is that in the long run he would regret nothing.

Months dragged by. It was only when Verdi announced – probably with a certain element of bluff – that he was applying for a post in Monza, seventy miles north east of Milan, that things began to happen.

A classic compromise was found. Ferrari was allowed to retain the post of organist; that of music director was thrown open to competition, as had been originally agreed. Ferrari decided to save face by not even applying. Verdi duly got the job. He did not just get the job; he stunned his examiner, who declared he was a good enough musician to be a *maestro* in Paris or London.

At last Verdi had status in the musical world. He had secured an appointment he did not want in a town he did not like. What is more, he was tied to a nine-year contract. That was a considerable commitment, and not one he had any intention of fulfilling.

Busseto, and Barezzi, must have thought they had finally secured the long-term services of their most talented young musician. Verdi had other ideas, but for the time being he kept them to himself.

What his contract did ensure, though, was a steady, if modest, income, and that allowed him to become a married man. On 4 May 1836, Margherita's birthday, Giuseppe Verdi, *maestro di musica*, married Margherita Barezzi. He was twenty-two; she was one year younger. Verdi's father Carlo was at the ceremony, along with Margherita's parents, but his mother was too ill to attend.

Barezzi threw a lavish party at his house opposite the town square in Busseto, attended by the entire Philharmonic Society, with the newly-weds seated at the head of the table.

A brief honeymoon (in Milan!), and it was down to work in Busseto for Verdi.

Portraits of the newly wedded couple were made, either on the wedding day itself or soon after. They were charcoal drawings done by Barezzi's brother. Verdi has a serious demeanour, looking off to his left, with the beard he wore all his life, and full straight hair parted on the right. His face has a softness to it, and one can see a glimpse of vulnerability about him. Not so Margherita, who fixes the artist with a direct gaze. There is a touch of humour in her face, as if she might break into a smile at any moment. Her most striking feature is her luxuriant hair, piled on either side of her head, and ornately on top of it.*

At only twenty-two years of age, Verdi was already something of a legend in Busseto, at least to his students. They were aware of the tussle that had been waged to secure him the top job, and he had earned the title of *maestro* that was now rightly his.

To say that Verdi was busy in his new role is an understatement. He wrote piece after piece to be performed in church – Masses, vespers and benedictions – and he taught his own music to the chorus and orchestra.

Every Sunday after Vespers, the Philharmonic Society band played his music in the town square.† The local people flocked to these performances, proud of the young man who had spent a decade in their town, and whose prodigious talent was nurtured locally.

---

* The drawing of Margherita is now lost. A portrait was painted from it after her death, highlighting her vivid red hair.

† As happens to this day, now with Verdi's seated statue looking down on the audience.

On top of this, he taught students in the music school, setting them exams and testing them. He was fortunate that his wife was a trained singer and teacher, allowing her to take on some of the duties.

Margherita soon fell pregnant, and ten months after the marriage, on 26 March 1837, she gave birth to a baby girl. The couple named their daughter Virginia Maria Luigia.

As if his duties as music director were not enough, every spare moment that Verdi had he spent answering his true calling. Perhaps Margherita – Ghita to her husband and family – was the only one who knew. Verdi was working on a new opera.

It is not clear to this day at what point he abandoned work on *Rocester* and began to write an entirely new opera, entitled *Oberto, Conte di San Bonifacio.* But he was soon making serious progress.

Serious enough to approach the opera house in Parma, the Teatro Regio di Parma, to try to persuade the director there to stage it. With characteristic but unjustified brio, Verdi announced a performance of his new opera in Parma for September 1837. He had to do some serious back-pedalling when the director of the opera house declared he could not risk putting on a new opera by an unknown composer.

Verdi turned instead to Milan and La Scala, with even less success. These were slights that Verdi would not forget. His relations with these two great opera houses remained strained for the rest of his life, even at one point leading to a total break. Verdi did not forgive easily.

Margherita was pregnant again within seven months of Virginia's birth, and a son was born to the couple on 11 July 1838. They named him Icilio Romano. The names of both their children, Virginia and Icilio, were taken from the glory days of ancient Rome, belonging to Roman martyrs, in a deliberate show of nationalism by Verdi and his wife.

The couple's joy was short lived. Just a month after Icilio's birth, Virginia died. She was only sixteen months.

Even in an era when infant mortality was commonplace, this was a devastating blow to the young couple. Maybe it was Virginia's death that galvanised Verdi. He was due two months' leave. He lost no time in taking his wife to Milan, leaving Icilio in the care of a wet nurse.

It was an unproductive stay. Try as he might, Verdi was unable to interest La Scala in his new opera. It was a forlorn hope in any case; the

---

Nor is it known whether any of the music he used for *Oberto* is remodelled from *Rocester*, since nothing of the earlier work has survived.

autumn season had long since been announced, and everybody con-
nected with the theatre was fully taken up with preparations.

To worsen Verdi's mood, Milan was in the throes of celebrating a
visit by the Emperor and Empress of Austria, paying an official visit to
the diamond in their northern Italian crown. Soldiers in ceremonial
uniform were on parade; there were plays, ballets and grand balls, and
everywhere was hung with the scarlet and gold of the Habsburgs.

Verdi and Margherita were unimpressed. Their shared nationalism had
already inspired the naming of their children, and they were certainly not
about to participate in festivities that they found profoundly distasteful.

One thing Verdi did do during the stay, however, was renew his musical contacts. There were plenty of musicians he could call on, friends
and colleagues from his days studying with Lavigna, and some of these
had contacts in high places.

For Verdi the contact in the highest place of all was Bartolomeo
Merelli, impresario and director of Europe's most prestigious opera
house, La Scala. He was also director of the Kärntnertor theatre in

Vienna, where Beethoven had frequently performed his compositions. Merelli was possibly the single most important impresario in Europe's musical world.

Through his contacts, Verdi's name was brought to the attention of Merelli. Verdi had by now many published compositions to his name, and it was more than likely Merelli was shown some of these, or might even have known about them already.

Word was brought back to Verdi that Merelli was impressed, though for the moment there was nothing he could do to help the young composer. La Scala's schedule was planned and under way.

Verdi needed no further encouragement. He was by now convinced he could make a career, earn a living, in Milan. He and Margherita returned to Busseto. His mind was made up. On 28 October 1838 Verdi handed in his notice and resigned as music director.

He was twenty-five, with a wife and child to support, in debt to his father-in-law (who once again had financed his latest trip to Milan), and in full-time employment with a steady, if small, income. That had now gone.

What gave him this unassailable confidence? He had completed his first opera, *Oberto*. He knew it was good. He was certain he would be able to get it staged at La Scala. And so, on 6 February 1839, Verdi, with his wife and son Icilio, who was just seven months old, left Busseto for the last time.

In Milan he was in no doubt that he would be able to establish himself as a composer of opera, the natural successor to Rossini; he would earn an ample living; his wife and son would live comfortably in the sophisticated city; they might even expand their family; and the future was assured.

He was wrong on all counts.

INTOLERABLE LOSSES

Giuseppe Verdi loved the company of women, and he had an undoubted eye for a pretty face. We have already seen how he flirted with his landlord's daughter in Milan, even taking her back to Busseto with him, causing her father to heap all manner of uncomplimentary epithets on his head.

To imagine that after marriage his roving eye might cease roving would be a presumption too far. He moved in musical circles, crowded with female musicians. In particular he now found himself drawn to writing for the voice – both songs and larger-scale works – and so his milieu was the world of opera, with its abundance of sopranos and mezzos.

One in particular had caught his attention. It was hardly surprising. She was the soprano of the moment, the most renowned in Italy. In the city of Milan, the home of Italian opera, she was feted, her name on the lips of all opera lovers. Her voice had a purity and beauty no one else's could match.

That was not all she was renowned for. The singing came first, of course. Giuseppina Strepponi had triumphed in Donizetti's *Lucia di Lammermoor* and *L'elisir d'amore*, as well as Bellini's *I puritani*. But she also had a remarkably colourful private life.

In February 1839 Giuseppina was twenty-three years of age, at the height of her fame and with a glittering career ahead of her. She was also the lover of several male opera singers and the mother of two illegitimate children. Her behaviour towards these infants – at least from a twenty-first-century perspective – seems extraordinary.

The first she had given birth to just a year earlier, in January 1838. It was a son, baptised Camillo Luigi Antonio. The birth register records the father as 'unidentified'. She was known to have had several affairs while on tour, and a more prolonged relationship with her agent. We can take it that she did not know who the father was. The baby was dispatched to a family in Florence. Giuseppina made no attempt to maintain contact, and as far as we know never saw her son again.

Within a matter of months she was pregnant again. In February 1839 she gave birth to a daughter, Giuseppa Faustina. The delivery took place six hours after she had come off stage. Although the pregnancy had been clearly visible, since she continued working right up to the birth, it appears there was a conspiracy to hide the pregnancy from the authorities. To give birth illegitimately was a crime.

When she was unable to perform, it was hinted she had suffered a miscarriage or stillbirth. The local newspaper reported she was recovering from 'a slight indisposition'.

Once again she could not be sure who the father was, though when word inevitably leaked out, her agent claimed paternity. And once again there was apparently not a trace of sentimentality in Giuseppina. The inconvenience of a new arrival could not be allowed to interrupt a flourishing career.

This time the baby was placed in a turnstile set into the wall of the Ospedale degli Innocenti (Hospital of the Innocents) in Florence. This was, in effect, a revolving door. The infant was deposited in the small doorway, the turnstile was rotated, and the bundle removed by nuns on the inner side of the wall out of sight. This unbearably poignant act was the sole means of escape for a woman who had sinned against the Roman Catholic church and who could not bear to take the consequences.

Did I say not a trace of sentimentality? Perhaps there was one small sign. She hung round her baby's neck a piece of string with half a coin attached. Two years later a married couple turned up at the hospital bearing the other half, which Giuseppina had passed to them, along with a sum of money.

Giuseppa thus had a home. But, as with her son, Giuseppina never saw her daughter again, or made any further attempt to contact her. We know nothing more of these two illegitimate children, other than the fact that Giuseppa lived to the age of eighty-six, dying in a mental hospital in 1925. You have to wonder if she ever knew the place her mother

held in musical history, due to the unique role she would play in the life
of Italy's greatest composer.

Exactly when Verdi first set eyes on La Strepponcina, as she was dubbed,
is not known. Nor do we know for certain when she first saw him. But
the mutual attraction was immediate.

Verdi was turning heads, and not just for his musical prowess. Several accounts describe him as immensely attractive, a blaze of creativity
in his eyes, his restless energy driven by unstoppable ambition. He
was married, which in the intense and emotional world of the theatre
might have been a challenge in itself, the more so since his wife was

cloistered at home caring for their son, who was less than a year old. The knowledge that Verdi was grieving for his daughter was likely to elicit emotional comfort from others.

As for Giuseppina, a portrait painted just a few years later shows a true beauty. A perfectly formed oval face, large eyes that were deeply dark and expressive, full lips, a long white neck and gently sloping shoulders. She was every inch the romantic heroine. Even allowing for flattery on the part of the artist, it is easy to sense her magnetism on stage and her allure off it.

It was inevitable, given the circles in which they moved, that Giuseppe and Giuseppina would meet, and perhaps inevitable too that a flame would spark. The creative artist and the interpreter, a shared passion for music and the opera; one, at twenty-three years of age, lauded in opera houses across the land, the other, three years older, on the brink of fame. They even shared a name!

At least Verdi himself was in no doubt he was on the brink of fame, and it seems Giuseppina was of the same view. She had heard talk of his compositions from fellow singers. She might even have tried them out herself. We know she was impressed because it was she who went to the all-powerful Bartolomeo Merelli and urged him to look again at Verdi's work, in particular his full-length opera *Oberto*. We can be certain, too, that she proposed Merelli award her the lead female role of Leonora, should he decide to put the opera into production.

Fate now intervened to give the young composer his first chance to make a real name for himself. The season at La Scala was going badly – for Merelli very badly indeed. Several singers had fallen ill. One had throat trouble; another's voice failed in mid-performance.

Merelli was having to cancel performances, reschedule others. Soon, the wealthy patrons of Milan began leaving the city for their summer residences. The season was turning into a financial disaster for Merelli. He needed something new, and something good, for the autumn.

There was an obvious solution, and it was Giuseppina who reminded him of it. Verdi's opera *Oberto*. Why was she able to persuade him to look again at *Oberto* without any apparent difficulty? Merelli was among Giuseppina's conquests. For a time she was his mistress; if that role had diminished in importance by this point, the relationship certainly had not ended. In fact it was rumoured in operatic circles that Merelli was the father of at least one of her illegitimate children.

Merelli did as Giuseppina asked, and we can imagine a certain sense of relief on his part at the discovery that the opera, as it stood, had merit.

In fact, with an alteration here and an amendment there, it might even be stageable.

Verdi, with his heightened sense of the dramatic, recounted to his French biographer Pougin more than forty years later how, as he was about to give up on Milan and return with his wife to Busseto, dejected, disappointed, disillusioned, he received a summons to La Scala, where the most powerful impresario in Italian opera awaited him.

> He told me in no uncertain terms that . . . he wanted to produce [Oberto] during the next season. If I accepted his offer, I would have to make some changes in the [vocal ranges] because he no longer would have all four of the same artists that he had had earlier.
>
> It was a good offer. Young, unknown, I happened to meet an impresario who dared to put a new work on stage without asking me for any kind of underwriting, which in any case I could not have given him. Merelli . . . offered to divide any receipts with me half and half, if he could sell the opera. Nor should I be under any illusion that this was a bad deal: it was for an opera by a beginner![11]

It most certainly was not a bad deal. In fact for Verdi it was to prove life transforming, and in more ways than one. A guarantee to stage his first completed opera on the most prestigious stage in Europe, half of any profits guaranteed. Verdi knew how fortunate he was. In collaboration with the librettist Temistocle Solera he set about making the changes Merelli wanted. Notoriously reluctant in later life to change what he had written, Verdi was aware that with Merelli's vast experience he should listen to his advice and learn from it.

Things did not, however, progress entirely smoothly. I said that earlier in the season several singers had suffered indispositions. One of them was none other than Giuseppina Strepponi herself. Two pregnancies in swift succession had taken their toll. Merelli had given her the role of Leonora and rehearsals were not going well. It must have been devastating for her to admit it to herself, but her voice was losing its lustre.

When an offer of less demanding work in Venice and Lucca came along, Giuseppina took it. La Scala was now too big a stage for her. She was forced to pull out of *Oberto*, and left Milan. Matters came to a head in Lucca: on the orders of five doctors, she took two months off.

What was actually going on in the celebrated soprano's life? In her revelatory biography of Giuseppina Strepponi, Gaia Servadio writes that the evidence points to Giuseppina suffering a miscarriage or abortion at about this time (after two full-term pregnancies so close together) – an abortion being more likely, since she would not perhaps have tolerated the prospect of yet another pregnancy. The doctors, Servadio believes, were bribed.

Servadio goes further. Given the complicated emotions that would afflict both Verdi and Giuseppina in later life over children in the extended Verdi family, coupled with the exhaustive lengths they went to to deceive others about their early relationship, she argues that 'it would be tempting to think that this pregnancy was due to Verdi'. She acknowledges, though, that we cannot even be fully certain that Giuseppina *was* pregnant. It is just that if she were, all speculation would fit.[12] It is a tempting, though unproven, hypothesis.

Given what was about to happen in Verdi's life, Giuseppina – whatever level their relationship might have reached – had reason to be grateful she was many miles absent from the young man who had captivated her.

Verdi, with the biggest challenge of his nascent career ahead of him, was about to be plunged to the depths of despair, yet again. His infant son, Icilio Romano, came down with a disease that even the doctors of Milan were unable to diagnose. For three weeks he lingered between life and death. On 22 October Icilio died, most probably of bronchial pneumonia. He was just fifteen months old.

Giuseppe Verdi and his wife Margherita had lost both their children in the space of fourteen months. Neither child had seen its second birthday.

Verdi was at least able to lose himself in his work. Margherita, away from her family, away from Busseto, simply shut herself indoors to grieve.

After a short and intensive period of rehearsal, *Oberto, Conte di San Bonifacio*, Verdi's first full-length opera, was premiered at La Scala on 17 November 1839, less than a month after Icilio's death. Margherita did not attend the most important night of her husband's career to date. It was not the moment to dress up in finery and feign enjoyment.

Verdi told later biographers that, between Act One and Act Two, he ran all the way from La Scala to their apartment to hug Ghita and tell her all was going well. Even given his predilection for the dramatic, one can easily imagine this most passionate of men doing that.

And in fact all really was going well. The audience thoroughly enjoyed the opening night of *Oberto*, a convoluted tale of love and betrayal among the aristocracy in medieval Italy. Verdi was called from the orchestra pit – the traditional place for the composer – several times during the performance to take applause, culminating in a triumphant curtain call at the close.

Oberto ran for fourteen performances – a good showing, and much to Merelli's relief. On the morning after the premiere he offered Verdi a

"*Verdi, with the biggest challenge of his nascent career ahead of him, was about to be plunged to the depths of despair, yet again.*"

contract for three further operas to be written at eight-month intervals. These would be performed either in Milan or Vienna – Merelli was of course operatic impresario in both cities.

Giuseppe Verdi had arrived on the world stage. He was no longer the provincial peasant, struggling to be accepted in the big city.

On the evening of 26 November, his father-in-law, Giovanni Barezzi, and his closest friend as a teenager, Giuseppe Demaldè, as well as other supporters from the Busseto Philharmonic Society, were in the La Scala audience for *Oberto*.

It must have been a joyous evening for them, to see 'their boy' up there on the stage of Europe's most prestigious opera house, and indeed it must have been a moment of unimaginable pride for the composer himself.

Not that you would believe it from his description of events more than thirty years later:

> *It won a success which, if not very notable, was at least great enough to warrant a certain number of performances, which Merelli thought he might increase by giving a few beyond those which had been subscribed.*[13]

A touch of false modesty, perhaps, from a composer who by then was world famous.

To his friends and colleagues it might have seemed that Giuseppe Verdi was assured of future fame and fortune – a success at La Scala, a contract for three further operas in his pocket – but that was not how it seemed to the composer himself.

Surprisingly, perhaps, he was seriously short of money. The cost of living, in particular for accommodation, was expensive in Milan. For that reason the apartment Verdi rented was unfurnished, the furniture having been brought from Busseto. Verdi had borrowed the money for a down-payment on the apartment from his father-in-law. In order to keep up with the rent, he needed to borrow again. This time he appealed to Merelli, against future payment. Merelli refused.

Verdi was thrown into despair. His first opera was being performed at La Scala, yet he had to suffer the humiliation of being unable to enjoy the lifestyle this should have allowed him, with requests for a loan turned down by the man who was effectively in charge of his career.

We know Verdi was deeply hurt because he told a biographer many years later that his wife saw his distress, and without telling him went out and pawned a 'few gold things of her own'.[14] He was deeply touched by this 'loving act', adding that he was quickly able to fulfil his promise to repay her.

Putting money troubles aside, he had work to do. Merelli handed him a libretto for the first of the three operas he was now contracted to write, a turgid melodrama with the title *Il proscritto* ('The Outcast').

Verdi set to work and found, somewhat bafflingly, that inspiration would not come. Perhaps not so bafflingly to us. He was grieving for the loss of his second child; his wife was cloistered in their apartment, deep in grief. The resolution of his financial problems depended on successful composition. He was a twenty-six-year-old man under intense pressure, on both a professional and an emotional level.

Was Giuseppina Strepponi also encroaching on his thought processes? Whatever level their relationship might or might not have reached, we can be certain that an emotional bond had formed between them.

She, so highly experienced, could have taught him a lot about stagecraft, about singers' needs, what they wanted from a composer, what they did not want. He for his part must have inspired her with his unquenchable ambition. On one of her absences from Milan she had sent him a small intimate portrait of herself. Was he careful to secrete it away from Margherita?

His creative juices temporarily stilled, Verdi was unexpectedly rescued by Merelli himself. The impresario found that he was missing an *opera buffa* for the coming season. He needed a piece of work that would make the audience laugh, some levity amid all the exaggerated melodrama of opera.

He handed Verdi a number of comic librettos, and told him to choose for himself which one to set. It was a remarkable act of confidence in the young composer, who had never tried his hand at comedy. Perhaps in an act of self-defence, a guard against possible failure, but more likely an early sign of the undoubted arrogance he would display in later years, Verdi declared them all worthless. Merelli, no doubt with a dismissive wave of the hand, told him to choose one, and get on with it.

Forty years later Verdi told his French biographer he had chosen the 'least bad'.[15] Given a new title, *Un giorno di regno* ('King for a Day') was an absurd tale of exchanged identities and thwarted love.

Verdi set to work in late May 1840, and once again struggled. This time he suffered physically as well. He developed a severe throat infection, giving him pulsating headaches and threatening to go down into his lungs, affecting his breathing. This was probably a psychosomatic

"Verdi had arrived on the world stage. He was no longer the provincial peasant, struggling to be accepted in the big city."

reaction to stress, something he would exhibit throughout his life at the beginning of the compositional process.

The opening night of the new opera was scheduled for 5 September on the stage of La Scala. To say time was short is an understatement. Three months to compose a full-length opera, rehearse the singers, make adjustments, rewrite here, cut or add there. All less than a year after the loss of his second child.

And it was a comedy! Anything less suitable for Verdi, given the circumstances of his life, it would be hard to imagine. What he could not know was that those circumstances were about to become much worse.

5

ANOTHER LOSS
AND A FIASCO

*I*n June 1840 Verdi's wife Margherita – his adored Ghita –
fell suddenly and seriously ill, so seriously that doctors could
do nothing to help her and warned Verdi she might die. He sent word
to his father-in-law in Busseto to come to Milan immediately.

Antonio Barezzi arrived in time to hold his daughter in his arms as
she died. Emotions still raw the following year, he wrote a harrowing
account in his diary:

> *Through a dreadful disease, perhaps unknown to the doctors, there
> died in my arms in Milan at noon on the day of Corpus Domini,
> my beloved daughter Margherita in the flower of her years and at the
> culmination of her good fortune, because [she was] married to the
> excellent young man Giuseppe Verdi, Maestro di Musica. I beg for
> peace for her pure soul, even as I weep over this tragic loss.*[16]

Margherita's fatal illness has been described variously as encephalitis
or rheumatic fever. It is impossible to know nearly two centuries later
exactly what the disease was or how she contracted it. We can be certain
only that it took her life with relentless speed.

As further evidence of the unquenchable admiration Barezzi had for
Verdi, even in writing about the tragedy of Ghita's death he finds words
to praise his son-in-law.

To summarise, then, the grim roll call of tragedy that had been inflicted on the young composer. As he approached his twenty-seventh birthday, Verdi had lost his two infant children and then his wife. From husband and father to childless widower in the blisteringly short period of one year and ten months.

Before I detail the devastating effect of all this on the young man, I want to pause to recount Verdi's own timetable of these multiple tragedies. It might seem somewhat heartless to challenge him regarding his memory of such awful events, but it is further evidence of the extraordinary lengths he went to in order to heighten the drama of his early life, and in so doing to wilfully, if mischievously, mislead future biographers. My brief, after all, is to reveal the man.*

His biographer Pougin (whose book was published in 1879 – nearly forty years after the events) quotes Verdi as telling him, 'A third coffin goes out of my house. I was alone . . . alone . . . In the short space of two months three persons dear to me had gone for ever; my family was destroyed.'

Two months? It seems Verdi was in no doubt, and had been in no doubt for some time. When the same account had appeared in a magazine interview ten years earlier, Verdi confirmed it was true: 'That's the true story of my life, absolutely and completely true.'[17]

Verdi had conflated the tragic events of twenty-two months into just two. Could he have been genuinely mistaken about the dates on which he had lost those dearest to him? Impossible, in my view. Could the writer have mistakenly omitted the word 'twenty'? Possible, but the same mistake in two accounts? And Verdi's assertion that it really did all happen within two months suggests he was challenged about it. The official Registers of Deaths give the actual dates spanning twenty-two months. But he is adamant.

If it was a wilful compression of the facts, why did Verdi do it? To make an already shocking story even more so. It was in the nature of the man. He was a dramatist. As his biographer Julian Budden puts it, '[It was] a fine feat of telescopic memory.'[18]

What we need be in no doubt about is the effect these multiple losses had on Verdi at the time. His boyhood friend Demaldè described him as sinking into so deep a depression that he gave up everything 'completely and for ever'. This included music. 'He thought of nothing but hiding himself in some dark place and living out his miserable existence.'[19]

---

* See Afterword, page 255.

Verdi meant it. He had had enough. It was as if the fates were conspiring against him, determined to thwart him in every area of his life. His personal life was in ruins. Not just one death, or even two, but three, with the loss of his wife meaning he could not even contemplate having more children.

And in his chosen profession of music? His first opera performed to a modicum of success – tantamount to failure in his eyes – and inspiration waning even before the latest loss. And he was supposed to be writing a comedy?

We can easily understand why he wanted to get out of Milan, leave the city far behind and return to his roots, back to the countryside of the Po valley where he felt truly at home (even if he had been less than complimentary about it in the past). Maybe now was the moment for a complete change of direction, to pursue the only other path that truly appealed to him. Farming and agriculture. Verdi the farmer, not the musician.

It would be a recurrent theme throughout his life. When music failed to give him the satisfaction he desired, or when others failed to accord it the esteem he felt it deserved, his thoughts would turn to his next love, agriculture.

Leave Milan is exactly what he now did. Significantly he did not return to Le Roncole, but to Busseto and the sanctuary of Barezzi's house. His relationship with both his parents was now distant. It was as if he had outgrown them, moved beyond the small world in which they existed.

In Busseto, by contrast, he knew he would be among like-minded people. He could converse on a more elevated level. He knew too that he would be cared for and protected, both emotionally and financially, even if there was the pain of all the memories of Ghita in the house where he had first met her and where they had lived together as man and wife.

Verdi's mental condition deteriorated, to the extent there was speculation that he was losing his sanity. No doubt to the anguish of his father-in-law, who had such faith in him as a musician, Verdi sent off an angry letter to Merelli telling him he was abandoning the opera he was supposed to be working on, and had no intention of returning to Milan.

One can only imagine the effect this had on the impresario, after all the problems he had had with singers and illness, postponements and cancellations. Now the young composer who was showing promise, in whom he had put his faith, had decided to throw it all in.

He knew, of course, the dreadful emotional pressure Verdi was under, and he must have weighed this up very carefully before deciding on his next course of action. It was in his own interests to play a strong hand, remind Verdi he was under contract to complete *Un giorno di regno*, and hold him to it. But that could deliver the *coup de grâce* to Verdi's mental fragility, and even if he did force Verdi to complete the opera, who could tell whether it would result in anything worthwhile?

But ultimately Merelli had no other option. Rehearsals were due to start in August, just weeks away, with the premiere on 5 September. The season was set. It was too late to cancel. He told Verdi in no uncertain terms he was contracted to complete the opera, and he intended to hold him to it.

I imagine Barezzi's encouragement ringing in his ears as the young composer set out once again for the city in which he had experienced so much personal tragedy. Back once more to the small apartment he had shared with his wife and infant son, and all the familiar furniture they had brought with them from Busseto. Alone now in the apartment in which Ghita and Icilio had died.

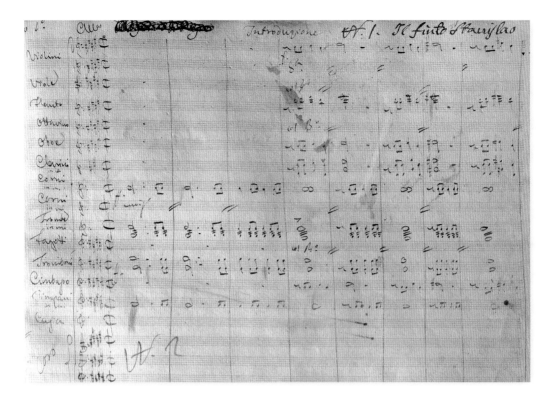

He also had with him a small box containing Margherita's locket, her wedding ring and a strand of her hair, which he kept with him for the rest of his life.

Under excruciatingly awful circumstances, Verdi set to work once more on *Un giorno*. As he completed each section, he supervised rehearsals. Tired, his emotions on a knife edge, just when he needed cooperation and enthusiasm from his singers, he did not receive it.

Two members of the cast, the lead tenor and soprano, both of whom had sung in *Oberto* the year before, made it clear that they were not happy. The soprano, in fact, told Merelli she wanted to pull out of the production altogether, requiring him to put out a statement saying she was recovering from an unspecified illness.

Given the fraught circumstances, it is a significant feat of musicianship that Verdi completed the full-length opera in time for the scheduled premiere of 5 September 1840.

It would be heart-warming to report that, on opening night on Europe's most prestigious operatic stage, singers and musicians rose to the occasion and gave Verdi the success he deserved, thus lifting him from the depths of personal despair and establishing him as the most talented young composer of opera in Italy.

The exact opposite happened. Extraordinary as it is to report, both lead singers at times did not even sing their arias, instead mouthing the words – to 'spare their voices', as one critic noted. Some of the arias were greeted with catcalls and whistles. Verdi, sitting with the orchestral players as was customary, heard it all.

The critics were merciless. 'A real mess', said the review in *La fama*. Others bemoaned the lack of humour and sparkle – a comic opera without comedy. Two critics mentioned the tragic personal circumstances under which Verdi had composed the opera, but compassion was not enough to save it.

Merelli had not just a flop on his hands, but a *fiasco*, in the full brutal sense of the Italian word. One can only imagine what was going through his mind when he made the decision to cancel the production *immediately*, after just a single performance. It simply cannot get worse than that for a composer, or indeed an impresario – except that an impresario can blame the composer; the composer cannot blame the impresario.

What, then, must have been going through Verdi's mind as he returned to his empty apartment after that one performance? If he was resolved before returning to Milan to give up composing, how much more determined must he have been that night to throw it all in and become a farmer?

The following day he was summoned to Merelli's office, fully expecting to be sped on his way to a life in agriculture. If that was not to happen, he would take matters into his own hand. He would ask for his contract to be cancelled, so that he could leave Milan. This is what he told Demaldè, who duly reported it in his memoirs.

But that is not quite the way things happened. Merelli had a problem. He had no choice but to cancel *Un giorno*, but he needed to put something in its place. It so happened that the scenery for *Oberto* was still in the warehouse, and many of the singers were still familiar with it.

He told Verdi he would re-stage *Oberto*, opening on 17 October, and he wanted Verdi to oversee it. Just as importantly – and posterity owes Merelli a debt for this – rather than attacking Verdi, criticising him, blaming him, he actually set about encouraging him, telling him not to let himself be defeated by one unhappy experience.

Verdi's suitably dramatic account of what transpired at the meeting, related to Pougin many years later, has him demanding that Merelli return his contract, with the impresario replying, 'Listen, Verdi, I cannot force you to compose! But my faith in you remains unshaken. Who knows whether you may or may not decide some day to begin to write again? Just let me know two months before a season, and I promise you that your opera will be given.'[20]

We can forgive Verdi if there is an element of exaggeration in his account. He was looking back on what he knew by then was a true turning point. The life of a farmer, at least for now, would have to be put on hold.

Verdi threw himself into overseeing a revival of his first opera. *Oberto* opened once again, on schedule, and the same audience that had booed and whistled *Un giorno* now applauded *Oberto*. The opera ran for a creditable seventeen performances.

I said this was a turning point for Verdi, but he – and we – know that only with the benefit of hindsight. His resolve to give up music was not entirely sublimated by the success of *Oberto*.

He was still reluctant to pick up his pen again. But what is of supreme importance – again evident only with hindsight – is that Verdi had learned lessons, lessons that could not have been learned in any other way than through the experience of total failure.

He acknowledged this nearly twenty years later in letters to close friends, one a publisher, the other a critic. Of course he is writing as a famous and successful composer, and the urge to dramatise is as irresistible as ever. There is also a large degree of self-pity. Nevertheless, the sheer rawness of what happened that night still consumes him.

> *[The audience] abused the opera of a poor, sick young man, harassed by the pressure of the schedule, and heartsick and torn by a horrible misfortune! Oh, if only the audience had – I do not say applauded, but had borne that opera in silence, I would not have had words enough to thank them.[21]*

But he gives back as good as he has received. What is particularly interesting about this next passage is the low esteem in which he holds his own profession, even when he is at the height of it.

> *I accept the whistles [of the audience], on the condition that I am not asked to give back anything in exchange for its applause. We poor gypsies, charlatans, and whatever-you-want-to-call-us, are forced to sell our efforts, our ideas, our ravings, [getting paid in] gold. For 3 lire the audience buys the right to whistle or applaud us. Our destiny is to resign ourselves to the situation. That is the whole story.[22]*

"The audience buys the right to whistle or applaud us. Our destiny is to resign ourselves to the situation."

Verdi

He goes on to say that the dreadful experience of that night taught him how to treat success or failure in the future:

> At twenty-five [sic] I already knew what 'the public' meant. From then on, successes have never made the blood rush to my head, and fiascos have never discouraged me. If I went on with this unfortunate career, it was because at twenty-five, it was too late for me to do anything else, and because I was not physically strong enough to go back to my fields.[23]

He might not always have put his own wise words into practice in later years, but these excerpts from his letters suggest he had recognised the all-important qualities necessary for the successful pursuit of a career as opera composer.

He had learned something else too from the fiasco of *Un giorno*. Comic opera was not for him. Comedy was not his *forte*. Drama: that was what came naturally, whether he was composing opera, describing his life, or writing letters.

It was a lesson well learned. It would be fifty-two years before he would compose a second comic opera.

6

'LITTLE BY LITTLE THE OPERA WAS COMPOSED'

What **happened next** in the life of the young composer is enshrined in legend – several legends, in fact. There are four different accounts of how he came to write the opera that changed his life – all originated from Verdi himself, three of them related at different times and to different friends and colleagues, who then wrote their own version of what he had said. They are all dramatic to a greater or lesser degree; Verdi's own account, unsurprisingly, is the most dramatic of them all.

His version comes, once again, in conversation with his French biographer Pougin many years after the event. With all the necessary cautions previously expressed – his predilection for exaggeration, a desire to enhance the drama, genuine mistakes of memory, or dubious details so enticing he has come to believe them himself – it is worth giving Verdi's account at length. It reveals as much about the man as it does the creation of his new opera.

The rerun of *Oberto* had done little to lift his spirits. Merelli told him that seventeen performances was a good run. Verdi quoted back at him a newspaper review that said the music, especially in the first act, seemed less thrilling this year than it was the year before.

He could not shake the depression that hung over him. He was still contemplating abandoning a musical career altogether. He remained under contract to Merelli but was earning nothing and was continually short of money.

He decided to move out of the apartment he had shared with his wife and son, and rented a single furnished room. He shipped all his furniture back to Busseto. He stayed in the darkened room for most of the day reading cheap novels. He saw practically no one. Verdi was consciously distancing himself from music and its world.

And then, as heavy snowflakes fell one winter evening in 1840, just a couple of months or so after the failure of *Il giorno*, Verdi was walking through the *galleria* that ran from La Scala down towards the cathedral, when who should he bump into but the impresario Merelli himself, walking from his home to the theatre.

Merelli took young Verdi by the arm and suggested he come with him to his office at La Scala. Verdi had nothing better to do, so allowed himself to be persuaded. As the two walked along, Merelli bemoaned the fact that he was once again in deep trouble. He had given a new libretto by Solera to the composer Otto Nicolai, who had had the gall to profess himself dissatisfied with it.

'Imagine,' said Merelli, 'a libretto by Solera, stupendous, magnificent! Extraordinary! Effective dramatic situations! Grand beautiful lines! But that crank of a composer refuses even to look at it. He says it is an impossible libretto! I don't know where to look. I need to find him another one right away.'[24]

Giuseppe Verdi to the rescue, at least in his own version of what transpired. He reminded Merelli that he had given him a libretto to work on, as the third opera he was under contract to write. It was called *Il proscritto*. He told Merelli he had not written a note of it. Would he like it back? He could give it to Nicolai.

'Oh bravo! That is a stroke of good luck!' Verdi quoted Merelli as saying.

Once in his office, Merelli sent an underling off in search of a second copy of *Il proscritto*. At the same time he reached into a drawer and out came the libretto by Solera that Nicolai had rejected.

'See, here is Solera's libretto! Such a beautiful plot! Imagine turning it down!' And then, tossing it across the desk to Verdi, the crucial words: 'Take it. Read it.'

'What in the devil do you want me to do with it?' Verdi retorted. 'No! No! I have no desire to read librettos.'

'Well, it's not going to hurt you. Take it home, read it, then bring it back to me.'[25]

That is Verdi's account of the single most momentous conversation of his life. It would be unwise to dismiss it. It is Verdi dramatising a meeting that we can be certain took place. And it becomes much more credible if we see it from Merelli's point of view.

He was genuinely in trouble over the new opera, given Nicolai's rejection of it. Nicolai was a composer who had had no great success with his operas to date.* *Oberto* had shown Merelli what Verdi was capable of, and who had been librettist of that? The same Solera whose libretto Nicolai had dismissed. Verdi and Solera had worked well on *Oberto*. What if Merelli could persuade Verdi to have a look at this new libretto?

Verdi got up to leave and Merelli handed him a huge sheaf of papers, which Verdi rolled up. He left for the short walk home. Is it too fanciful to imagine Merelli punching the air in a small gesture of triumph, or allowing himself a smile of satisfaction that he had persuaded Verdi at least to take a look at Solera's libretto?

As he walked home through the snow, Verdi described how he felt 'a kind of indefinable, sick feeling, all over, an immense sadness, an agitation that made my heart swell!'[26] This is a prelude to the best-known part of this legendary tale, better known perhaps than any other single moment in the creative process in Verdi's long and productive life.

I shall let Verdi tell it himself, in words noted down by Pougin:

I went to my place and, with an almost violent gesture, I threw the manuscript on the table, and stood straight in front of it. The bundle of pages, falling on the table, opened by itself. Without knowing why, I stared at the page before me and saw the line 'Va, pensiero sull'ali dorate' ['Fly, thoughts, on golden wings']. I ran through the lines that followed and got a tremendous impression from them, all the more moving because they were almost a paraphrase of the Bible, which I always loved to read.

I read one section; I read another. Then, firm in my decision not to compose again, I forced myself to close the manuscript and go to bed. But YES! Nabucco was racing through my head! I could not sleep. I got up and read the libretto, not once, not twice, but three times, so that in the morning, you might say, I knew Solera's whole libretto from memory.[27]

Temistocle Solera.

* His best-known opera, *Die lustigen Weiber von Windsor* ('The Merry Wives of Windsor'), was still some years off.

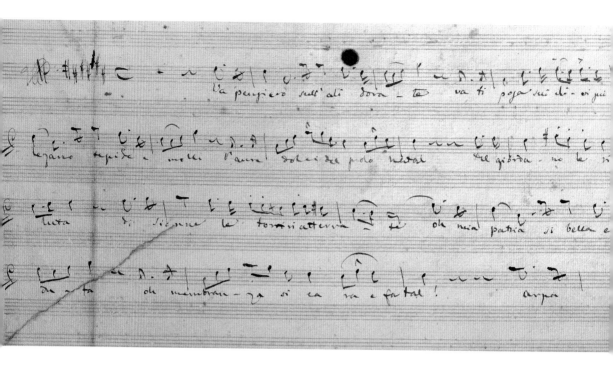

Above

Handwritten score of the beginning of the 'Chorus of the Hebrew Slaves'.

Credible? That he tossed the rolled-up pages onto the table and they fell open at the words that would become the most famous lines of music he would write in his entire career? A sleepless night, at the end of which he could recite practically the whole libretto?

In fact Verdi himself unwittingly casts doubt on his own version by telling a rather different story to another friend. According to that version, when he got home with the rolled-up libretto, he threw it in a corner, where it stayed untouched for a full five months, while he spent his time devouring trashy novels.

Only then did he begrudgingly pick it up, go to the piano, and set the scene in which the main female character dies. But it was enough:

The ice was broken. Like a man emerging from a dark, dank jail to breathe the pure country air, Verdi again found himself in the atmosphere he adored. Three months from then, Nabucco *was finished, composed, and exactly as it is today.*[28]

Well, not entirely. That scene was later dropped, and Verdi would be making changes right up to the first performance, and after.

But a legend is a legend, and no legend exists without some truth at the base of it. The story of the pages falling open at what became

'The Chorus of the Hebrew Slaves' has most certainly stuck. Go to any performance of *Nabucco* in any opera house in the world, and you will surely read it in the programme.

In fact Verdi's own account, as told to Pougin, does not end there. After the almost certainly inflated claim that by morning he knew Solera's whole libretto from memory, Verdi said he was still resolved not to compose again, and the next day duly returned to La Scala and gave the manuscript back to Merelli.

But Merelli was not taking no for an answer.

> *'Beautiful, eh?' [Merelli] said to me.*
> *'Very. Very beautiful.'*
> *'All right, then, set it to music!'*
> *'Not a chance! I would not even dream of it. I don't want any-thing to do with it.'*
> *'Set it to music! Set it to music!'*
> *And, saying this, Merelli took the libretto, stuck it in the pocket of my overcoat, took me by the shoulders, and, with a big shove, rushed me out of his office. – Not just that; he closed the door in my face and locked it!*
> *What was I to do?*
> *I went back home with* Nabucco *in my pocket. One day, one line; one day, another; now one note, then a phrase . . . little by little the opera was composed.*[29]

It is a beguiling account. The reluctant young composer, the former composer, resolved to compose no more, being forcibly talked into it by Europe's most powerful theatrical impresario. Perhaps he did protest too much. Perhaps he protested only a little.

It does not matter. The final sentences are without doubt entirely true. It was a slow process, but little by little Verdi composed his *Nabucco*.

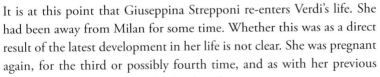

It is at this point that Giuseppina Strepponi re-enters Verdi's life. She had been away from Milan for some time. Whether this was as a direct result of the latest development in her life is not clear. She was pregnant again, for the third or possibly fourth time, and as with her previous pregnancies it was not entirely clear by whom.

Nor is it clear whether Verdi was aware of this. What is certain is that he wrote the part of the main female protagonist, Abigaille, with Giuseppina in mind. He wanted her in his opera, and he made this clear to Merelli. Merelli did not refuse him. La Strepponcina, even if her voice was not what it once was, remained box-office gold.

The opening night of *Nabucco* was scheduled for 9 March 1842. Just four months before this Giuseppina gave birth to a girl, who was baptised Adelina Rosa Maria Theresia Carolina. As with her previous children, Giuseppina gave her baby away, this time to a married couple who she paid to take the child, and she had no further contact with her. There is no evidence of how she reacted – if indeed she knew – when Adelina died of dysentery eleven months later.

Despite the fact that Giuseppina's voice had deteriorated significantly, Verdi was still determined she would sing the role of Abigaille. Before each full rehearsal, he rehearsed her separately at the piano. He had written an enormously complex part, with some death-defying leaps of two octaves in one of the arias.

Given what was at stake – a brand new opera by a young composer whose last effort had resulted in a fiasco, being staged at La Scala in front of the most discerning audience in Italy – it is hardly surprising that there was plenty of tension in the air.

Things did not go entirely smoothly even between Verdi and his librettist, though he was able to make light of it when recounting it years later to Pougin.

Solera had written a love duet in Act Three, which Verdi thought slowed the pace of the action too much. Instead he wanted the High Priest Zaccaria to prophesy that God would destroy Babylon. 'Here,' said Verdi, handing Solera a Bible, 'you already have the words. They are in here.'

The two men argued, then Verdi – as he recounted it – locked the door of his apartment, put the key in his pocket, and told Solera he was not leaving until he had written it. There was an 'ugly' moment, said Verdi, as he saw 'a fire of rage' burning in Solera's eyes, 'for the poet was a large man who could quickly have done away with that obstinate composer'.

But all ended well. 'After a moment [Solera] sat down at the writing table, and fifteen minutes later the Prophecy was written.'[30] To this day Zaccaria's Prophecy, following 'The Chorus of the Hebrew Slaves', remains one of the most dramatic passages in the entire opera.

Only twelve days were available for rehearsals before opening night on 9 March – far too few for such a complex production. As rehearsals progressed, problems multiplied without being solved.

The biggest concern was Giuseppina's voice. Verdi was by this point genuinely worried that it was in such a poor state that the whole opera might have to be postponed; it was too late for another singer to step in. Rumours began to fly. Verdi had not wanted her to sing in the first place, but Merelli insisted; Merelli had not wanted her to sing in the first place, but Verdi insisted. Blame for inevitable failure was already being apportioned, even before the opening night.

There was confusion over the entrance of the onstage band. Verdi seemed unable to convince its leader of the right cue. Costumes had been rather haphazardly made and were hardly likely to impress the audience. The stage scenery had been borrowed from a ballet production and hurriedly repainted.

Verdi himself was making changes right up to the dress rehearsal, and at the very last minute – after the dress rehearsal and before the first performance – composed an overture. One can imagine the orchestral players' consternation. For those of a superstitious disposition, perhaps the most worrying omen was that the dress rehearsal went superbly. Everything came together. Giuseppina proved she could still sing; even the band entered on cue. At the final curtain, stagehands roared their approval and beat the floor with their tools.

Everything was in place for a disastrous opening night. Verdi took his customary place in the orchestra, between cellos and harpsichord. He reported later that one of the cellists, anticipating success, leaned forward to him and said, '*Maestrino*, I wish I were in your place this evening.'

We have only Verdi's account of the first performance of *Nabucco*, as told to his publisher and friend Tito Ricordi many years later, quoted in Pougin. If there is any element of exaggeration in it, he can surely be forgiven.

The overture began with portentous chords, followed by a clashing of cymbals and runs on the strings, then the chords again, before a hushed passage full of tension, punctuated by *fortissimo* chords. Verdi then quotes 'The Chorus of the Hebrew Slaves', before any other tune from the opera. He knows what he has created. This was music on an altogether different level – not just from anything Verdi had composed but from anything that had ever been heard at La Scala. And he had written the overture in an hour or so on the day of the first performance.

There was furious applause even as the curtain went up. It barely stopped. Each dramatic moment was greeted with applause and cheers. We have to smile as Verdi told Ricordi he was so nervous that when everyone stood up, shouting and screaming, at the end of Act One, he thought they were protesting: 'At first, I believed that they were making

"This was music on an altogether different level – not just from anything Verdi had composed but from anything that had ever been heard at La Scala."

fun of the poor composer, and that they were about to jump on me and do me harm.'[31]

I wonder if he genuinely thought that. I can see those twinkling eyes and turned-up lips as he played the poor put-upon composer.

The reviews were unanimous: 'noisy and enormously well received'; 'the universal agreement of the audience was beyond dispute'; 'a surprising effect that moves listeners and causes them to applaud and shout with enthusiasm'.[32]

Several critics reported that Verdi and the singers were called out onto the stage again and again. Verdi, sometimes alone, sometimes with singers, received 'loud, endless applause offered by an ecstatic audience'.

There was relief all round that Giuseppina's voice had held up to the end; the other singers rose to the occasion, and the orchestra was on top form. It was the success that had so far eluded Verdi, that had been so long in coming. From fiasco to triumph in a single night.

After the premiere Verdi walked home with the one man who had stood by him through thick and thin, professionally and in the darkest hours of his young life. Antonio Barezzi had been in the audience at La Scala when Verdi was booed off stage for *Un giorno*. He was there too for the triumph of *Nabucco*.

As they walked, Verdi confessed to his father-in-law he had not expected such a triumph, even though the dress rehearsal had shown him how good it could be. Barezzi must have smiled quietly to himself, his early judgement of Verdi's musical prowess thoroughly vindicated. It is conjecture, but surely Ghita's name must have passed the men's lips, and how she would have relished her husband's success.

Overnight Verdi was the toast of Milan. As Italian opera aficionados do, when they accept one of their own, they applauded and celebrated every aspect of the man:

> *The night [after the premiere] no one in Milan slept; the next day the masterpiece was the sole topic of conversation. Everyone was talking about Verdi; and even fashion and cuisine borrowed his name, making hats* alla Verdi, *shawls* alla Verdi, *and sauces* alla Verdi. *From every city in Italy impresarios hurried to beg the new* maestro *to write something just for them, and made him the biggest possible offers.*[33]

Nabucco ran for the scheduled eight performances, and then a further fifty-seven between August and September. That was a record for La Scala, unmatched by either Donizetti or Rossini.

G. VERDI
NABUCCO

Opera completa per Pianoforte

EDIZIONI RICORDI

(PRINTED IN ITALY)

Verdi was finally able to put his in-built scepticism, his natural cynicism, behind him. He told Ricordi years later he knew that night that his career as operatic composer was assured:

> *With this opera you can truly say that my artistic career began. And although I had to fight against many obstacles, it is certain all the same that* Nabucco *was born under a lucky star, so lucky that even all the things that could have gone wrong [did not do so, but] helped to make it a success.*[34]

Verdi the operatic composer was on his way, but what of Verdi the man? *Nabucco,* and indeed what came before, changed Verdi both professionally and personally. Giuseppina gives a fascinating insight into the sort of man the young composer was now.

During those fraught rehearsals leading up to opening night, with Giuseppina struggling to master the role of Abigaille, she described Verdi as cold, deeply mistrustful of men and God, a man who seemed to have turned into stone.

That is understandable, given the tension he was under. But it is also easy to see how his experiences, at home and at work, had changed him for ever. He had lost his wife and two infant children; he had composed two operas, one achieving a modicum of success, the other an outright disaster. He felt he had been manipulated by the musical world – impresarios and singers – ignored by God, used by anyone who thought he could be useful to them.

That had now changed. This was a new Verdi. This was a Verdi who knew his own mind, who knew what he wanted. From now on nothing would stand between him and his aims. That would be the hallmark of the man Giuseppe Verdi had become.

7

THE GALLEY YEARS

No other opera by Verdi is so beset with legend as *Nabucco*. It is easy to understand why. Verdi was little known before that fateful opening night. None of his acquaintances were reminiscing about him at this stage; that came later. Had *Nabucco* failed, and Verdi carried out his threat to give up composing, we would be hard pushed to establish more than a few concrete facts about his early life and works.

We know relatively little about the compositional process of the opera itself, and what we do know comes from Verdi himself many decades later. It was therefore inevitable, given what a turning point it represented for the composer, that the story of *Nabucco*'s origins would become ever more embellished.

The most potent of these, and one that persists to this day, is the place *Nabucco* holds – and the fundamental role it played – in the struggle for Italian independence. There is some truth in the legend, but it is both overstated and chronologically incorrect.

Put simply, the plot of *Nabucco* – the yearning of the Israelites held captive in Babylon for their native land – could be seen with very little stretch of the imagination to represent the longing of Italians to be free of Austrian domination. In writing *Nabucco*, Verdi gave voice to an oppressed people (two oppressed peoples, one biblical, one very contemporary), and in so doing became the figurehead of Italy's struggle for independence.

In particular it was 'The Chorus of the Hebrew Slaves' – those words at which the libretto fell open so fortuitously when Verdi threw the pages down on the kitchen table – that symbolised the struggle.

Legend has it that on the opening-night the audience, immediately recognising the import of that chorus and the direct relevance of the words to their own situation, stood as it was sung, and immediately demanded an encore.

This is not true, but it was to become true at later performances. At the time Verdi was writing *Nabucco*, there was no such country as Italy. It was a hodgepodge of kingdoms, duchies and states, ruled first by the French, and then after the Congress of Vienna by Austria.[*] Discontent there certainly was. Milan was in effect an Austrian city, with the authorities imposing absolute rule from the Habsburg capital of Vienna. The emperor was a supreme monarch, appointed by God. But a coherent campaign for Italian independence was still twenty years in the future.

We have to add to this the fact that Verdi himself did not select the plot of *Nabucco*; it was chosen for him. Once the fight for independence had been won, it was very easy to look back and see the opera as crystallising the desire for Italian independence, but this was not at the forefront of Verdi's mind while he was working on it – not least because the man himself was hardly the political firebrand he was later made out to be.

Giuseppe Verdi was most certainly a patriot. He had believed in Italian independence from a young age, even if it was no more than an idealised vision of a barely attainable future. I have described how he and his wife deliberately eschewed Habsburg influences in their early years in Milan. They wore Italian fashion. Verdi, as soon as he was mature enough to do so, grew a full beard.

Officially such beards were frowned upon (there were even attempts to ban them) and the Habsburg authorities instructed men to grow elaborate moustaches and military whiskers, in keeping with the Habsburg style that was prevalent in Vienna, despite being an impossible order to enforce. Verdi kept a full beard all his life, but certainly in these early years that was as far as his anti-Habsburg protests went.

---

[*] We have seen how, technically, Verdi was born a Frenchman.

That said, I do not want to underestimate the impact of 'Va, pensiero'. It is a remarkable piece of writing. The melody is disarmingly simple and for the most part it is sung in unison, which gives great power and emotion to the words of longing expressed by the Israelites. It is also not an exaggeration to say that for the first time in any opera the chorus plays as important a role as any of the lead singers.

No less a figure than Rossini (who correctly predicted that Verdi would soon equal, and then eclipse, him) described 'Va, pensiero' as not so much a chorus, more an aria for sopranos, altos, tenors and basses. Perhaps the boldest stroke of originality is that it ends quietly, with a long note fading away. No wonder that, in later years, the Habsburg authorities had such trouble banning it; it is hardly a rousing call to arms.

I described at the end of the last chapter how Verdi was now a changed man, a man who 'seemed to have turned into stone', in Giuseppina's memorable words, following the deaths of his wife and children, and the fiasco of *Un giorno*. He was in fact changing in more ways than he could have imagined.

The success of *Nabucco* opened doors for Verdi. Suddenly he found he had friends everywhere: 'They needed to tell him how they had always loved him. They all wanted to press his hand, to walk arm in arm with him, to address him as *Tu*.'[35]

The nineteenth-century Viennese fashion for salon culture had spread south to Milan, but whereas in Vienna this had largely been musical (the likes of Mozart and Beethoven owed their careers to successful salon matinées and soirées), in Milan there was a political edge. Aristocratic salons were the meeting places of intellectuals – poets, playwrights, authors, thinkers, artists, musicians – and the talk over card games and billiards was of a united Italy, free of Austrian domination.

The most prestigious of these salons was held in the home of Countess Clara Maffei. The countess was herself a radical thinker – more so than her more conservative husband – and she encouraged free-thinking intellectuals of the day to gather in her salon.

Before *Nabucco* Verdi could not have hoped for entry into Countess Maffei's salon. After it, the countess was in open competition with other aristocrats to secure Verdi as a regular visitor. Here, Verdi found himself lauded, his head filled with revolutionary ideals.

Most evenings after a day's work, he would call in at the Maffei salon, though it is interesting that the only documented comment about this period is how it was noted that Verdi would fight hard to win at

"The success of Nabucco opened doors for Verdi. Suddenly he found he had friends everywhere."

cards, and argue over disputed points. Verdi the political revolutionary was still some way off.

It is at about this time that Verdi's relationship with Giuseppina Strepponi developed further. We cannot be entirely sure when. Given the extraordinary lengths both went to in later years to discourage or actively mislead biographers, and even friends, we will probably never be able to state with absolute certainty when they began to live together.

The success of *Nabucco* undoubtedly went a considerable way to cementing their relationship. Verdi, as we have seen, was deeply worried about Giuseppina's ability to carry off the role of Abigaille. In fact she not only did so, but did so with considerable aplomb.

Her performances in the initial run earned positive reviews as much for her efforts as for the quality of her singing. One critic said she 'worked miracles', although her voice was weak and she was in need of a rest. She herself was under no illusion. 'I sang, or rather, I dragged myself to the end of the performances,' she wrote in a letter.

Giuseppina did not take part when the opera was revived later in the year. Verdi made substantial changes to accommodate the new soprano. He also cut the scene of Abigaille's death, the first part of the opera he wrote. It is this revised version of the opera that is performed to this day.

One might expect Giuseppina's professional problems – the fact that her singing voice was now in decline, which would inevitably lead to the end of her stage career – to spill over into her relationship with Verdi, and it is possible that to an extent they did. Mary Jane Phillips-Matz suggests that Verdi might have fallen in love at this stage with another patroness of the arts, Donna Emilia Morosini.

Several of his letters to Donna Emilia have survived, and the language is intense and intimate, in contrast to the words he uses to describe Giuseppina:

> *What is the lovable Peppina doing? and my dear Bigettina? A kiss to the second and nothing to the first. I have some important accounts to settle with Peppina. She won't get away from me.*

There is tantalisingly little information about Verdi's relationship with Donna Emilia, which, given what we know of Verdi's methods, should not surprise us. However deep, or brief, the relationship might have been, though, it was to Giuseppina that he turned when he wanted advice, on all matters from the artistic to the financial. If there is a hint

in those letters that the relationship might not have been entirely plain sailing, certainly there was no major fracture, and it was to survive the many vicissitudes that lay ahead.

For the immediate future, Verdi had work to do. From struggling to persuade Merelli to stage his operas, suddenly he could hardly keep up with demand. As early as the day of the third performance of *Nabucco*, Merelli summoned Verdi to his office and told him he was commissioning him to write a new opera as the centrepiece of the next season at La Scala. The terms? 'Here is a blank contract. After a success like yours I cannot dictate conditions; it is up to you to set them. Fill out this contract; whatever you write in will be yours.'[36]

After just two performances of his third opera, Verdi had overtaken Italy's two greatest living operatic composers, Rossini and Donizetti, to become the most in-demand composer of opera in Italy.

Evidence, though, that he was still a provincial at heart, unused to negotiating at this exalted level, comes from his decision (as reported to Pougin) to consult Giuseppina over what to do. How much money should he demand?

Giuseppina's advice was not to undersell himself, but at the same time not to make too extravagant a demand. She suggested he should ask for the same amount Bellini had been paid for *Norma* more than a decade earlier, namely 8,000 Austrian lire (at the time the most ever paid for an opera). Verdi upped the figure slightly and wrote 9,000 lire* in the blank space.[37]

Verdi himself chose the subject: *I Lombardi alla prima crociata* ('The Lombards on the First Crusade'), a tale of jealousy and revenge, wrapped up in the First Crusade to liberate Jerusalem. The parallels with *Nabucco* are obvious. In the earlier opera the Israelites are being held captive in Babylon; in *I Lombardi* the Lombards intend to liberate Jerusalem from the infidels. Again Verdi gives a crucial role to the chorus; the almost hymn-like *'O signore, dal tetto natio'* ('O Lord, who in our native home') is clearly modelled on *'Va, pensiero'*.

In almost every respect Verdi is consciously setting out to repeat the successful formula of *Nabucco*. Once again he chose Solera to write the libretto, and once again, when he wasn't satisfied with a certain passage, he subjected the writer to the same disciplinary tactic he had used previously. Solera has left a captivating account of what a taskmaster Verdi had become:

> *'Here I need a warm phrase.' [Verdi told him.] 'You find it. Sit down and think and write. I'll run over to the theatre and come back later.' And he took his hat and left, turning the key in the lock from the outside. His idea of locking me in the room was a real fixation with him.*

But Solera now had the measure of Verdi. After jotting down half a line, and then another half, he got up and opened a cupboard. Half a dozen bottles of wine stood inside –

> *seeming to invite me to taste them. I took one and opened it. Getting back to work, I toasted every line I wrote, welcoming it with a good swig of wine.*[38]

---

*Other accounts give the sums as 10,000 lire, increased by Verdi to 12,000.

Solera recounts how Verdi, on returning, noticed how his eyes were shining brightly and put it down to inspiration rather than alcohol. Together the two of them completed the aria, where the dying crusader promises his lover they will be reunited in heaven – Verdi improvising the lines and 'gesturing like an actor in a cheap theatre'.

Even if we allow Solera a measure of poetic licence (would Verdi really not have noticed the open bottle of wine and its effect on his librettist?), the anecdote offers a fascinating insight into how Verdi worked, coming up with words as well as notes when the moment demanded and inspiration struck. Perhaps we should not be surprised that Solera, twice locked into a room by the impatient composer, gave Verdi the nickname 'The Tyrant' and would not collaborate with him again after *I Lombardi*.

The premiere of *I Lombardi* was set for 11 February 1843, a mere five months after the end of the phenomenally successful run of *Nabucco*. Verdi – as with *Nabucco*, and in a pattern repeated throughout his life – was tense, irritable, argumentative, his health teetering on the brink of serious illness during the compositional process.

But this, as I have intimated, was a different Verdi. He had the success of *Nabucco* behind him. He had lived through the inestimable sorrow of losing his wife and two infant children. He was now a 'man of stone'. He knew his art, and he alone knew it; no one else would be allowed to trespass on his territory.

That resolve was about to be tested. As was customary with every new public production, the Austrian censors – Austrian, not Italian, since northern Italy was governed from Vienna (in itself certain to offend Verdi) – demanded to see the libretto of *I Lombardi*. They rejected it on numerous grounds.

The senior censor, the Austrian Archbishop of Milan, objected to the staging of Christian processions, the depiction of crusaders, the scene showing the baptism of an infidel, and above all to the singing of an aria beginning with the sacred words 'Ave Maria'. All these were sacrilegious, and he wrote to the Milan chief of police ordering him to ban the opera. For good measure he wrote directly to the Emperor too, denouncing Merelli and La Scala for 'licentiousness' and 'failure to show respect for the faith'.

Verdi's opera, it seems, was doomed. But the Archbishop had reckoned without the single-minded and determined man that Verdi had become. The chief of police – Italian-born, but a protégé of Chancellor Metternich and an Austrian sympathiser to his fingertips – summoned Merelli, Verdi and Solera to his office. Verdi said no. He simply refused to go.

"Verdi knew his art, and he alone knew it; no one else would be allowed to trespass on his territory."

G. VERDI.

I Lombardi
ALLA PRIMA CROCIATA

OPERA COMPLETA

PER

Canto

E

Pianoforte

Edizioni Ricordi

A Edel

As he told Pougin many years later, 'My position is this: I will not change a word or a note. It will be performed as it is, or it will not be performed at all.'

So it was just Merelli and Solera who appeared before the chief of police. Merelli, clearly emboldened not only by Verdi's resolve but also by the anticipation of the opera-going public for the new opera by Verdi, decided attack was the best form of defence.

He dismissed the Archbishop's letter with a wave of the hand, then told the police chief the opera was beyond the point of no return. Rehearsals were almost over, the scenery painted, costumes ready. Cast and orchestra were united in their praise for the work, and the public had secured their tickets for what was certain to be a triumph. The composer, he said, refused to make any changes.

His final argument contained an implied threat. If the opera were to be cancelled, the police chief alone would bear full responsibility for the consequences.

Merelli and Solera must have been dumbfounded by the police chief's reaction. He listened, then stood, and stated clearly he would never be 'the one to clip the wings of this young man, who promises so much to the art of music. Go ahead. I will take responsibility for what happens.'

If Merelli's tactic had been to go on the attack, that of the police chief was to kill the impresario – and through him Verdi himself – with kindness. To save face, one minor change was asked for and agreed. Giselda's heartfelt prayer in Act One should begin with the words 'Salve Maria', rather than 'Ave Maria'. It was the smallest of concessions.

With the ever-present caveat that this is Verdi's own account related forty years after the event, and describing a meeting at which he was not present, the composer had, in effect, seen off the censor. It was not the last time he would have to do so in his long career, but it was a very useful lesson in what could be achieved by a firm stance. 'Intractability' is a trait that henceforth can be accurately applied to Giuseppe Verdi.

I Lombardi opened on schedule and was the triumph Merelli had predicted. An audience that wanted a *Nabucco* Mark Two got exactly what it desired, right down to an emotional and patriotic chorus.

The opera remained in the repertory for years, even decades. Verdi substantially reworked it to be performed in French in Paris (with the new title *Jérusalem*), and it was the first of his operas to be performed in the United States. And so Verdi himself might be surprised to find that it is rarely performed today. But even in his day critics were less enthusiastic than the opera-going public and have remained so, pointing out

Left

Cover of the sheet music of the opera *I Lombardi alla prima crociata*.

its inconsistencies, even banalities of plot, and some lacklustre musical writing amid very few striking moments. Comparisons with *Nabucco* might have served it well at its birth, but cause it to suffer now.

Not that that impinged on Verdi at the time. He basked in praise and glory. A poet[*] published a paean extolling *Nabucco* and *I Lombardi* as the two tiers of Verdi's 'double crown' that he would wear as he conquered the world.

> *Onward, O young man, on this difficult path. Fearless, you must dare to risk everything and hurry to climb the highest peak of fame, where immortality is found. Do not let unanimous acclaim make you proud. May you live in peace and happiness.*

If there had remained the smallest shred of doubt, there was none now. Verdi had proved himself not once but twice. The road ahead was clear. More operas. Many more operas. In under a decade, beginning with *Nabucco*, he would compose thirteen operas. That is an extraordinary rate of more than one opera a year. But it would not be easy. There would be failures as well as successes. His health would suffer, even to the extent that his life would be in danger.

Verdi, many decades later, would describe these as his 'galley years' (*anni di galera*). One might expect the ageing and famous composer to look back with pride on his early achievements and capacity for hard work. But by then cynicism had taken over. He had never really liked his profession – or, more accurately, the myriad personalities he had to deal with to see one of his creations come to life. Symphonies would have been so much easier than operas.

There would be personal problems too. He was not yet thirty years of age, but it seemed he had already endured a lifetime of trauma and tragedy. If he hoped that now, with two major successes behind him, life would become altogether more congenial, he was to be much mistaken.

---

[*] Count Ottavio Tasca.

'SIGNOR MAESTRO'

Despite his blaming all and sundry for the pressure they put him under during this period, Verdi's claims about 'galley years' were disingenuous. Certainly this was a composer producing at a prolific rate. Thirteen operas in under a decade; twenty--seven operas (not counting rewrites) in a lifetime. Yet not purely (as he later implied) because he was pushed by others to compose, but because he quite simply needed to compose, in the same way that he needed to breathe.

It is a phenomenal achievement. Twenty-seven operas in a composing career of a little over fifty years represents an average of just over one opera every two years, the majority of them firmly in the repertory and performed around the world to this day. I can think of no other operatic composer of true stature who can come close to equalling such a record. Certainly Verdi's rival Wagner, with his eleven (mature) operas – I shall examine the extent of their rivalry in a later chapter – is way behind, as is his successor Giacomo Puccini with thirteen.

The operas poured from Verdi's pen – *Ernani, I due Foscari, Giovanna d'Arco, Attila, Macbeth* – and he seemed to be constantly on the move between Milan, Venice, Rome and Naples, rehearsing one opera in one city, supervising performances of another work in another. Even for a young man it was to prove too much.

A vivid description of just how far he was pushing himself was given by a young musician who attended a rehearsal of *Giovanna d'Arco* in Milan:

> *It makes me very sad to see [Verdi] wearing himself out. He shouts as if in desperation. He stamps his foot so much that he seems to be playing an organ with pedals. He sweats so much that drops fall on the score.*[39]

The young man was Emanuele Muzio, who came to know Verdi by virtue of the fact that his own musical talents were nurtured by Antonio Barezzi, the same music patron who had done so much to encourage Verdi and had become his father-in-law.

The similarities do not end there. When Muzio made clear his intention to apply to study at the Milan Conservatory, Barezzi assured him that if he failed to gain entrance, funds would be raised to allow him to study privately.

Musical history repeated itself. Just as Verdi had been rejected by the Milan Conservatory, so was Muzio. Exactly how Muzio managed to acquire Verdi as a teacher is not known (almost certainly through the Barezzi connection) but it was a relationship made in heaven.

Muzio, eight years younger than Verdi, was the only pupil Verdi ever took on. Realising just what a great musician Verdi was, Muzio took it on himself to act in every respect as the composer's helper, soon proving himself indispensable.[*]

That the younger man was totally in awe of Verdi was soon apparent. To him Verdi was from the start, and would remain, the 'Signor Maestro'. One can imagine Verdi, at thirty-one years of age, swelling with pride every time he heard the words.

Muzio wrote to their mutual benefactor Barezzi that 'My Signor Maestro has a breadth of spirit, a generosity, a wisdom, a heart that (to draw a comparison) one would have to set beside yours and say that they are the most generous hearts in the whole world.'

In another letter to Barezzi, he is even more effusive, with an unfortunately accurate assessment of his own musical talents:

If you could see us, I seem more like a friend, rather than his pupil. We are always together at dinner, in the cafés, when we play cards (but just for one hour from twelve to one); all in all, he doesn't go anywhere without me at his side. In the house he has a big table and we both write there together, and so I always have his advice. As for myself, I will not be able to abandon him . . . If it were not for the Signor Maestro, what would I be? A poor devil who would not know how to do anything.

In that last self-deprecating sentence, Muzio showed he was under no illusions about his own abilities. He was to go on to write two operas,

---

[*] Julian Budden compares the relationship to that between Beethoven and Ferdinand Ries, a totally apt comparison.

both of which reached the stage but failed to remain there. One imagines just an hour in the company of Verdi was enough to convince Muzio that his future lay not as a composer of opera, but in the shadow of a truly great one.

Constantly in Verdi's company, Muzio would watch the 'Signor Maestro' at work, take mundane matters off his hands, run errands, do chores, whatever the great man needed to assist his creative process.

Even more to his credit, Muzio used what musical talents he had in the service of his master. He would later make piano reductions* of many of Verdi's operas, and conduct performances too, including premieres in the United States and elsewhere.

The relationship between the two men was to last, literally, a lifetime. So close was it that Verdi was to appoint Muzio as one of the executors of his will, and was devastated (as we shall see) when the younger man died before him.

At around this time another individual entered Verdi's life, and in a certain way the relationship mirrored that with Muzio, at least in so far as it was very much Verdi who was in control.

Francesco Maria Piave, a Venetian born and bred, was introduced to Verdi by one of the directors of Venice's opera house, La Fenice. Three years older than Verdi, he was something of a polymath. Journalist, translator, as well as resident poet and stage manager at La Fenice, he had also tried his hand at opera – albeit only once – with a libretto for the prolific operatic composer Giovanni Pacini.

Verdi, meanwhile, having dispensed with Solera (or maybe it was Solera, not wishing to be locked into a room for a third time, who dispensed with Verdi), was a composer in search of a librettist.

It was to be an unlikely collaboration. In the first place it was Barezzi, no less, who later drew comparisons with the little lamented Solera. Piave, he wrote, was 'a big, jolly young man like Solera'.[40] Not, one imagines, characteristics likely to endear him to the serious, even somewhat humourless, intensely hard-working Verdi.

Then there was his sheer lack of experience. Just a single libretto to his name, for a composer who had already written fifty operas, and

---

* It was customary then, as now, for opera scores to be reduced to a single piano part to allow for rehearsals to take place without engaging a full orchestra.

Left

Francesco Maria Piave.

whose fame at that time Verdi could only hope to emulate, even if musical history would accord him little or no recognition.[†]

Also counting against Piave, as far as Verdi was concerned, was the
fact that he was a Venetian through and through, born on the glass-pro-
ducing island of Murano to a local official who owned a glass factory.

[†] Pacini would go on to compose more than seventy operas, making him
(with Handel) one of the most prolific operatic composers in musical history.
Although they were enormously popular in his day, none of his operas has
found a regular place in the repertory.

Verdi did not like Venice, though he recognised its qualities, and given the prestige of its opera house, La Fenice, he could not avoid going there. 'Venice is beautiful, it's poetic, it's divine, but . . . I would not stay here voluntarily,' he wrote.[41]

The simple reason was that the climate of Venice – damp, chilly, with a foggy mist that hung over the city in the winter months – was the worst possible for a man prone to chronic throat infections. After one particularly bad spell, he told a friend that if he stayed there much longer he would get consumption.

Why, then, did Verdi decide to work with Piave? Because, put concisely, Verdi was now a man of stone, and Piave was an individual as easy to manipulate, and dominate, as a piece of clay.

Verdi quickly understood that with Piave he could get exactly what he wanted. If a line written by Piave did not precisely fit his needs, he commanded him to go away and try again. Verdi would not accept a single word or a line unless he considered it perfect from a musical and dramatic point of view. And Piave, like putty, was content to be moulded in any way Verdi wished.

From now on the man of stone would assume total control of every aspect of his operas. It is not much of an exaggeration to say that to a large extent Verdi became his own librettist. Even if he did not originate the words, he was merciless in reworking them, or ordering them to be reworked, until he got exactly what he wanted.

None of his librettists felt the force of Verdi's dominating personality more than Piave. Biographers have used words like 'bully' and 'enslave' to characterise Verdi's treatment of Piave, and they are hardly an exaggeration: 'Verdi always harried [Piave] unmercifully . . . [but] Piave rewarded him with doglike devotion, and the two remained on terms of sincere friendship,' writes one.[42]

The first opera the two were to collaborate on was *Ernani*, commissioned by the Teatro La Fenice in Venice for the new Carnival season. It was fortunate the relationship did not end before it had even started.

Verdi was soon demanding changes in the libretto, and Piave – for the first and last time – plucked up the nerve to resist. Verdi went straight to the top, writing to the management of La Fenice, to complain about his librettist. This seems even more cruel when you consider Piave was actually employed by the theatre.

The letter is worth quoting, though, for more than the light it throws on the relationship between the two men. In it Verdi spells out exactly how he sees the collaboration between composer and librettist, and thus

Teatro La Fenice, the opera house in Venice, in 1837.

gives us an invaluable insight into his working method. No surprise that for him the composer is all important; the librettist there merely to do the composer's will. As for his description of himself, that word 'disingenuous' is once again apt.

> *As for me, I would never want to trouble a poet [by asking him] to change a single line [!] . . . Even though I myself have very limited experience, I go to the theatre all year round, just the same, and I pay very careful attention. I have seen as clear as day that so many works would not have failed had there been a better distribution of the set pieces, if the effects had been better calculated, if the musical forms had been clearer . . . in a word, if poet and composer had been more experienced. So many times a recitative that is too long, a phrase or a sentence that would be exquisite in a book, and even in a play, make people laugh in an opera.*

Strip away the false modesty, and this offers an unequalled understanding of the aims and methods of Verdi the composer, penned by the man himself. To sum up what he says in a single sentence, it is the audience that is paramount. At all costs, and whatever it takes, the audience must be entertained.

Which, with the new season at La Fenice, the audience was most certainly not, and it was Verdi himself who was failing to entertain them. The season opened on 26 December 1843 with Verdi's opera *I Lombardi*. It was, in his own words, which were written 'one hour after midnight', in fact 'not a quarter of an hour since the curtain fell, one of the really classic *fiascos*'. [43]

This was all the more galling since its premiere in Milan eleven months earlier had been such a success, and Verdi returned swiftly to his hotel to nurse his wounds. For once he was not exaggerating by using the word 'fiasco'. Only one short aria was applauded; every other set piece was either whistled at or tolerated in silence.

The problem, as Verdi made blisteringly clear to the management of La Fenice, was with the singers, especially the tenor, who was also contracted to sing the lead role in *Ernani*. Verdi took a hard line: sack him, he ordered La Fenice, or I break my contract.

The management hit back, refusing to release him from his contract. Eventually a compromise was reached, with a new tenor found and the opening night put back, but Verdi was in ill-health and emotional turmoil. Disputes with the management, the notoriously fickle Venetian public with their blood up, and a first collaboration with a new librettist – all combined to push Verdi close to a nervous breakdown.

Matters were made even worse when the new tenor arrived late from Spain and it became swiftly apparent he had not learned the role. Verdi was in despair, all his pre-premiere demons in full flow.

It probably was not much of an exaggeration when he wrote to the critic Luigi Toccagni shortly before opening night:

> *I am writing to you with tears in my eyes, and I cannot wait to leave here. Add to this a slight fever that strikes me every evening, and you will see how 'well' I am . . . If* Ernani *were to fail, I would blow my brains out. I could not bear the idea . . . Night is coming, and I am in desperation. Say hello to all my men and women friends, and tell them to think of me. Love me, but really love me.*

This is an anguished cry from a man who really has plumbed the depths of his emotions. Even if the suicide threat was no more than a turn of phrase – how can we know? – the thought of giving it all up, perhaps realising that long-held ambition to become a man of the soil, must have been at the forefront of his mind.

Not for the first, or last, time in his career, he need not have worried. *Ernani* was a triumph – against the odds. In fact Verdi had had good reason to be worried. He himself was still orchestrating the score just days before the opening night; the scenery was not ready; the lead soprano was singing flat; the volatile Spanish tenor complaining of hoarseness.

But it seems the fickle Venetian audience was ready to make amends for *I Lombardi*. It was as though it was willing *Ernani* to succeed. Succeed it most certainly did. After the first performance, on 9 March 1844, instead of Verdi skulking back to his hotel alone and depressed, this time he had a band following him, playing his music and shouting his name. The Venetians had taken this tale, which was adapted from Victor Hugo, of bandits and brigands in the Pyrenees to its heart. Characteristically, he himself described the premiere as 'fairly successful'.

It was a personal triumph for Verdi, and it came at exactly the moment he needed it. If there had been two people involved in the creation of *Ernani*, it was Verdi alone who soaked up the adulation. But he knew he had found a librettist who was a seriously good writer, who was prepared to allow him total control, and with whom Verdi knew he could work easily.

Francesco Maria Piave would go on to write librettos for nine more operas by Verdi, including two of the most popular he was ever to write: *Rigoletto* (1851) and *La traviata* (1853). That does not mean either found its way easily onto the stage.

I quoted earlier a biographer as describing the relationship between the two men as one of 'sincere friendship'. Mary Jane Phillips-Matz goes further. She describes Piave as 'someone Verdi loved'.

Verdi might have harried Piave, pressurised him, made unreasonable demands, even bullied him, but when Piave needed him, Verdi was there.

At the height of their collaboration, in 1870, Piave suffered a stroke that left him paralysed and unable to speak. Verdi stepped into the breach, asking – 'bludgeoning', according to one biographer [44] – a number of composers to contribute to an album of pieces to be sold to raise funds for Piave's wife and daughter. He also gave the considerable sum of 10,000 lire to the daughter.

Piave was unable to work again. When he died six years later at the age of sixty-five, Verdi paid for his funeral and arranged for him to be buried in Milan's Monumental Cemetery, final resting place of many Italian artists and musicians.

Earlier proof of how close the two men were came at the same time that they were collaborating on their first opera, *Ernani*. Verdi had

"It seems the fickle Venetian audience was ready to make amends. It was as though it was willing Ernani to succeed."

formed an intimate relationship with a woman in Venice, and we know about it only because he confided in Piave.

In letters to his librettist, he refers to her as 'that Angel whom you know' and 'the woman I like'. Several names have been put forward as the woman with whom Verdi had an affair (which would last, on and off, for six years), ranging from a variety of singers to members of aristocratic families whom Verdi met at salons in the palaces of Venice. Her identity, though, has never been firmly established.

Giuseppina Strepponi, at the time, was in Verona.

9

VERDI, MAN OF PROPERTY

The success of *Ernani* was not a portent of things to come. The operas that followed either achieved a modicum of success, or were outright failures, and the pressure was telling on Giuseppe Verdi.

From Muzio's letters to Barezzi back in Busseto we learn that Verdi was working so hard he was at breaking point. As well as rehearsing one opera while supervising performances of another, he was also dealing with business correspondence and various interviews and meetings during the morning. His day began at eight and he regularly worked through until after midnight. His only break came when he and Muzio took two hours off at midday for lunch.

Through the early months of 1845 the intense pressure manifested itself in health problems. His stomach and digestion were playing up; he complained of severe headaches, even rheumatism. And that old bugbear, a sore throat, seemed permanently with him. For a man of thirty-one, he was not in good condition.

As with all Verdi's operas, his newest creation, *Giovanna d'Arco* (a retelling of the legend of Joan of Arc) had a difficult birth. Problems with singers, as well as with the orchestra, which Muzio described as 'mean and small', scenery and costumes once again not ready. All familiar territory for the frustrated and anxious composer.

It was at rehearsals for this opera that Muzio gave the vivid description of Verdi sweating and shouting.[*] That was when he was able to attend; he missed several rehearsals due to ill-health.

On opening night at La Scala on 15 February 1845 Muzio described the audience as 'restless'. Nevertheless on the whole the opera was well received and enjoyed a respectable run of seventeen performances.

But while the audiences might have given it their approval, the critics were less effusive. Several wrote that Verdi was repeating himself, that he had run out of new ideas, and that the single quality most absent was inspiration.

Verdi, in a poor frame of mind already, was deeply wounded by the criticism. Looking for a scapegoat, he turned on the one man to whom he owed so much, the impresario Bartolomeo Merelli.

He accused Merelli, in essence, of putting his works and reputation at risk by demanding changes that were not necessary, employing singers who were not up to the job, mounting inferior productions with scenery and costumes not ready, promising that he would stage a particular opera and then omitting it from the season.

There was some truth in all these accusations, and matters came to a head when Verdi discovered that Merelli was secretly negotiating with the publisher Ricordi to sell his share in the rights to *Giovanna d'Arco*.

It was the last straw. Verdi had had enough of La Scala and Merelli. Whether or not there was a face-to-face confrontation between the two men, we do not know. Given Verdi's state of mind, it is more than likely, though if it did happen neither man spoke about it in later years.

Verdi vowed there and then that he would never again speak to Merelli, and that he would not set foot on the stage of La Scala as long as Merelli was there. This, to the man who had stood by him after the fiasco of *Un giorno di regno*, who had encouraged him to write *Nabucco* – in fact, without whose nurture Verdi might well have given up a musical career altogether.

It was no idle threat. Verdi would have nothing to do with La Scala – the most prestigious opera house in Italy, indeed in Europe – for almost twenty-five years. When, world famous, he did return, Merelli had long since gone into retirement.

---

[*] See page 72.

It was at about this time that another side to Verdi's character emerged. He had a fondness for property, and once money started to come in following the success of *Ernani*, he began to indulge that fondness.

Perhaps it was the insecurity of his childhood, seeing his father the innkeeper serving customers food and drink, being always at the mercy of wealthier landowners and landlords, that instilled in Verdi the desire to become a landowner himself.

And so, as soon as he was able, Verdi bought some property. In May 1844 he acquired a substantial holding just a stone's throw from his home village of Le Roncole – a farmhouse, outbuildings and arable land. The total cost of 29,800 lire was to be paid in four instalments over two and a half years.

For a man with Verdi's confidence in his own abilities, and the inevitable success of his operas, this might seem a sensible arrangement. In fact it would put him under financial pressure, at least in the short term, and loans that would later be made in both directions were to become a cause of considerable friction between Verdi and his father.

Matters were exacerbated when, less than a year and a half later, in October 1845, Verdi extended his property portfolio. This time, after lengthy negotiations, he became the owner of the Palazzo Cavalli, an elegant townhouse in the main street of Busseto.

He had, in a sense, come home, and the people of Busseto were delighted to welcome him back. That welcome would not last, though. The Palazzo would become the catalyst for an ugly little dispute between Verdi and the Bussetans, who had always regarded him as one of their own.

This latest purchase had put him even deeper in debt, and he was ill equipped – financially and emotionally – to handle it. On the financial front, his income always seemed to fall short of his expectations. Opera-house managers drove hard bargains. What might seem a beneficial arrangement to a musician with limited experience of finance and contracts could turn out to be very different when the small print came into play – percentages, box-office receipts, ancillary costs. If Verdi was prone to complain that he never seemed to receive as much income as his contracts suggested he might expect, he was not entirely wrong.

More seriously, he was certainly not in the right frame of mind to be mortgaging himself up to the hilt with extravagant property purchases. Muzio wrote to Barezzi that the Signor Maestro was still intending to give up an operatic career after another year at most. Verdi himself wrote to a friend that he hated the 'accursed notes' he had to write, and would not be happy until 'I shall have finished this career that I abhor.'

'Disingenuous.' That word again. But once again it applies. He clearly did not 'abhor' his chosen profession or consider the musical notes he wrote 'accursed'. He might have hated all the rigmarole and complications that went with operatic composition. However, when it came to composing, he simply had no choice in the matter. There might be less complicated genres, but fate had decreed that for Giuseppe Verdi it had to be opera.

If he really did intend to give up music, how did he expect to earn an income to meet the payments on his properties? It must have weighed on his mind as the new year dawned. Certainly he gave himself time to reflect. For at least the first six months of 1846 he did absolutely no work at all, which meant no income, relying on Muzio to take care of anything that needed taking care of – including himself.

Verdi was actually very unwell, so unwell in fact that he was forced to cancel a proposed trip to London. All his old physical complaints –

some real, some surely psychosomatic – had returned to incapacitate him. Muzio wrote to Barezzi that he was deeply worried about how thin and sickly looking the Signor Maestro had become, and took it on himself to look after him, to make sure he was adequately fed and that his physical needs were catered for.

By the summer he was well enough to travel – just a short distance to the spa town of Recoaro in the Italian Alps just north of Verona. Still no composing.

The first hint that that might be about to change came when Piave wrote to him to ask a favour. Would Verdi mind awfully if he offered the libretto he had written based on Byron's poem 'The Corsair' (*Il corsaro*) to another composer, since Verdi (who had asked him to write it) was apparently not intending to set it?

Verdi's reply is a classic, revealing perfectly to us a man who lets off steam at full force with that ever-present twinkle. Insult after insult is delivered in a way unlikely to give offence, particularly when there is genuine sincerity in there too. Proof of that comes in the final line, a clear indication that, although Verdi might be done with music, music was not yet done with him.

> *What? You've either gone mad or are going mad! That* Corsaro *which I have so cherished, which cost me so much thought, and which you yourself have versified with more care than usual? . . . And I should cede it to you? . . . And you don't even tell me where it is for or for whom? . . . Away with you, off to the hospital and have your head examined . . . If you had been any other person I wouldn't even have bothered to answer . . . but the friend,* Francesco Maria Piave, *whose care, lavished on me with more than fraternal heart during the period of my illness, I shall never forget. To him I cannot cannot [sic] deny this wish . . . If you want this* Corsaro *I yield it to you, on condition, however, that you must make me another libretto with the same love with which you made this one.*[45]

Little could Verdi know just how brilliantly Piave would respond over the coming years to that demand in the final sentence of his letter. For the immediate future, though, he was to make Piave's life a misery.

Verdi was under contract to the opera house in Florence, the Teatro della Pergola, to provide an opera, and to the surprise of those around him he decided now was the moment to honour it. His health had improved, and the absence from composing had clearly caused a renewed stirring of creativity.

"There might be less complicated genres, but fate had decreed that for Giuseppe Verdi it had to be opera."

He decided there were three possibilities: a play by Schiller, a play by Grillparzer or Shakespeare's *Macbeth*. He made the decision on the basis of which singers were available, but really there was no contest.

To say that Verdi was obsessed with Shakespeare would not be much of an overstatement. For practically his entire adult life it was his ambition to write an opera based on *King Lear*. More than one librettist adapted the play, or portions of it, for him, but he was never satisfied. For more than fifty years he spoke of his *Re Lear*, but not a note of music was ever written.

As well as *Lear*, at several times in his life he discussed setting *Hamlet*, *Cymbeline* and *Antony and Cleopatra* to music. None ever materialised.

He did, however, set three Shakespeare plays, each time creating a work of genius. *Otello* and *Falstaff* lie ahead. Right now, recovering from serious illness, still in half a mind to give up composing altogether, certainly not in the right frame of mind to write, he set about turning *Macbeth* into opera.

Piave, as that letter intimated, was Verdi's chosen librettist, and once again it was as well that Piave possessed an accommodating nature. Verdi drove him relentlessly. To begin with, he himself wrote a detailed dramatisation of the text and sent it to Piave.

When Piave began to submit verses to him, Verdi scrutinised every word. Nothing was overlooked; nothing escaped his control. He constantly ordered Piave to adhere to Shakespeare's text, and admonished him when he strayed from it.

During the autumn and winter of 1846 Verdi subjected Piave to a barrage of letters. On the one hand he demanded more words; on the other those that Piave had already submitted were not good enough, or not sufficiently faithful to the original.

It was clear that Verdi was now operating on a different musical level. His ambition for *Macbeth* was greater than for any of his previous works. Driven by his unquenchable admiration for Shakespeare, he was determined that this opera would do full justice to the great playwright. He wrote to Piave:

> *This tragedy is one of the greatest creations of the human spirit. If we cannot make something great out of it, let us at least do something out of the ordinary . . . There must not be a single useless word: everything must say something.*[46]

Verdi might just as well have written that 'if we cannot make something great out of it, it is entirely your fault, not mine'. Still, Piave continued

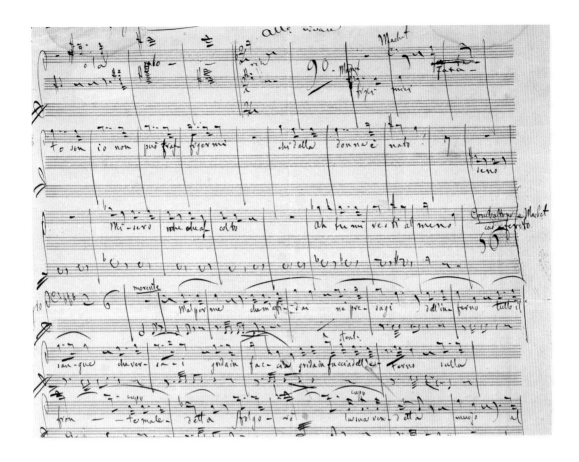

Above

Handwritten score of
the aria 'Trusting in the
prophecies of Hell' from
Verdi's *Macbeth* (1847).

to feed his libretto to Verdi. He received little gratitude. In fact, late on in the process Verdi sacked him, complaining the verses Piave had provided him with were impossible to set to music.

In a calculated snub, Piave's name was left off the first printed edition of the opera. Piave, deeply dismayed, would no doubt be gladdened to know his name would later be restored, though he would not live to see it, and he is to this day credited with writing the libretto.

Verdi was no kinder to his singers. The soprano engaged to sing the role of Lady Macbeth, Marianna Barbieri-Nini, has left a riveting account of rehearsals. In all, she says, there were more than one hundred rehearsal sessions. Exaggeration? Probably not, particularly given what she goes on to report.

'Verdi, implacable, did not care if he wearied the artists, and tormented them for hours on end with the same piece.' Until he was completely satisfied, she says, he would not go on to the next scene.

Right

Act One, Scene Two of
Verdi's *Macbeth*, from
a performance at the
Théâtre Lyrique in 1865.

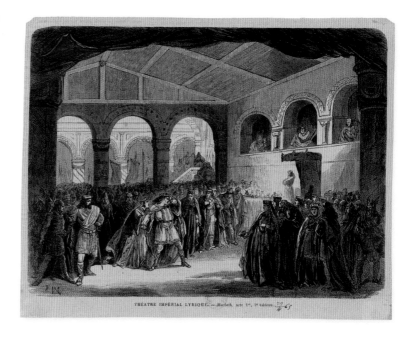

This is Verdi the creative genius, and he does not care whether the singers and musicians love him or loathe him. It seems the latter was nearer to the mark. 'He was not much loved by those who worked for him,' according to Barbieri-Nini, 'for not a word of encouragement ever left his lips. Never a heartfelt "bravo", not even when the orchestra or choir believed they had done their utmost to please him.'

She herself felt the brunt of Verdi's obsessive control. The composer had, it seems, become expert in the behaviour of sleepwalkers:

> *The sleepwalking scene took me three months of study. For three months, morning and night, I sought to imitate those who speak while sleeping, articulating words almost without moving their lips, and leaving the rest of their face immobile, including the eyes. It drove me crazy.*

And her punchline:

> *As for the duet with the baritone that begins 'Fatal mia donna! Un murmure', you may think I am exaggerating, but it was rehearsed more than one and hundred and fifty times, so that it might be closer to 'speech' than 'singing'.*[47]

Exaggerating? Again, probably not.

A further example of just how deeply Verdi involved himself in every aspect of the opera is his insistence that the appearance of Banquo's ghost during the banquet should be achieved by having the actor rise from underneath the stage through a trapdoor, and that he should have an ashen face, rumpled hair and several wounds on his neck.

Verdi's opera *Macbeth* opened at the Teatro della Pergola in Florence on 14 March 1847. So much publicity was there ahead of the opening night, such a degree of anticipation, that the theatre had to open its doors at four o'clock in the afternoon, fully four hours before the curtain was due to rise. Even an individual as close to Verdi as Antonio Barezzi had to pay an extra premium to secure his reserved seat.

How was *Macbeth* received? Just how successful was it? If we believe Verdi, king of the understatement, 'The opera was not a fiasco.'[48] It certainly was not. For a start, it was constantly interrupted by calls for encores, beginning with the opening chorus of the witches.

Barbieri-Nini, again, gives us a description of Verdi's nervousness, prowling around her anxiously as she waited to go on to sing the crucial sleepwalking scene. He need not have worried. It was, she says, greeted with a storm of applause. As for the duet *'Fatal mia donna!'*, which had been rehearsed so many times, it too had to be repeated before the opera could continue.

We owe to Barbieri-Nini a marvellous account of the effect his opera's reception had on the composer himself. Verdi came to her dressing room, she reports, gesturing with his hands because he was unable to speak at all. She too, she admits, was laughing and crying, also unable to speak. Verdi's eyes were red with tears. He took her hands, grasped them tightly between his own, and then rushed out of the room without uttering a word.

Verdi and his soprano shared a carriage back to the Hôtel Suisse, where they were staying, and a huge crowd accompanied them on the short journey. The same thing happened on the second night. During this performance Verdi was called onto the stage 'countless times', and the carriage back to the hotel afterwards was accompanied by a crowd who 'yelled like the damned'.[49]

The momentum continued. A group of Verdi's admirers had had a golden crown inscribed with the words 'from the Florentines to Giuseppe Verdi'. It was presented to him by Barbieri-Nini on the third night. After this third performance, he received a further accolade, both touching and extraordinary. As Verdi mounted his carriage, a group unhitched the horses and pulled it back themselves to the hotel.

Verdi had the success he so badly needed, and which he had worked so hard to achieve. It allowed him to fulfil a promise he had made to himself around a year or so earlier. This was not Verdi the taskmaster berating singers and librettists; this was Verdi giving back to the man to whom he owed so much.

He wrote to his father-in-law, Antonio Barezzi, apologising for not having done this before, and informing him he was dedicating *Macbeth* to him. His letter gives us a useful indication of just how highly he regarded his new opera.

> *Now here is this* Macbeth, *which I love much more than my other operas and which I therefore consider more worthy to be presented to you. It is offered from the heart: may it be accepted by the heart* and be a testimony for all time to the gratitude and love borne to you by your most affectionate G. Verdi.[50]

A family friend in Busseto was in the room when Barezzi read the letter. 'Weeping profusely and deeply moved, [Barezzi] exclaimed: "I recognised his goodness and talent [even] when he was a boy and protected him as best I could, and he has not let me down."'

Barezzi was correct on all counts. His reply was unstinting in its gratitude and praise for his son-in-law:

> *Your gift is extremely precious to me. Your recognition of me will always remain engraved in my heart. Deign to receive in exchange the hot tears of love that I shed for you, the only tribute that I can offer you. Love me, O my adored son of my heart, as I love you, and receive a thousand kisses.*

I say 'unstinting', but there was one small hint in Barezzi's reply that suggested there was a cloud of sorts hanging over his relationship with his son-in-law, and it involved his domestic arrangements. I shall return to this shortly.

For the moment, though, Verdi savoured the success of *Macbeth*, and Barezzi was thoroughly entitled to bask in reflected glory. It was time now for Verdi to spread his wings, as it were. London had been beckoning for some time; the moment to cross the Channel had arrived.

---

* This may have been a conscious replication of Beethoven's words of dedication on the manuscript of his *Missa Solemnis*: 'From the heart, may it return to the heart' (*Von Herzen, möge es wieder zu Herzen gehn*).

10

QUEEN VICTORIA
IS NOT AMUSED

The three works that Verdi had been considering as possible subjects for a new opera, before he decided on *Macbeth*, included an intense drama by Schiller entitled *Die Räuber* ('The Robbers'). It was this that attracted him most, and he worked intensively to complete it in time for its scheduled premiere in London in July 1847.

After the success of *Ernani* some years earlier in London, which had established his reputation in the British capital, Verdi had been contracted to provide a new work for Her Majesty's Theatre – home of opera in London – which he himself would conduct, but ill-health – and, frankly, a lack of desire to cross the Channel – had led to him cancelling the trip.

With a renewed energy and a desire to fulfil his commitments, even if it meant taking him away from home, he worked furiously on Schiller's drama, with Muzio at his side to assist. The opera would be called *I masnadieri* ('The Robbers'), with the libretto entrusted to Verdi's old friend Andrea Maffei, poet and experienced translator, and thus well equipped to handle the German prose.

After a lengthy journey north through Europe – it was almost as if Verdi was trying to put off the inevitable – he and Muzio arrived in London on 5 June 1847. Verdi, we can now see, was a man who liked his creature comforts and the familiarity of home customs. Muzio was no different.

London was 'chaos' and 'a Babylonia', Muzio wrote home to Barezzi. He described London as the most expensive city in the world, noisy and confused, and he and the Signor Maestro as two lost souls.

The apartment Muzio had rented near the theatre was small and cramped. If the weather turned warm, he wrote, they would surely suffocate. As for the climate (Muzio now seeming rather to enjoy his heightened invective), it was the worst in the world, the air poisoned by smoke. The only time they could breathe was in the early morning, before the English lit their fires. That did not help: the smoke burned their eyes, and 'softened and blackened the skin'.

Muzio was no doubt reflecting his master's views when he wrote, 'Long live our sun, which I used to love but which I now worship – now that I am in these fogs and in this smoke, which suffocates me and blinds my spirit.'

To deepen their woes, they were unable to communicate with their servants, neither side speaking the other's language, added to which the servants were 'rougher than rocks'. Before their arrival they had been assured French was widely spoken in London. It turned out this was entirely untrue.

Barezzi must have put on a wry smile as he read that Verdi and Muzio were 'two poor devils who are not all right and are not comfortable'.

If Muzio is to be believed, the effects of all this were more than merely cosmetic. He quotes Verdi as saying the cold weather, the fog, the food and wine, *everything*, had left him with no desire to do anything. 'And that is that.'

It was all taking its toll. 'The humid heavy air acts very powerfully on [Verdi's] nervous system and makes him crazier and more melancholy than usual,' Muzio wrote, which suggests that Verdi's habitual health problems associated with forthcoming premieres might have been troubling him once again, exacerbated by the English weather – in fact, by all things English.

Verdi's humour was not improved by the fact that he was feted everywhere he went. His fame had preceded him. Far from enjoying this, he hated it. He did not want to be recognised or approached in any way. He made a point of turning down invitations, Muzio in effect acting as a barrier between him and the cream of London society.

Higher, even, than the cream. Queen Victoria, no less, let it be known that she wished to meet Maestro Verdi. The Maestro had no hesitation in turning her down, to the surprise of London's press and aristocracy, and no doubt to the consternation of the faithful Muzio.

Not that there was much time to socialise. Despite Verdi's apparent lack of enthusiasm for work, Muzio reported that the two of them got up at five in the morning, started work at six, and kept working for twelve hours, with scarcely a break.

To add to Verdi's troubles there were, as always, problems with singers. To sing the lead soprano role of Amalia, the London impresario Benjamin Lumley had signed none other than Jenny Lind, the leading soprano of her day, and beloved of London audiences. But there was doubt over whether the Swedish Nightingale could arrive in London in sufficient time to learn the role.

When she did finally reach London and begin rehearsals, Muzio wrote of her musical prowess glowingly, albeit not entirely without criticism, but as for other aspects of her character he was ungallant in the extreme:

> *La Lind is a perfect and profound musician; she sight-reads any piece of music whatever . . . her voice is a bit sharp at the top and weak at the bottom . . . She has an agility like no other singer, but she performs too many trills and effects that were pleasing to audiences in the last century, but are not acceptable in 1847.*

He then gives vent to opinions that do him little credit:

> *Her face is ugly, serious, and there is something Nordic about it that makes it very unattractive to me. She has a huge nose . . . the Nordic complexion, and very very large hands and feet.*

But, he notes, she shares one characteristic with the Maestro:

> *She hates the theatre and the stage. She says that she is unhappy and that she will find happiness and a little bit of pleasure when she no longer has to deal with people in the theatre and the theatre itself. In this she is very much in agreement with the Maestro.*

The portents, all in all, were not good for Verdi's new opera, scheduled to open on 22 July. Matters were made worse by the theatre management insisting he conduct his own work, as was customary in London. Verdi refused, right up until 18 July, only relenting at the last minute. It would be the first time he had ever wielded the baton at the premiere of one of his operas.

The date of the opening night had actually been chosen by Queen Victoria, who made known her intention to attend. It was the day on which Parliament rose for the summer, and the Queen, who was pregnant at the time, was about to leave for the calm of the countryside.

The fact that the royal couple would be at the premiere ensured the most exclusive turnout that London could offer. The Duke of Wellington, the Duke of Cambridge, practically every member of the House of Lords, the cream of London society, the exiled Prince Louis Bonaparte of France . . . there had rarely, if ever, been an audience like it. One suspects, given the mood he was in, the least impressed person there was Giuseppe Verdi himself.

With Verdi conducting, and the Swedish Nightingale on exquisite form, the opening night was a triumph. Muzio wrote at length to Barezzi, describing how Verdi was honoured with an ovation as he appeared at the conductor's chair, and was called out again and again to take solo bows.

'From the prelude to the last finale,' he wrote, 'there was nothing but applause, [shouts of] "Evviva", curtain calls, and encores.' From the moment the orchestra filed into the pit, the audience erupted with cheers. There were cries of 'Viva Verdi', and – in Muzio's eccentric and endearing spelling – 'Bietifol'.

Jenny Lind herself declared she had never heard music so beautiful, or sung a role that fitted her so perfectly.

All of which makes it hard to believe that one critic, Henry Fother-gill Chorley of the *Athenaeum*, described it as 'the worst opera ever to have been given at Her Majesty's Theatre'.[51]

Even more wounding, had it been made public, was the reaction of the monarch herself. She most definitely was not amused. 'A new opera by Signor Verdi . . . the music very noisy and trivial,' she wrote in her diary.

The shared opinion of critic and Queen is the one that prevailed. It seems Verdi, despite the cheering and plaudits, knew the opera was not one of his best. 'It did not create a furore,' he wrote to Clara Maffei with characteristic understatement, given Muzio's description of the au-dience's ecstatic reaction.

He offered no explanation for what he perceived to be the opera's lack of success; he attempted no rewrite or explanation. He was just keen to leave *I masnadieri* behind, and with it London too. He conducted just two performances before handing the baton over. After two further performances the opera closed.

Verdi had fulfilled his obligations. Time to leave London and head to Paris, where a certain Giuseppina Strepponi had rented an apartment.

There was a sound musical reason for Verdi to go to Paris. For the last two years, the directors of the Paris Opéra had been urging him to create a work for them to stage. Now that he was actually in the city, they were able to put a proposal to him face to face.

Clearly reluctant to take on too much work, Verdi managed to negotiate a highly favourable contract. It stipulated that he would provide a 'new' work by November 1847, but he secured their agreement for him to adapt his earlier opera *I Lombardi alla prima crociata* to a French libretto.

There would be some alterations to the characters, and some new passages, including a ballet, would be written, but the new opera, to be entitled *Jérusalem*, would be largely similar to the earlier work. Yet Verdi was to be paid the same sum he would have received if he had created an entirely new opera.

Muzio, knowing the Signor Maestro as intimately as he did, would not have been surprised that, after London, Verdi dispatched him to Milan and travelled on to Paris on his own. But he did express surprise that Verdi did not immediately return to Milan once he had completed *Jérusalem*. This was because Verdi himself had said he would stay in Paris for a month at most, but after that the days became weeks and the weeks months. No one back home was in any doubt as to why. His musical circle in Busseto knew full well that Giuseppina was in Paris, and Verdi made no secret of his address in letters – just round the corner from where Giuseppina was living.

Giuseppina, accepting that her performing days were over, had started a new phase of her career. The previous autumn she had moved to Paris to give singing lessons. Twice a week, from 3 p.m. to 5 p.m. on Tuesdays and Fridays, she gave classes to ladies, both professional singers and amateurs.

She taught her pupils to sing in the specifically Verdian style, stating that he had created a new form of opera, far removed from the works

of Bellini, Cherubini, Donizetti, Rossini. She even staged recitals of his music – singers accompanied at the piano – in her apartment. She was, in effect, carrying the torch for Giuseppe Verdi's music.

We might imagine that, reunited with the woman who had already shared so much of his life (and who was to go on to share so much more), Verdi would have found some calm and relaxation in Paris, particularly since the work he needed to do on *Jérusalem* was not particularly arduous.

Indeed he might have done, though that is not the face he presented to others:

> *I have a real hatred for the boulevards . . . I see friends, enemies, priests, friars, soldiers, spies, beggars . . . in other words a little of everything. And I do my best to avoid them.*

London, Paris, it seems nowhere outside Italy was entirely to his satisfaction. Once again, though, the private Verdi differs from the one he wanted others to see. Giuseppina, with her calmness and elegance, her spirit and sense of humour, proved the perfect foil to Verdi's mood swings and general grumpiness. In private we can be certain that he led a happier life than the one he showed to the outside world.

We know that Giuseppina arranged soirées, introducing Verdi to people who might prove useful to him. There seems to have been no attempt to disguise the intimacy between them, even when it came to matters of work.

Verdi and Giuseppina actually cooperated on *Jérusalem*. In one passage on the original manuscript, their hands alternate, and it is a passage so intensely romantic that it cannot have been by accident. It must have been their intention that it should be discovered.

[Strepponi's hand]	*I have lost all!*
[Verdi's hand]	*No, I am still left you! And it will be for life!*
[Strepponi's hand]	*Angel from heaven! . . . May I die in the arms of a husband!*
[Verdi's hand]	*Let me die with you! My death will be . . .*
[Strepponi's hand]	*. . . sweet.*[52]

The split in the last line must have raised eyebrows, as it was surely intended to do.

Some time between the middle of November 1847 and Christmas they received a visitor, and both Verdi and Giuseppina must have braced themselves, fearing a certain amount of tension or at the very least discomfort.

Antonio Barezzi wrote to his son-in-law to say he was coming to Paris. It was an overdue visit; Barezzi had intended to visit Verdi in London, but had been unable to do so. The last time he had seen him was in Florence for the premiere of *Macbeth*.

I suggested at the end of the last chapter that there was the hint of a cloud hanging over Barezzi's relationship with Verdi. We cannot be certain of it, but in the first sentence of that letter thanking Verdi for the dedication of *Macbeth*, Barezzi wrote, 'Dearest Son-in-Law, if my heart were not unfortunately immensely troubled . . .'

What might that mean? Could it be that Barezzi had learned Giuseppina was staying secretly in the Hôtel Suisse in Florence, and that this was the first time he had realised that his son-in-law was involved in an intimate relationship with another woman?

Shortly before opening night of *Macbeth*, a printer's boy was sent to Verdi's rooms in the hotel with proofs of the libretto. In a letter the boy, Salvatore Landi, later wrote that he found 'Verdi and his wife', and that Verdi gave him an extraordinarily large tip.

Phillips-Matz says there is no reason to doubt Landi's account, since he need not have written the letter in the first place.

Giuseppina's biographer disagrees. In the first place, she says it was a hotel porter who 'surprised the Maestro in his room with his wife'. She goes on to say it was highly unlikely that Giuseppina would have abandoned her pupils in Paris, and that surely Verdi would not have allowed such a situation to exist, knowing his father-in-law was in Florence for the premiere.

She suggests the woman in question was one of Verdi's many female admirers, of which there was no shortage, given that he was 'such a desirable single man . . . wonderful, extremely good-looking, brooding and interesting'.[53]

What both biographers agree on is that once Barezzi became aware of the relationship (whenever that was), he must have been intensely disappointed in Verdi's choice of companion. Giuseppina, known to have been involved in a number of relationships that had led to several illegitimate births, was at the very least socially unacceptable. In his mind, Barezzi must have compared her to his own dearly loved and deeply mourned daughter, and she could not have emerged from the comparison with any credit.

This was surely the couple's main concern as they prepared themselves for Barezzi's Paris visit. Giuseppina, realising she could do nothing to erase her past reputation, decided to put on as good a show as she could.

She played the perfect hostess. She gave dinner parties, lauding Barezzi to her friends and conspicuously tending to his needs as much as she did to Verdi's. She took him into her classes so he could see her professionalism and the esteem in which she was held by her pupils.

It seems to have worked, judging by a letter Barezzi wrote to Verdi once he returned to Busseto. He had nothing but good things to say about Giuseppina, and let his son-in-law know he had spread her praises widely:

> *Since my arrival in Busseto from Paris, I have not let one single day go by without telling people about the great things I saw during my trip, and the welcome I got there from you, from Signora Peppina, and from your other friends; and I assure you that those memories*

"In private we can be certain that Verdi led a happier life than the one he showed to the outside world."

*will always remain engraved in my heart . . . You give me hope that
I will get a letter from Signora Peppina, and I have to tell you that
I am waiting anxiously for it, and in the meantime give her my
regards, and her women too, whom I found so kind.*

If Verdi and Giuseppina thought any problems that might arise from
their relationship were now a thing of the past, they were to be disabused
of the notion before too long. As the intimacy between them became
more generally known in Busseto, so resentment towards them grew. For
now, though, other matters were about to intervene, which worked to
their temporary advantage.

Verdi continued to put off his return to Milan for one reason or another. In fact in early February he gave Muzio a date for his return, and
did not let Muzio know he was not coming until the actual day Muzio
expected to see him.

Not long after that a return to Milan became an impossibility – at
least for a few tumultuous weeks. The year was 1848, the year of revolutions across Europe, and the spark was lit in Paris.

11

'The Hour of Liberation Has Sounded'

Years of discontent came to a head in Paris in February 1848, when a popular uprising forced the abdication of King Louis-Philippe. Paris was not alone. Revolutionary fervour rapidly spread across Europe. Soon there were barricades in the streets of the great capitals of Europe – Paris, Vienna, Berlin. There were protests in dozens of towns and cities across the continent.

The Enlightenment, a revolution in ideas that had swept Europe in the preceding century, now became a popular movement in the streets. The divine right of kings no longer went unchallenged. No longer could the Church control the laws people obeyed, or the thoughts they were allowed to think.

The people of Europe had had enough of oppression and dictatorial rule. They wanted to be free to say what they wanted and be ruled by politicians they trusted. They wanted, in other words, democracy, and nowhere more so than in Vienna, seat of the Habsburg emperor.

There was anarchy on the streets. The capital of empire was reduced to disorder. The man who had ruled as an oppressive chancellor for nearly thirty years, Prince Clemens von Metternich, had lost control. The city had seen nothing like it. Troops were ordered onto the streets, but could not restore order. Then the seemingly impossible happened. Metternich was forced to flee the capital with his wife. The emperor followed him before the year was out.

The Austro-Hungarian empire was disintegrating, with even Hungary proclaiming itself an independent kingdom. Revolution spread through the disparate parts of the empire, affecting not just Austrians and Hungarians, but Slovenes, Poles, Czechs, Croats, Slovaks, Ukrainians, Romanians, Serbs – and Italians.

Giuseppe Verdi, in Paris, was following events keenly. Always an Italian nationalist, if not a particularly ardent one, he now believed Italy's hour had come. It was time to force the Austrians out of northern Italy and for Italians to assert control over their own land. A unified Italy, from the Alps in the north to Sicily in the south, still seemed an unattainable dream, but who could be sure?

As early as 11 February, with the uprising in Paris barely under way, Verdi wrote to a friend, 'Now it is our turn.'[54] He might have been more than five hundred miles away from Milan, but his instincts proved correct.

The people of Milan took their lead from the Parisians, although tensions had been rising since the start of the new year. In a concerted action typical of the Milanese character, practically the entire city gave up smoking. It was a move designed to hit the tobacco trade, a government monopoly that sent millions of lire in tax to the government in Vienna.

On the morning of 3 January, groups of Austrian soldiers swaggered past cafés in the colonnade, ostentatiously smoking. At first they were greeted with boos and catcalls. But it soon turned ugly. The Milanese gathered in crowds and began pelting them with stones. The soldiers collectively panicked. They charged the crowds, bayonets fixed, and opened fire. At least five were killed and more than fifty injured.

Riots and demonstrations spread across the city. The head of the occupying Austrian army, the authoritarian General Radetzky von Radetz – revered by the Viennese governing classes, despised in Italy[*] – ordered the soldiers to put the uprising down.

But this was not a conventional battle in open fields that could be fought by soldiers trained on the parade ground. Barricades went up in narrow streets, manned by men, women and children. The people of Milan fought for their freedom in front of the doors of their houses and shops.

---

[*] He was to be immortalised later in the year by Johann Strauss the Elder's composition of the Radetzky March to celebrate his victory over the Piedmontese army at the Battle of Custoza.

For five days the Milanese harried the Austrian troops, gaining control of the streets and keeping it. Radetzky, all his military training and experience reduced to nothing by an undisciplined but passionate populace, finally accepted defeat and ordered his troops to withdraw. The episode has gone down in history as the Five Days of Milan (*Cinque giornate di Milano*).

Verdi, hearing of events in Italy, left as soon as he could for Milan, even if he had no intention of making it a prolonged stay. He wanted to see for himself what was happening. He was not the only Italian to return from Paris. Giuseppina's eccentric aristocratic friend and fellow singer, Princess Cristina Belgiojoso, entered Milan (so it was said) at the head of a volunteer corps of a hundred and sixty men, astride a white horse, dressed as Joan of Arc and carrying a French tricolour.

Verdi had missed the action, but was overjoyed to find himself in a liberated city. The barricades were still in place, and he took joy in touring them. He must have learned from colleagues at La Scala how even the opera house had been a scene of protest against Austrian rule. On the evening of 17 March the Austrian ballerina Fanny Elssler had been booed on stage and fainted. She hastily left Milan for the safety of Vienna.

On 21 April Verdi wrote a long letter to Piave in Venice – more accurately, to 'Citizen Piave', national guard in the newly proclaimed Venetian Republic. This is a Verdi we have not encountered before. To call the letter joyous is an understatement. His excitement bursts from every word. He himself acknowledges that he is a new man.

Most importantly, there is more than a hint not just of an interest in politics, but of Verdi himself taking part in political activity, something that would have a dramatic effect on his life a little more than a decade later. Almost inevitably, he sees a chance to denigrate his own profession, though I suspect, as always, this is rather tongue in cheek.

The letter reveals so much of Verdi's character, it is worth quoting at some length:

> *Dear Piave*
>
> *You can imagine whether I wanted to remain in Paris, after hearing there was a revolution in Milan. I left the moment I heard the news, but I could see nothing but these stupendous barricades. Honour to these heroes! Honour to all Italy, which in this moment is truly great!*
>
> *The hour of her liberation has sounded, you may be convinced of that. It is the people who want it: and when the people want something there is no absolute power that can resist them.*

Those who want to impose themselves on us by sheer force can do what they want, they can conspire as much as they like, but they will not succeed in cheating the people out of their rights. Yes, another few months and Italy will be free, united, republican. What else should it be?

You speak to me of music!! What has got into you? Do you think that I want to bother myself now with notes, with sounds? There is and must be only one music welcome to the ears of Italians in 1848. The music of the cannon! I would not write a note of music for all the gold in the world . . .

This is Verdi the democrat, the people's champion. He then goes on to congratulate Piave on having taken up arms on behalf of Venice, and expresses a desire to do likewise – except for him it would have to be as a 'tribune'.

You are a national guard! I like your being only a plain soldier! . . . I, too, if I could have enlisted, would want to be a simple soldier, but now I can be only a tribune, and a wretched tribune, because I am only occasionally eloquent . . .

Verdi's use of the word 'tribune' is especially interesting. Tribunes were elected officials in ancient Rome, 'elected' being the operative word. He is deliberately using a word associated with the governance of ancient Rome, as if he sees the future of Italy becoming a reflection of the past. Remember, his only son was named Icilio, a name from the days of ancient Rome.

And that phrase 'because I am only occasionally eloquent' – disingenuous to a fault, coming from a man who could write words as eloquent as many a librettist or poet, and music whose eloquence (he surely knew) was unmatched!

There is a reference in the letter to work in hand – '[I have to write] two operas' – of which more in a moment, but first I have to quote the final words of the letter. Here is a Verdi unbounded in his joy, and it is clear that he is as surprised by this as we are. The disparaging self-mockery, the often false modesty, the ever-present twinkle in the eye – all these give way to unbridled jubilation.

If you could see me now, you would not recognise me any more. I no longer have that glum look that frightened you! I am drunk with joy! Imagine that there are no more Germans [sic] *here!! You know how*

much I liked them! Addio, addio, say hello to everyone. A thousand good wishes . . .[55]

As for those two operas Verdi mentioned he had to write, one would enhance his reputation, albeit only briefly; the other would rank as one of his most humiliating failures.

It was failure that came first. Verdi's mind was on other things. In early 1848, as the barricades were going up across Europe and Verdi began to envision an independent Italy, he had been reminded by the Milanese publisher Francesco Lucca that he was under contract to provide an opera, which he had as yet failed to do.

It was the last thing he needed. 'You speak to me of music? Do you think I want to be bothered with notes,' as he wrote to Piave. Then he remembered *Il corsaro*, the opera on which he had done considerable work a couple of years earlier before abandoning composition to get over his ill-health at a spa. It was this opera that he had written angrily to Piave about, when Piave asked his permission to offer the libretto to another publisher.

With neither head nor heart fully engaged, Verdi completed *Il corsaro*. The subject matter, Byron's epic poem about the privateer Conrad, no longer interested him. He was dissatisfied with Piave's libretto, but made no attempt to ask for changes. He had mentally moved on from the project.

Nevertheless he sent the score to Lucca, with a terse note asserting that this ended any obligation he had. To Lucca's credit – and he was a man Verdi disliked and would not become involved with again – he secured an opening at the Teatro Grande in Trieste, one of Italy's finest opera houses.*

Lucca also secured the services of a fine cast of singers, including Marianna Barbieri-Nini, who had excelled in the role of Lady Macbeth, to sing the leading female role. Verdi took a surprisingly close interest in the production of the opera, given his lukewarm approach to composing it. He wrote at length to Barbieri-Nini with instructions on how to handle key moments.

But there, in essence, was the problem. He *wrote* to her. Not once did he leave Paris to attend rehearsals, entrusting the entire production to Emanuele Muzio. Opening night was set for 25 October. When the time came, he pleaded a heavy cold that prevented him from leaving Paris – where, by now, he was openly living with Giuseppina Strepponi.

There was another reason why he might have decided to remain in Paris. Trieste was the one city in northern Italy that had remained under the control of the Austrians. The flames of revolution had not spread as far east as the city, which stood at the extreme north-eastern point of the Adriatic, in the heart of land that formed part of the Austro-Hungarian empire.

The fact that the composer was not at the opening night of his opera (a truly rare occurrence in the land of opera) upset all factions. Italians opposed to Austrian rule, Italians supportive of Austrian rule – Verdi was the man they wanted on their side. However disruptive his actual presence might have been, it would have been far better for him to be there than stay away.

---

* Within hours of Verdi's death in January 1901, the theatre was renamed the Teatro Lirico Giuseppe Verdi.

The audience on opening night vented their frustration at Verdi's absence on his opera. Throughout it was met by stony silence. A critic wrote that the only reason there were no catcalls or whistles was because the audience was blessed with an innate kindness. This might have been overly sympathetic to the audience but made its point.

Verdi, back in Paris, was untroubled. As far as he was concerned *Il corsaro* was already history. He made no attempt to correct or rewrite any passages. He was unconcerned if it passed into oblivion. Which it did, and where it remains largely to this day; it was given its first performance in Britain in 1966, and in the United States as recently as 1981.

Verdi was more fortunate with the second opera he composed in the year of revolution. For a start, it was an entirely new project, directly linked to current events in Europe. It was Verdi's decision to compose an opera that would reflect Italy's desire to rid itself of Austrian occupation. More than that, it was his profound hope that the new opera would actually further the Italian cause.

To that end he decided to adapt a recent French drama about a medieval battle, and reset it in twelfth-century Italy. He gave it the title *La battaglia di Legnano* ('The Battle of Legnano'). It was no coincidence that the city of Legnano, a short distance north-west of Milan, was still occupied by the Austrians.

Verdi worked on the opera in the autumn and winter of 1848. Rehearsals began at the turn of the new year, with an opening date of 27 January 1849. Verdi had offered the opera to his publisher, Tito Ricordi, who had replaced Lucca in Verdi's affections, and would remain his preferred publisher for decades to come.

Ricordi placed the work with the opera house in Rome, the Teatro Argentina. Again, no coincidence. Inevitably, it was not long before the Habsburg government in Vienna began to reassert its authority, and, one by one, cities that had freed themselves from the Austrians were re-occupied. Rome, though, the largest, remained under Italian control. In fact there were plans to declare Rome a republic, something that would actually happen just two weeks after the premiere of Verdi's new opera. Time, as well as history, was on Verdi's side.

This time Verdi made no mistake about where he should be. He was in Rome, and it was as if his presence there practically guaranteed success for the opera even before it had opened. He could scarcely walk along the street without being besieged. Habitually reluctant to receive public acclaim, in Rome he did not demur. Maybe he had learned his lesson from Trieste.

So enthusiastic were his supporters that they demanded the theatre open the dress rehearsal to the public, threatening to force entry if they were refused. Their wish was granted, though it seems that failed to calm their ardour.

The Teatro Argentina was virtually under siege in the days leading up to the first performance. Tickets were sold out long in advance. As for the first performance itself, Muzio reported back to Barezzi in Busseto:

> *The people wanted to attend at any cost, and they broke into the theatre, packing it as full as an egg. Maestro Verdi was called on stage twenty times. The next day there was not a box seat, a ticket, or a libretto of the opera to be found anywhere. Everything was sold out!*

Verdi, knowing he needed a success, had stuck to a formula that had served him well. His setting of *'Viva Italia! Sacro un patto tutti stringe i figli suoi'* ('Long live Italy! A sacred pact unites all its children'), which recurs throughout the opera in both vocal and instrumental form, appealed to exactly the same patriotic instincts as 'The Chorus of the Hebrew Slaves' in *Nabucco*.

On opening night, the final act had to be encored in its entirety. On subsequent nights, the scene in which the heroic slayer of Barbarossa is borne in on a litter and dies amid the acclamations of the people was encored.

Verdi had his success – or so it seemed. In fact the very quality that gave *La battaglia* its instant success also served to undermine it. Although Rome declared itself a republic, it was always beleaguered by the Austrians and the French, and it fell in the summer of 1849. The northern cities that had defied the Austrians were re-occupied.

Once the Austrians were back in control, the dreaded censor once again had control of what was performed on the public stage. The chances of *La battaglia* passing his scrutiny unchanged were nil. It was not long before this *succès fou* for Verdi left the stage, and as time and events moved on, it would not return. Like *Il corsaro*, it was consigned to near oblivion, not reaching the stage in Britain until 1960 and the United States until 1976.

But if time and events had moved on, so had Giuseppe Verdi. In May 1848, he had left Paris briefly and returned to Busseto, where he made a purchase that was to transform his life.

12

VERDI SETS TONGUES WAGGING

Verdi was not fond of big cities. He expressed dislike for both London and Paris, and tolerated Milan only because he had no choice. The most famous composer in Italy, internationally renowned, still hankered for a rural life. In mid-1848, between those two most recent operas, neither of which did much to enhance his career, he decided to do something about it.

In April, he returned home for a short visit. It had been a while since he had been to Le Roncole to see his parents; he also caught up with his father-in-law Antonio Barezzi and close friends such as Demaldè in Busseto.

But that was not the prime motive for his return to that small corner of the Po valley, the land where he had grown up and where he always felt most at home. By this point Verdi had earned a substantial amount of money. Financial problems from his property purchases were in the past. It has been suggested that he could have retired completely at this point in his life, had he wanted to do so. Given how many times he had hinted at this in letters to friends, along with withering comments about his profession, it is perhaps surprising he did not do so. (We can at least be grateful for that.)

It was now that he made a major decision about how to spend the surplus money he had accrued. First, he sold the property he had earlier acquired at Il Pulgaro. On 8 May 1848 he signed the deeds on a substantial property, the Villa Sant'Agata. It comprised a farmhouse, outbuildings and several acres of arable land.

It might well have been Verdi's intention at some point soon to realise – finally – his dream of giving up music and becoming a farmer. At the very least it would provide him with a retreat from the world for which he had developed such distaste. It was secluded, private, and he must have known – even if only subconsciously – that to have a home like that as his base could only nurture and encourage his creativity.

Sant'Agata could not have been better situated, for a number of reasons. Its north-east corner bordered the mighty Po river, whose waters irrigated the soil. Its south-eastern corner touched the smaller Ongina river, its south-western corner the Arda river. With such natural irrigation, the soil was wonderfully fertile.

The estate was just a stone's throw from Le Roncole, and even closer to Busseto. Its location had one other aspect that appealed to Verdi. The Ongina river, which runs roughly north–south, formed the border between Piacenza province to the west and Parma province to the east.

It soon became local legend that the deciding factor in Verdi's decision to purchase the estate was the fact that it lay on the western bank of the Ongina, thus falling within Piacenza province. Verdi, it will be recalled, had long since fallen out with the Teatro Regio di Parma (see page 30). Why would he therefore want to live within Parma province? Verdi was a man who did not forgive a slight.

The main farmhouse at Sant'Agata needed substantial work, and from the time he bought the property Verdi began renovations. He would continue them for the best part of the half-century that he lived there.

A year after completing his purchase, Verdi moved his parents into the Villa Sant'Agata, and began making preparations to return to Busseto. He now owned two substantial properties – the Palazzo Cavalli in the centre of Busseto, and the Villa Sant'Agata just a short distance away in the heart of the countryside.

There was no need any more for Verdi to rent apartments in Paris or Milan, or anywhere else he happened to be working. It was a miserable existence, in any case, having to live in towns or cities he disliked. From now on, he decided, people could come to him, rather than the other way round. And he could now choose whether to live in the town or the countryside.

There was another reason for the return to Busseto. He had decided to make a very substantial change in the way he lived. He knew it would not be totally straightforward, that there would be bumps along the way. But even he could not have imagined just how difficult life would become.

In the intervening year between purchasing Sant'Agata and returning to Busseto, Verdi had lived with Giuseppina in Paris as man and wife. It was a state of affairs he wanted to continue. In Paris it had been the perfectly natural thing to do, arousing no comment at all. That was how Verdi wanted it to be in Busseto.

Verdi decided to make the move first on his own, left Paris and Giuseppina, and moved into the Palazzo Cavalli on 29 July 1849. It is easy to imagine the excitement in the town at the return of its most famous son. For twenty years, the talk in cafés, on the street, in salons, had been of how the boy who had played on the organ at Sunday service had gone on to conquer the world of opera, feted in the great opera houses of Europe.

The excitement, however, was not mutual. In those intervening twenty years Verdi had become a stranger to the Bussetans. They might have thought they knew him, but he was no longer the ambitious young man, inexperienced in worldly affairs. Now, with his return, they wanted to rekindle the intimacy, but he did not.

What Verdi wanted was peace and quiet, as he confided in a letter to his publisher; to be left alone to get on with his life. That might be as a composer of more operas, or it might be as a landowner and farmer at Sant'Agata. Either way, his plans did not include an involvement in local affairs.

It has to be said that if Verdi hankered after the quiet life, he did not necessarily go about achieving it in the right way. It was soon local gossip that within days of arriving back in Busseto, he had taken a carriage ride to a villa just outside Busseto, which was the summer residence of a certain baroness he was rumoured to have had an affair with many years earlier. He arrived, the wagging tongues said, to find her ensconced with her lover. It was Barezzi himself, closer than anyone to Verdi, who apparently told his friends Verdi was shocked and disappointed and the relationship was definitively over.

We find the same ambivalence in his relationship to the woman he had decided to share his life with. There was no doubting his intention to bring Giuseppina to Busseto – with all the risks that that entailed – yet, judging by the letters that passed between them, he was hardly playing the part of the ardent suitor.

"What Verdi wanted was peace and quiet; to be left alone to get on with his life."

Giuseppina was in Florence, where she was making financial arrangements for the education of her illegitimate son Camillo.* From there she intended to go to Parma, and from there to Busseto to join Verdi.

Verdi wrote to her in Florence, and as well as habitual moans about most things, he had clearly suggested in his letter that it would be best if he sent someone to meet her in Parma and escort her to Busseto. She replies with horror – mock, maybe, but she is clearly upset that he does not say he will come personally to Parma to meet her.

> *You tell me about the ugly countryside, the bad service, and on top of that you tell me: 'If you don't like it, I'll have you accompanied (N.B. I'll* have you *accompanied!) wherever you like.' But what the devil! Do people forget how to love in Busseto, and to write with a little bit of affection?'* [56]

Just in case he hasn't got the message, she adds an unambiguous P.S.: 'Don't send anybody else, but come yourself to fetch me from Parma, for I should be very embarrassed to be presented at your house by anyone other than yourself.' Endearingly, and clearly in jest, she calls him an 'ugly, wretched monster!'

In that single additional sentence, Giuseppina articulates the fears the two of them must have discussed in Paris, when Verdi made it clear he wanted her to live with him in Busseto.

It is worth pausing for a moment to see this state of affairs through Giuseppina's eyes. That letter was written days before her thirty-fourth birthday. In probably lengthy, possibly fraught, conversations with Verdi in Paris, she had agreed to come to Busseto to live with him.

In so doing, she was effectively giving up the life she had worked so hard to build up. She was leaving Paris, which she had made her home, where she had established a career for herself as a singing teacher, having accepted her life on the operatic stage was over, where she had friends and an active social life. She was, in her biographer's words, 'burning her only bridge'. [57]

What was she leaving all this for? As that single sentence in her letter shows, it was an uncertain future. She was – and she knew this would be general knowledge in Busseto – Verdi's mistress, and also the mother of several illegitimate children. As well as this, she had, in effect, replaced

---

* It is not known whether she saw the boy, now aged eleven, or maintained any personal contact with him.

Above

Villa Sant'Agata, Verdi's
home for nearly half a
century.

a much-loved young woman, a Bussetan born and bred, daughter of one of the town's most prominent and respected citizens, who had died tragically young, along with the two children she had borne Verdi.

Verdi himself must have reassured her in Paris that he would be able to control events. With his reputation, with his fame, he would make sure her life was a good one, accepted by everyone as the woman who shared *his* life. She, clearly, still had her doubts.

Verdi at least did the noble thing and went to Parma to fetch his Peppina. In an open carriage, on 14 September 1849, the two of them rode into the main street of Busseto, the Via Roma.

The Via Roma (then, as now) is a colonnaded street, its elegant arcades separated by decorated pillars. Were there many pairs of eyes blinking behind shutters, straining for a first glimpse of the woman their most famous son had brought home?

Palazzo Cavalli was built round an internal courtyard, its frontage overlooking the Via Roma. The couple was thus able to enter the building unseen, but the windows of the main rooms on the first floor gave out over the Via Roma. One can imagine Verdi fastening the shutters as soon as he and Giuseppina entered their new home.

If the people of Busseto were looking forward to involving Verdi in local life, they were soon to be disappointed. He deliberately sought out solitude, as he made clear in a letter to Piave:

> *We eat here, we sleep, we work. I have two young horses to take us for a drive – and that is all. The life that I lead is an extremely solitary one. I do not visit anyone's house, and I receive no one excepting my father-in-law and my brother-in-law.* *You, however, can do whatever you want!!! You can go to the café, to the bar, wherever the devil you like.*

"If the people of Busseto were looking forward to involving Verdi in local life, they were soon to be disappointed."

If Verdi seemed envious of the lifestyle Piave was able to enjoy, he had it in his power to correct matters. Invitations poured in for Verdi from the moment of his arrival back in Busseto – for him, at least, not Giuseppina. He turned them all down.

In another letter, written slightly later, he wrote:

> *I have lived all this time [since leaving Paris] in a country place, far from every human contact, without news, without reading any newspapers, etc. It is a life that turns men into animals, but at least it is quiet.*

One is tempted to say he had only himself to blame. This was the life he had chosen for himself and his Peppina.

For some days, maybe even for the first few weeks, Giuseppina stayed cloistered in the Palazzo Cavalli. When, finally, she ventured out, she found herself ignored by the locals. Her greetings went unanswered. She was left in no doubt that she was unwelcome.

In the evening, with alcohol flowing in the cafés and bars of the Via Roma, insults were shouted beneath the Palazzo Cavalli. It is a local legend, repeated to this day, that on one or more occasions, stones were thrown up at the first-floor windows.[†]

It was a difficult state of affairs, made worse by the loyalty of even such a friend and admirer of Verdi as his father-in-law being sorely tested. To have seen and met Giuseppina in Paris was one thing. Here, in his home town, it was entirely different.

---

[*] Margherita Barezzi's brother Giovannino, who had always enjoyed a close relationship with Verdi.

[†] When my wife Nula and I visited Busseto in October 2016, we heard this from several people, who were eager to show us those first-floor windows, the shutters still firmly closed.

Worst of all for Verdi, his own parents left him in no doubt that they thoroughly disapproved of his living arrangements. His mother had even had a bed moved from the Palazzo Cavalli to Sant'Agata in the hope that her son would abandon his mistress and come and live with his parents in the country.

It was the beginning of a period of tension between Verdi and his parents, which would worsen as time passed.

Meanwhile, there was work to be done. Verdi, to his chagrin and despite all his earlier intentions to give up composition, had an opera to write. In the event it would involve almost as much drama offstage as on.

The opera house at Naples, the Teatro San Carlo, reminded Verdi he was under contract to write an opera for them, which had been delayed due to the upheavals of the 1848 uprisings. The librettist they had contracted was the same Salvatore Cammarano with whom Verdi had worked on *La battaglia di Legnano*, the official librettist at the Teatro San Carlo.

Verdi had previously found Cammarano congenial to work with, and had approved of the libretto he had provided. But the librettist was now in something of a state. Knowing Verdi was reluctant to fulfil his obligation, Cammarano wrote pleadingly to him.

The opera house had informed him that if the opera was not ready to stage by the end of the year 1849, they would slap a fine on him. If he was unable to pay it, they would put him in prison. With a wife and six children to support, he wrote to Verdi, begging him to agree to write the opera.

Verdi acquiesced, but with ill grace: 'I will write the opera for Naples next year *for your sake alone*. It will rob me of two hours peace every day and of my health.'[58]

After initial problems with the censor, Verdi and Cammarano agreed they would adapt a Schiller play, stripping it of all political overtones, and concentrating on domesticity and relationships. They retitled it *Luisa Miller*.

Verdi took a keen interest – as he always did – in the writing of the libretto, making a raft of suggestions to Cammarano, but clearly evident in his correspondence is a respect for the librettist, which he was no doubt pleased to see was reciprocated.

Cammarano wrote to him: '[It is] my firm opinion that when [an opera] has two authors they must at least be like brothers, and that if

Poetry should not be the servant of Music, still less should it tyrannise over her.'[59] Verdi probably could not have put it better himself.

If Cammarano had at least avoided a fine and possible imprisonment, things were not looking good in any other respect. Verdi arrived in Naples to supervise rehearsals to find a letter from Cammarano warning him that the Teatro San Carlo was in serious financial trouble. Cammarano advised Verdi that as yet he had received no payment, and that Verdi would do well to demand the advance due to him – one third of his fee – as soon as he set foot in Naples.

This the composer did. The theatre refused to pay. Verdi countered by threatening to suspend rehearsals. The theatre went on the attack. If Verdi did that, they would invoke a law whereby he would be detained and prevented from leaving the city. Verdi escalated the dispute by saying that, in that case, he would seek asylum aboard a French warship anchored in the Bay of Naples, and take his score with him.

Perhaps both sides realised the absurdity of the level to which matters had escalated. The theatre assured Verdi he would be paid in full, if not entirely on the date due, and Verdi allowed himself to be mollified.

There was the usual trouble with singers, but *Luisa Miller* opened on schedule just before the turn of the year, on 8 December 1849. It was well received, and productions of it were staged over the next two years in Venice, Florence and Milan. It was seen in Philadelphia in 1852 and London in 1858.

Verdi was pleased to be done with Naples. As he returned home he caught a heavy cold, perhaps the final unwelcome gift from a city he had no desire to see ever again.

Verdi had now fallen out with the managements of three of Italy's major opera houses – La Scala in Milan, the Teatro Regio di Parma and the Teatro San Carlo in Naples. For a lesser operatic composer this would have been fatal. But Verdi knew these opera houses needed him more than he needed them, and he would make them pay for their intransigence.

Neither Parma nor Naples would ever see the premiere of another Verdi opera, and Milan would have to wait another thirty-five years before it did so.

It was, once again, a changed Giuseppe Verdi who returned to Busseto after just three performances of *Luisa Miller*. The euphoria of 1848 had dissipated. The cities liberated from the Austrians had all been retaken

The first edition vocal
score of *Luisa Miller*,
illustrating the death
of Luisa.

and reoccupied. An independent Italy remained a dream. Verdi was disillusioned with politics. Not for him any longer heady discussions and
arguments in salons of the nobility.

In a sense Verdi was withdrawing into himself. It would not last for
ever; before too long he would re-emerge onto the political scene. But
for now the isolated life he was leading in Busseto with Giuseppina
suited him, even if it meant deprivations for her and tensions in relationships that had once meant so much to him.

This change in mood found its way into Verdi's music too. *Luisa
Miller* was unlike any of his fourteen previous operas. Gone are the big
set-piece scenes. This is an altogether more intimate work, but no less
dramatic for that. It is drama on a smaller scale.

Two families from different social strata, one in a middle-class home,
the other in a castle; two fathers, with different aspirations for their children; these are as close to 'ordinary' people as Verdi ever portrayed in
an opera. There are no political overtones; it is a drama of individuals,
set in scenes of domesticity. There is love, thwarted love, duplicity and
death, and for these themes Verdi had found a new style of music.

Rather than simply accompanying the singers, the orchestra plays an
independent role, as if it, too, were a character. But he uses fewer musicians, or rather deploys them in a different way. There is a 'symphonic'
feel to the music, evident from the opening notes of the overture.

It is unlike any overture Verdi had written to date. There is no hint
of any of the themes or melodies to come. Instead it is based on rhythms

that modulate and intensify. The clarinet has a soaring phrase near the start, and re-emerges at key points in the work, as if it were another singer.

This is a Verdi who has, consciously or subconsciously, moved on. He has entered a new phase, both musically and as a human being. The operas he would embark on next would prove to be his greatest and best loved, and they would owe little, or nothing, to his past works.

Similarly, as a man, Verdi was about to enter a new phase of his life. From now on, he determined to be less beholden to theatre managements. He would be his own man; he would choose his own subjects. This applied to censorship too. I believe Verdi had an innate belief, an understanding even, that censorship would one day end, or at least become so diluted as to be ineffective. If the events of 1848 could take place, who could tell what else might one day follow?

And so for his next opera, almost in defiance, he chose a story that he asked his long-standing librettist Piave to adapt from a French play entitled *Le pasteur*.

Under the new title, *Stiffelio*, it included practically everything that could be guaranteed to offend the censor, politics aside. A Protestant pastor, verses from the Bible sung on stage, the depiction of a religious rite, an adulteress portrayed sympathetically by her husband who actually speaks of forgiveness, an altar, pulpit and church benches – and to cap it all, singers dressed in normal everyday clothes. Verdi even included elements of sacred music in his score.

He could not have set his opera up for more of a mauling by the censor if he had tried. And that was what it got. When it had its premiere in Trieste, where it was certainly better received than the last work he had staged there, it had been purged of all religious references and bore little relation to what Verdi had written.

Verdi, giving it up for lost – 'castrated' he called it – wrote a new version called *Aroldo*, and ordered the original *Stiffelio* to be destroyed. Fortunately for posterity *Aroldo* swiftly vanished, and *Stiffelio* – as Verdi wrote it – survived, to be regarded today as a major achievement. It was to prove to be the forerunner of some of his greatest works, containing dramatic elements and contrasting characters that would come to fruition in later works such as *Otello* and *Don Carlos*.

For now, though, Verdi retreated once more to the quiet cloistered life in Busseto with Giuseppina. It would not remain quiet for long. He was about to enter a truly turbulent period in his private life. In his professional life, however, his most productive and successful period was about to begin. The galley years were over.

13

THE OPERA IS 'REPUGNANT, IMMORAL, OBSCENE'

*E*ven before *Stiffelio,* Verdi had read a play by Victor Hugo called *Le roi s'amuse* and thought it might make a strong plot for an opera. In fact, writing to Piave, he described it as 'the greatest drama of modern times', [60] and urged him to start work on a libretto.

Verdi had been approached by La Fenice, the Venice opera house (with which he was still on good terms) to provide a new opera for the forthcoming season. Verdi had accepted, and decided to work once again with Piave, who was chief librettist at La Fenice. That way, Verdi calculated, the path to opening night should be made somewhat smoother. He could not have known how wrong he was.

It is easy to see why Hugo's story so captivated Verdi. It is packed with drama, difficult relationships, ambiguous characters, a love affair, a curse that hangs over the whole story, and ultimately murder. The most dissolute character, a relentless womaniser and rapist, is a monarch, King Francis I of France. The man who mocks him and comes to despise him is not only a court jester – there is barely a rung on the social ladder low enough for him – but a hunchback too. In other words, Hugo completely subverts convention. Unfortunately for Verdi, what had been accepted in print was deemed scandalous on stage.

When *Le roi s'amuse* was first staged, it caused outrage in Paris, was banned after just one performance and was not staged again for another fifty years. If Verdi thought that the Austrian censors in control of Italian theatre would be any more lenient, he was to be sorely disabused of the notion.

In fact, he was aware of the potential problem of securing approval for his opera, but considered it easily dealt with. The solution lay with Piave. He was chief librettist at La Fenice; he was on good terms with the management. Verdi instructed him to speak to them and get clearance from them first, which would make the censors' approval all the easier to obtain. Piave, ever obedient, said he would, and reassured Verdi that from an informal conversation he had already had with one of the management, he did not expect any difficulty.

Piave submitted his libretto to the board of La Fenice. The new title was *La maledizione* ('The Curse'), which Piave – perhaps to mollify the board – confessed he did not like, suggesting it could be changed.

Then he settled in to wait for the board's response, aware that back in Busseto Verdi was waiting somewhat anxiously too. He must have been shocked rigid when the board came back to him, objecting to the libretto on a raft of grounds: the King of France was falsely portrayed, his immoral actions would never have been committed by a divinely appointed monarch, and all in all the story was cruel, violent and immoral.

It was a devastating ruling, appearing to shut the door on the new opera; it was beyond saving. Piave objected as strongly as he was able, to no avail. He passed the bad news on to Verdi.

In a stinging letter to the board of La Fenice, Verdi put the blame entirely on the hapless Piave, stating that on the librettist's assurance that there would be no problems, he had already done a substantial amount of work on the opera, in fact most of it was already completed. And his letter contained a clear threat: 'If I now were forced to take on another subject, I would not have enough time to undertake such a study, and I could not write an opera which would satisfy my conscience.'

The board realised they would have to compromise, or they would have no opera. They took a similar step to Piave, misguidedly assuring Verdi that the censor would raise no objections.

The Public Order Office, the censors, reacted even more strongly than the board of La Fenice. The plot of the proposed opera was 'repugnant' and 'immoral', replete with 'obscene triviality'. It was so far from being acceptable, wrote the Director of the Public Order Office, that it was not only banned absolutely, but changes of any kind were prohibited.

La maledizione, Verdi's new opera, was dead in the water. But this time he was not going to take it lying down. He was no longer the Verdi

"Verdi's new opera was dead in the water. But he was not going to take it lying down. He was no longer the Verdi who could be pushed around."

who could be pushed around, who agreed to adapt his creations to satisfy the whim of petty officials with no idea of what constituted art.

He went on the attack. He refused the theatre's entreaties to rework the opera in the hope that that might make it acceptable to the censors. He wrote to the secretary of the theatre's board: 'I tell you particularly, and in a friendly way, that even if they shower me with gold, or throw me in prison, I absolutely cannot set a new libretto.'

Verdi's frustration is understandable. As is the fact that his usual psychosomatic problems were rearing up to torment him: throat problems, chest problems, stomach problems. 'Whatever did I do when I accepted that contract?' he wrote to a friend.

There was deadlock. The censors stood firm. Verdi would not attempt any sort of rewrite. La Fenice was in danger of losing the opening production of its new season. With just two weeks to go, posters and programmes about to be printed, Verdi tore up his contract and La Fenice had no opera.

Fortunately for the history of music, the story was not yet over. Remarkably, of the three protagonists (Verdi, the theatre, the censors) it appears it was the censors who ultimately backed down – one in particular, albeit ever so slightly.

Piave, along with a board member from La Fenice, went to see the most senior of the censors, the Director of Public Order. Between them, a compromise was hammered out. The chief censor allowed the plot to stand in its original form, but the main character could no longer be a monarch. He allowed the jester to remain deformed, but the kidnapping of his daughter would have to be handled in a way that 'conforms to the demands for [decency] on stage'.

That last demand was suitably vague, the other stipulations not so severe, and Piave thought Verdi might just possibly agree to the changes. He immediately left for Busseto to see Verdi. We can only imagine how relieved Piave must have been to find the composer in a mood that suggested a satisfactory outcome might not be beyond the bounds of possibility.

Better than that, at their very first meeting Verdi agreed that the setting of the story should be changed from the royal court in France to a small independent duchy; the king should now be an anonymous duke whose name would not be revealed; certain other names would change; decency would prevail; and – perhaps most importantly for Verdi – the opera would now be the last of the season, giving him more time to complete it.

In a move obviously calculated to appease Verdi, he alone was allowed to decide on the handling of the crucial denouement, when the jester discovers that the body in the sack is that of his daughter.

One other change in particular was also made. It is not clear exactly when this was decided, how it came about, or who suggested it. The opera adapted from *Le roi s'amuse* began life as *La maledizione*, then became *Il duca di Vendôme*, and then in a letter to Piave on 14 January 1851 Verdi first used the name of the jester, the name that would prevail, that would secure its place in operatic history as Verdi's greatest creation to date, one of the best loved he would ever write, and a firm fixture in opera houses around the world to this day and beyond: *Rigoletto*.

Despite stomach problems, despite a private life that was threatening to spiral out of control (of which more in the next chapter), Verdi worked long and hard hours, setting the words provided by Piave as soon as he received them – words that had been passed by the censor.

On 26 January Piave wrote to Verdi in colourful and excited language:

Dear Verdi, Te Deum laudamus! Gloria in excelsis Deo! Allelujah! Allelujah! *At last yesterday at three in the afternoon our* Rigoletto *reached the directors safe and sound, with no broken bones and no amputations.*

Verdi still had the last act to complete and orchestrate. Ten days later, he wrote to Piave: 'Today I finished the opera.' It had taken its toll though. Ever suspicious, Verdi feared that the management of La Fenice might now try to bring the performance forward, but he wanted enough time for the singers to learn their parts, and for there to be sufficient rehearsal.

He might have been exaggerating, but probably not by much, when he wrote to the management stating that the sheer effort of completing the opera had left him really ill, and that if they tried to make any scheduling changes whatsoever he would send them doctors' certificates.

Interestingly, at the same time his business sense did not leave him. He sent a letter to his publisher Ricordi confirming that La Fenice had the right to stage the opera, but only in Venice. The score would be Ricordi's 'own, absolute property', but only on payment of:

. . . fourteen thousand francs in 700 gold napoleons of 20 francs each . . . You will have to pay me 300 of the 700 gold napoleons (and not 400) immediately after [Rigoletto] *is staged, and you will make this amount available to me at the Poste Restante in Cremona as I return from Venice. You will pay me the rest in monthly payments of*

50 napoleons beginning on the first of next April and continuing in the same way on the first of each month until it is paid.

In an era before agents came on the scene, Verdi was more than capable of negotiating for himself!

Verdi arrived in Venice to supervise rehearsals, well aware that after weeks of fraught negotiations, setbacks, unreasonable demands, he was now very much in the driving seat. The season at La Fenice was not going well; audiences were disappointed, and this was reflected in low ticket sales. Piave wrote to Verdi that *Rigoletto* was awaited as the 'salvation' of the season.

Now it was Verdi's turn to make demands. He got the singers he wanted and the rehearsal time he demanded. Still, with just three weeks until opening night, there was a lot of work to do.

Piave had secured for Verdi the two warmest and sunniest rooms in the city's finest hotel, the Hotel Europa, and had had a piano installed

FIGURINI dell'Opera RIGOLETTO del Maestro G. VERDI

Gilda
Atto III Scena IV e seguenti

Gilda
Atto III Scena I. II e III.

Gilda

Duca
Atto III Scena I. e seguenti.

Duca.

Duca
in costume borghese

Rigoletto.
Atto I Scena III.

Rigoletto
Atto I Scena VII.

C.te di Monterone.

Giovanna.

C.te di Ceprano, Marullo, Borsa.
Coro e Ballerini (variando i Colori.)

C.sa di Ceprano
e Ballerine (variando i Colori.)

Paggio
della Duchessa.

Alabardieri. Usciere.

C.te di Ceprano, Marullo, Bursa.
e Coro (Colori variati.)

Maddalena.

Sparafucile.

Paggi delle Dame
Colori variati.)

Servi di Corte.

Paggi del Duca.

MILANO
DALL' I. R. STABILIMENTO NAZIONALE PRIVILEGIATO DI
GIOVANNI RICORDI
Contrada degli Omenoni N. 1720, e sotto il portico a fianco dell' I. R. Teatro alla Scala.
Firenze, G. Ricordi e Jouhaud.

for Verdi's use. Now it was down to the hard work of getting the new opera ready for opening night on 11 March 1851.

Verdi himself was in no doubt about the worth of this new opera – why else would he have fought so hard to bring it to fruition in the form he wanted? He was aware that in the original play Victor Hugo had turned convention on its head. Verdi himself, in a letter to Piave, used fine understatement when he described his opera as 'somewhat revolutionary . . . and therefore newer, both in its form and style'.

A ruler (even if now a duke rather a king) was the villain, a hunchback jester the hero. The word 'hero', though, is too simplistic a description for Rigoletto. He is a father full of love for his daughter, and yet with a thirst for revenge so strong he is prepared to plot murder. Verdi himself said of him, 'I thought it would be beautiful to portray this extremely deformed and ridiculous character who is inwardly passionate and full of love.'[61]

The duke, handsome and with an unquenchable desire for seduction – at whatever cost to the woman or her family, or indeed her husband – is portrayed as shallow and immoral. To him Verdi gives the aria that runs through the whole work, and is possibly the most instantly memorable he was ever to write. He banned his singers from whistling it in the street before opening night, because he did not want to spoil the surprise of it. But those (from his day to this) who consider it a fine example of Verdi's tunefulness, should remember he composed 'La donna è mobile' as a pastiche, a piece deliberately designed to be shallow and trivial, to reflect the character of the duke.

Even Sparafucile, the murderer, has a certain dignity. As for the main female part, Gilda, Rigoletto's daughter, she is torn between love and virtue, allowing herself to be seduced even though she knows the pain it will cause her father. She is thus caught in a dilemma. She must either lie to him, or hurt him beyond measure.

At every point in the opera, the music perfectly captures the sentiment, the conflicts of emotion, duplicity, duality, and moments of utmost tenderness. Gilda's aria, 'Caro nome', is almost as well known as 'La donna è mobile'; and the duet in which father and daughter remember her mother, now in heaven, is one of the most moving moments in all Verdi opera. And over everything hangs the curse, uttered by Monterone – another father whose daughter has been seduced by the duke.

This was an opera unlike any Verdi had written before. He knew it; so did the audience. The opening night was a total triumph. Some critics, as always, found fault, perhaps unsurprisingly, with the 'violence'

Left

Costumes designed for the premiere of *Rigoletto* at the Teatro La Fenice.

and 'licentiousness', one reporting that the audience left the theatre 'empty and disgusted at such a horrendous and nauseating spectacle'.

One wonders if he was at the same opera as another critic, who wrote that the

> composer was hailed, called out, acclaimed after almost every piece, and two numbers even had to be repeated . . . it is stupendous, admirable . . . it cries out to you, it instils passion in you . . . it strikes you with sweet, ingenious passages. There was never such powerful eloquence in sound.

A plaudit came from an unlikely quarter. The author of the original, Victor Hugo, who had castigated an earlier adaptation by Verdi and Piave of his play *Hernani* as *Ernani* in 1844 as 'a clumsy counterfeit', now wrote that he regretted his earlier reaction. For particular praise he singled out the Quartet near the start of Act Three of *Rigoletto*, in which four voices blend with vastly different emotions. It caused Hugo to remark, perspicaciously, that he could only wish there was a way of making four characters express different sentiments simultaneously in spoken drama.*

The opening night presaged an extraordinarily successful early life for *Rigoletto*. In the same year, it was produced in Rome, Trieste, Verona, Bergamo and Treviso. The following year saw productions in Turin, Florence, Padua, Genoa, Bologna, Parma and its first showing outside Italy at the prestigious Kärtnertortheater in Vienna. Many other Italian cities followed, and it soon began to travel further afield.

By the end of 1853 it had been seen in Corfu and Budapest, as well as in Austria (again), Malta, Germany, Russia, Portugal, Spain, England, Scotland and Poland. It went on to Gibraltar, Alexandria, Bucharest and Constantinople. *Rigoletto* crossed the Atlantic in 1854, to be seen in New York and San Francisco, as well as in Havana and Montevideo.

Giuseppe Verdi was now world famous, an achievement not lost on his fellow countrymen. If, in the past, he had aroused mixed emotions both professionally and personally, that was now forgotten – at least for the time being. Almost all Italians with even a modicum of interest in the arts were proud of their musical son.

---

* This remarkable piece of writing was undoubtedly inspired by the Quartet in Act One of Beethoven's *Fidelio*, and remains a source of inspiration to this day. A performance of it by four retired operatic singers, and their conflicting emotions, formed the plot of the 1999 play *Quartet* by Ronald Harwood, and the subsequent film.

Above

An early edition of the vocal score for 'Bella figlia dell'amore' from Act Three.

It was well over a decade since Verdi had had an unqualified success on home soil; that had been *Macbeth* in 1847. But this was on an altogether different scale. Verdi the composer had grown and matured, entering now not just his most productive years, but composing operas of a kind neither Italy nor the world had ever heard or seen before.

With *Rigoletto*, Verdi eclipsed all who had gone before him. Names such as Bellini, Donizetti, and especially Rossini, were still revered, but Verdi had now unquestionably surpassed them. At the age of just thirty-seven, who could tell what masterpieces might lie in the future?

It was a valid question, and one that Verdi would answer again and again in his long life. Yet with the benefit of hindsight, we can see now that Verdi's achievement with *Rigoletto* was all the more remarkable, given the turmoil that beset other aspects of his life.

While he was writing it, while he was castigating Piave with letter after letter, while he was fighting the management of La Fenice and then the censors, his private life – away from all the tensions of trying to create an opera and get it to the stage – was in turmoil.

Amid all the excitement and publicity surrounding the opening night of *Rigoletto*, the presence of local and regional dignitaries, Verdi's legion of supporters determined to ensure the opera's success, one man was missing.

Verdi's most loyal supporter, the man who was the first to recognise his genius, who nurtured and supported him from the very start, who loved him like a son, Antonio Barezzi, refused to go to Venice to attend the opening night.

Verdi was hurt and confused. But really he should not have been. Barezzi was not alone in distancing himself from Verdi; in fact there were many who now openly shunned him. He might have been hurt and confused, but he could not plead ignorance. He knew exactly what he had done to offend them.

14

A Rift in the Verdi Family

Verdi was living in sin and the people of Busseto did not like it. I have already described how Giuseppina was shunned when she stepped outside the Palazzo Cavalli, insults were hurled, even stones thrown up at the windows. Giuseppina had tried going to church, but found herself sitting alone.

It was a difficult situation, and one that Verdi was doing nothing to improve. To have brought her to Busseto in the first place – an unmarried mother of illegitimate children – was a provocation to the deeply conservative Bussetans. Now he was cloistering himself inside the four walls of the Palazzo Cavalli with the woman who was his mistress. Or was she? Was she perhaps his wife? It might seem a bizarre question to ask, but there was genuine doubt.

To Barezzi he had refused to state whether or not he had married Giuseppina, and his father-in-law relayed that refusal to family and friends. 'Who knows whether she is or is not my wife?' Verdi wrote to Barezzi. 'And if she were, who knows what particular motives, what reasons we have for not making that public?'[62]

It was entirely within Verdi's power to resolve matters, to reassure Barezzi and others. He could, obviously, have married Giuseppina. Given her colourful past it might be expected that she would never attain the popularity and esteem that, say, a local bride would receive (or Margherita had possessed), but he could reasonably argue that both he and she inhabited the same professional world, had fallen in love while working together, and had decided to spend the rest of their lives as husband and wife.

Given Verdi's fame as the local boy who had accomplished so much, and indeed Giuseppina's reputation as a former star singer, that would surely have been enough to still wagging tongues.

Or he could have gone on a charm offensive. He could have invited family and friends round to his house to meet the woman he shared it with. Giuseppina was a sophisticated woman, used to the salons of Milan and other great Italian cities. She could most certainly have held her own in Busseto.

On arrival back in Busseto, Verdi had been inundated with invitations. He could have accepted them, brought Giuseppina along on his arm, introduced her around, generally behaved as a married man, even if the relationship had not – as yet – been formalised.

He did none of these things. He made it a deliberate policy to keep Giuseppina cloistered within the four walls of the Cavalli, and to remain cloistered there with her.

In a period of roughly a year and eight months, apart from occasional trips to Paris and Florence, it is believed Giuseppina virtually did not set foot outside the Cavalli. It is possible that she might have gone to church in a nearby village, to avoid ostracism in Busseto.

It was Barezzi first who made known his misgivings to Verdi. He sent him notes asking why he was not welcome at the Cavalli, why he was not invited to come and see the young man he admired so much, and meet his partner. In that same twenty-month period Barezzi had not once seen Giuseppina. It must have been all the more galling, given that Barezzi's house was just a few yards away, on the other side of the Via Roma to the Cavalli.

It looks as if Verdi was not only shunning his former father-in-law, the man to whom he owed so much on a personal level, but cutting him out of his professional life as well. A heartfelt sentence in a letter Barezzi wrote to Verdi – the letter has not survived, probably because Verdi destroyed it, but Verdi quotes the sentence in his reply – reads: 'I understand perfectly that I am not the man to take care of [important matters], because my time has already run out; but I could still handle little things.'

To have upset the man who stood by him loyally through thick and thin, who had been there for him every inch of the way, comforting him after the death of his wife and children, encouraging him after the

failure of *Il giorno*, helping him in so many ways, including financially, must have taken some doing. Verdi had achieved it.

Precisely why Verdi allowed this to happen, *caused* it to happen, we cannot know. It is possible Giuseppina herself may have had a hand in it, perhaps giving Verdi an ultimatum along the lines of 'It's me or them'. It seems unlikely; we are left with the conclusion that Verdi, for reasons best known to him, did not make it easy for himself, or others.

Verdi had also become estranged from Barezzi's son, Giovannino, though it seems it was Giovannino who was the instigator. Verdi and he had been close friends for many years. As younger men they had spent a lot of time together, socialising and even carousing in Milan. Verdi asked his brother-in-law to take over the administration of Sant'Agata in the interim between his parents leaving and he and Giuseppina moving in.

To Verdi's shock and disappointment, Giovannino refused to set foot inside Sant'Agata. The young man, who had been such a comfort to Verdi after Margherita's death, had clearly now taken his father's side. Verdi tried to make light of it, or at least to find a way to excuse his friend:

> I gave him a wide-ranging, written power of attorney, and he never set foot even once in Sant'Agata. I do not reprove him for this. He was perfectly right. He had his own affairs, which are quite important, and because of that, he could not take care of mine.

It is a fair assumption that there were families in Busseto with eligible daughters, young women whose hopeful parents envisaged them becoming the bride of the famous composer.

But it was not to be. Verdi had chosen a way of life calculated to offend. Even if he was unaware of that on first arriving in Busseto (unlikely though that would be), he would have been in no doubt as soon as the insults began. Giuseppina at least would have left him in no doubt.

There were two other people whom Verdi had upset, and the word 'upset' is an understatement. They were wounded to the core by his behaviour, which they found deeply hurtful, incomprehensible and immoral. They were Carlo and Luigia Verdi, his parents.

Relations between Verdi and his parents had been tense for some time. Breaking the rule that one should never do business with family, loans had been going backwards and forwards between Verdi and his father – in both directions – with Carlo berating his son several times for overreaching himself. Verdi, naturally, was irritated by his father's interference.

Despite the many words written about their famous son, Carlo and Luigia Verdi remain shadowy figures. In all the interviews Verdi gave, the biographers and journalists he spoke to, he makes very little reference to his parents, stressing only the poverty of his childhood and how hard his father worked at the *osteria*.

In possibly his most extensive interview, to his French biographer Arthur Pougin, there are only two indirect references to Carlo and Luigia, neither of them in quotation marks.

Pougin describes them as 'an honest and industrious young couple', Carlo going off to Busseto every week 'to obtain the stores which he required . . . returning on foot, carrying on his shoulders the two baskets which he brought back to the village'. As for the child, he was 'brought up by his mother, who adored him'.[63]

And that is it. No further mention, not even when the acquisition of the spinet for the eight-year-old boy is described. Nor are their deaths recorded in conversation between Verdi and Pougin. Given what was about to happen between Verdi and his parents, this is perhaps unsurprising.

"As far as the world is concerned, Carlo Verdi has to be one thing, and Giuseppe Verdi something else."
Verdi on his father

Unsurprising, too, that Verdi's behaviour had so upset his father. He was, by all accounts, a deeply religious man. Giuseppina was later to describe him as going to Mass daily, then returning to church in the evening to recite the rosary. We have no evidence of Carlo attending his son's operas on a regular basis, even when his fame was firmly established. No basking in reflected glory for Carlo Verdi.

There is some evidence Luigia tried to heal the growing rift with her only surviving child. She stayed for a while with her son at the Palazzo Cavalli when Giuseppina was away, and I have already recounted how she had one of the beds moved to Sant'Agata in the hope he would move in there to be with his parents.

Not only was that out of the question as far as Verdi was concerned, but he then took truly drastic action to prevent any further interference from them. In January 1851 he decided to cut himself off from his parents, not just by refusing to see them, but by engaging a lawyer to draw up a document of legal separation.

Proof that this was not just a sudden action on impulse, in later years he referred back to the separation as an act of 'emancipation'. In fact the legal document proved difficult to draw up. It seems Carlo was assuring friends that he and his son were reconciled.

Verdi reacted angrily. His words, in a letter to the lawyer, are bitter and uncompromising:

> From a trusted source I have heard that my father is going around peddling the story that things have been settled between us . . . I want to repeat to you . . . that I intend to be separated from my father in my residence and in my business. To sum up, I can only repeat what I told you yesterday in person: as far as the world is concerned, Carlo Verdi has to be one thing, and Giuseppe Verdi something else.

If Verdi was laying down the law, literally, over the major matter of a formal break with his parents, proof of just how petty he was being at the same time came in a letter he wrote to the lawyer just two weeks later:

> I let my mother have the rights to the chicken-yard while we were together; now that we are separated it is quite natural that this right should revert to me. About fifteen days ago the Brunelli woman asked me to whom she should bring the produce from the chicken-yard, I answered: Here in the house in Busseto. That is the whole story! I did not give this order out of stinginess, but because I do not want to let my parents have any rights, either small or large.

And three days later:

> *My father never had any right over the chicken-yard; and if you persuade my mother to accept for the moment a gift of money to compensate her [for loss of income from the chicken-yard], it would be absolutely improper and ridiculous for my father to come forward with some claim over this, too.*

These letters were written at the end of January and early February 1851, at *exactly* the time Verdi was struggling with *Rigoletto*, after arguing with the management of La Fenice, confronting the censors, in constant touch with Piave over the libretto, worried about the quality of singers available – all the problems associated with bringing an opera to the stage.

In the midst of rehearsals with the singers, coaching them privately at the piano as well as directing them on stage, Verdi was at the same time making sure his parents no longer derived any benefit from the chickens at Sant'Agata.

He was to go even further. He ordered the lawyer to insert a clause into the document of separation instructing his parents to leave Sant'Agata by 11 March, or at the latest 11 May. He was throwing his parents out of the farmhouse they had helped him to buy.

Financial matters between father and son were at this stage complicated. Each owed the other money. Transactions, it appears, were many and not all were documented. But it remained a fact that Carlo Verdi had loaned his son money to buy Sant'Agata, and there is no evidence Verdi repaid any of it.

As part of the legal agreement, Verdi took it on himself to find a house for his parents to rent. This he did – a house that was actually smaller than tenant houses on the Sant'Agata estate. Verdi lent his father money to secure the lease, but two months later demanded it back.

All this tension was taking its toll, and not just on Verdi. On 25 March – two weeks exactly after the premiere of *Rigoletto* – he wrote to Piave:

> *My mother . . . is still sick! I foresee new disasters with my father! I am not well!! I feel tired, as exhausted as if they had drained off half my blood. I still have a bit of stomach ache and a cough.*

Verdi, another triumph under his belt, the pre-eminent operatic composer in Europe, was at this stage thirty-seven years of age. His father was sixty-five and his mother sixty-three. To quote Phillips-Matz, 'At an age when they might have hoped to share their son's fame and enjoy it

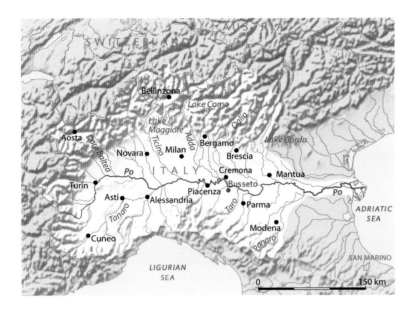

with him, they saw him getting ready to move his mistress into Sant'
Agata, even as Carlo Verdi was going deeper into debt daily.'

There was the added strain of his mother's illness, possibly brought
on, and certainly exacerbated, by the continuing strain of estrangement
and forcible eviction by her own son.

None of this went unnoticed and unremarked on in the small close-
knit town of Busseto. Every step in the escalating dispute between Verdi
and his parents must have been general knowledge, and in a society
where love and respect for parents is a given, Verdi would have come off
far worse than his parents in the eyes of his fellow Bussetans.

We really do have to pause for a moment to try to understand what
it was that drove Verdi to such extreme lengths. The familiar tensions of
writing a new opera would not in themselves be enough to cause such
seemingly irrational behaviour.

Even Giuseppina was unhappy with him. In a letter to Piave while
he and Verdi were in Venice for *Rigoletto*, she wrote, 'I beg you to put
a lot of effort into educating Verdi, so that he comes back to Busseto a
little bit less of a Bear!!!'

Part of the reason might be that Verdi was harbouring a secret. It
involved the woman to whom he had referred as 'that Angel whom you
know' in a letter to Piave when they were working on *Ernani* together.

It seems that, despite living with Giuseppina in Busseto, the other
relationship might not have been entirely over. In the same letter to

Piave in Venice in which he talks of his mother's illness and future disasters with his father, he ends with the words: 'Give my greetings to the Angel you know about. Addio Addio.'

We know no further details, because Piave successfully guarded Verdi's secret. We can state with certainty that the 'Angel' did not come to Busseto. That would have been entirely out of the question, even with Strepponi absent on one of her trips. Another woman simply would not have been able to enter or leave the Palazzo Cavalli unnoticed.

Did Verdi arrange a secret rendezvous either close to home, or in Venice, or at some point in between? We cannot totally rule it out, but again it is unlikely. There would, surely, have been too much at stake for a man who was already the target of malicious gossip in the town where he lived.

We can, however, state that the woman, the 'Angel', makes no further appearance in Verdi's life. Whether it was he or she who terminated the relationship, we cannot know. Most likely, Verdi realised that it would be impossible to continue with it.

And so, even if the strain of this contributed to Verdi's behaviour, it is unlikely to have caused him lasting pain. The affair – if that was what it was – was over.

We need to look further afield in trying to explain Verdi's actions at this crucial juncture in his life. In particular, why was his father so offended by his actions? Why was Verdi so determined to keep Giuseppina cloistered in the Cavalli, knowing the antagonism he was building up?

Could it be that Giuseppina was pregnant?

15

A QUESTION OF IDENTITY

hat follows is an amalgam of fact and speculation. Speculation in a biography, I believe, is permitted when it is made clear that it is speculation, and where it is based on known fact.

For what follows I am heavily indebted to Verdi's most comprehensive biographer, Mary Jane Phillips-Matz, who carried out more extensive research in Busseto and the surrounding area than any other modern biographer, to the extent of living in Busseto, befriending and speaking to local people, hearing their stories and legends of Verdi, and examining records there and in other towns that had never before been made public. I shall tell this particular story largely as she tells it.

On 14 April 1851, at half past nine in the evening, a newborn baby girl was placed in the turnstile set into the wall at the Ospedale Maggiore in Cremona. The bell was rung, the turnstile revolved, and the nuns took the baby in.

Unusually for an abandoned baby, the nuns found a name for the baby inside the basket, and the following day she was baptised Santa Streppini. In every section of the baptismal register, in answer to details such as name of father, name of mother, and so on, is the word 'unknown'.*

---

* After exhaustive searching, Phillips-Matz found this document in a locked cabinet of the lowest storage cellar of Cremona City Hospital, not, as might be expected, in the parish records office. It is a fair assumption that it had been hidden there.

"The relationship between Verdi and Giuseppina might have been somewhat relaxed as far as other relationships were concerned."

Was Giuseppina Strepponi the baby's mother? We know that she had given up three earlier babies to foster parents, one of them placed in the turnstile in Florence, so to have placed this new baby in the turnstile would not have been an unlikely action for her to take.

Clearly the name 'Streppini' is just a single letter away from 'Strepponi', and again using false names closely resembling her own is not something alien to Giuseppina. Her illegitimate son was registered under the name 'Sterponi', while Giuseppina herself used the invented name 'Spillottini' when she wanted to receive letters in secret.

This new infant was placed with foster parents under the name Santa Stropellini. Yet another invented name, clearly and carefully entered into the register.

Phillips-Matz established, after exhaustive research, that none of these invented names appeared in any other official record for the entire first half of the nineteenth century. In other words, at the time these illegitimate babies were born, there was no other family in the Po valley with any of those family names. The invention of them, then, was obviously done with great care, to ensure there could be no confusion with any other family.

The foster parents with whom Santa was placed were smallholders living on a farm near the Sant'Agata estate. From it they could clearly see the Sant'Agata villa; one of the family would later do gardening work for Verdi.

Santa lived with her foster parents until she was fifteen. She was then formally adopted by their daughter and her husband, an unusual course of action that might be interpreted as a move to keep the child in the family. The husband's mother was a similar age to Verdi and had been a friend of his when both were growing up in Busseto.

Santa and her new foster parents continued to live in the smallholding on the edge of Verdi's Sant'Agata estate. Clearly (and unlike Strepponi's earlier children) great care had been taken in the placing of this child. Was it made to ensure she lived close to Giuseppina? We cannot be sure, since there is no record of any further contact between the two of them. But it does seem plausible.

If Giuseppina was indeed Santa's mother, then she would have become pregnant around the end of June or early July 1850. Towards the end of the year, she would not have been able to conceal it. It was at this time that relations between Verdi and his parents reached breaking point. Could it have been the discovery of Giuseppina's pregnancy that caused it? It would certainly explain Verdi's reluctance to have visitors to the Palazzo Cavalli in Busseto. It would also explain why she remained cloistered within the building for such a long period.

If we accept the proposition that Santa was Giuseppina's daughter, it leads naturally to the assumption that Verdi was the father. He was living with her at the Palazzo Cavalli in Busseto at the time, of course. It is therefore unthinkable that she could have become pregnant by someone else – or, if she had, that Verdi would have allowed his relationship with her to continue.

At the very least, it might explain the rift between him and his parents. It might also go some way to explaining his complicated relationship with Giuseppina. Were they married or weren't they? If they were, had he become stepfather to her other illegitimate children, as Italian law demanded? Given his international fame and reputation, the potential scandal that would have ensued was surely out of the question.

There are a lot of 'ifs', and no conclusive evidence that Giuseppina was Santa's mother or Verdi her father. But the circumstantial evidence, it has to be admitted, is strong on both counts.

To add to this, we have local legend. Phillips-Matz, who lived with Bussetans of a later generation, was told time and time again that Santa's father was Verdi and her mother Giuseppina, and that this knowledge had been handed down through the generations.

There is more, and it concerns Verdi, though not this time Giuseppina. In late May 1850 a boy was born in Busseto, named Giuseppe, and placed in the turnstile in the same hospital in Cremona where Santa would be put almost a year later.

Giuseppe was placed with foster parents in Busseto, where he would live and grow up. When he was old enough to understand, Giuseppe was told that he was Verdi's illegitimate son, and that his mother was one of the maids in the Palazzo Cavalli when Verdi and Giuseppina were living there.

It is certainly possible. At this stage in their lives, the relationship between Verdi and Giuseppina, while not being entirely open, might have been somewhat relaxed as far as other relationships were concerned. We know Verdi had affairs; there was the 'Angel' in Venice and the baroness who lived outside Busseto, and there were surely more.

Once again, it was local legend that Giuseppe's father was Verdi, and once again this was passed down the generations.

We know, too, that in the run-up to *Rigoletto* Verdi was under intense pressure, both professionally and in his private life. The letter to Piave that I quoted in the last chapter, where he says he feels tired, 'as exhausted as if they had drained off half my blood', was written less than three weeks before Santa was born.

Exactly two weeks after Santa was placed in the turnstile, Verdi wrote again to Piave. After criticising his father, who 'does not want to leave me free and at peace', there are these heartfelt words:

> *I assure you that I am at a fork in the road that is so dreadful that I do not know how to get out of it. But it is better not to mention certain things to you, and it is useless for me to tell you about my troubles, [for] you cannot help me.*

If only he had told Piave. What was the 'fork in the road'? We can only surmise. It might have referred to *Rigoletto*, or it might have referred to something more personal.

To take conjecture even further, we can look at Verdi's artistic creations, his operas. It has not been lost on biographers that through many of them run strong father–daughter relationships.

Even before Santa's appearance on the scene, we have the illegitimate Abigaille in *Nabucco*, a role that Verdi was determined Giuseppina would sing. There is a tender duet between father and daughter in Act Three of *Luisa Miller*. The strongest portrayal to date of a father–daughter relationship comes in *Rigoletto*; in fact it forms the whole basis of the drama. As I have shown, it is entirely possible that Giuseppina was pregnant while Verdi was working on *Rigoletto*.

Still to come is *La traviata*, in which Violetta begs her lover's father to embrace her as a daughter. Beyond that, there is the great father–daughter recognition scene in *Simon Boccanegra*; father comforts daughter in Act One of *La forza del destino*; and on Verdi's mind throughout most of his adult life is his desire to write an opera based on *King Lear*, with the searing relationship between the king and his daughter Cordelia at its heart.

We can, naturally, conclude nothing from any of this. In fact one can quite reasonably point out that three of those operas were composed before Santa was born, so even if he were the father, how would Verdi know he had a daughter?

Nor must we forget that Verdi was a father who had lost two children – one a daughter – in infancy.

Taking everything together, the circumstantial evidence that Santa was the daughter of Verdi and Giuseppina is strong, perhaps even overwhelming. Phillips-Matz concludes that they were indeed her parents, while accepting there is no definitive proof.

Giuseppina's biographer Gaia Servadio disagrees. She points to the fact that Giuseppina had a brief physical relationship with the composer Donizetti when she was in her mid-twenties. Seven years later Donizetti died of syphilis. He had already lost his wife, whom it's thought he infected, and Servadio suggests he caused physical harm to Giuseppina, leaving her sterile by the age of twenty-eight.[*]

The opera critic Andrew Porter, in an article for the *Financial Times* following the publication of Phillips-Matz's biography, writes, 'There is no *proof*, only pointers toward the probability that the composer of those poignant father–daughter duets lived with a load of guilt.'[64]

He suggests, though, that a man of Verdi's 'stern fearless character' would have been more likely to defy the world and 'boldly and lovingly acknowledge his love-child'. In the close-knit and deeply devout community of Busseto in the 1850s, he would certainly have had to be fearless, given the damage that would have done to his reputation.

We have not yet heard from the woman at the centre of all this, Giuseppina Strepponi herself. We have precious little to go on, in fact just a couple of sentences in a single letter. They do not resolve the issue; indeed in some sense they add to the uncertainty.

Depending on the reading of her words, they could be said to refute the proposition that Santa was their daughter. Conversely her use of the future tense, and the words that follow in parenthesis, could be said to give the theory credence. Either way, Giuseppina's words offer us an insight into the extraordinary hold she clearly had over Verdi.

On 3 January 1853, while she was in Livorno and he was in Rome, Giuseppina wrote to Verdi:

> *We will not have children (since God perhaps is punishing me for my sins by preventing me from enjoying any legitimate joy before I die)! Well, having no children by me, you will not, I hope, give me the sorrow of having any by another woman. Now, without children, you have a fortune more than sufficient to provide for your needs and even for a bit of luxury. We adore the country and in the country one spends little [money] – and there is great pleasure.*[65]

This lends credence to Servadio's theory that Giuseppina was incapable of having children, for whatever reason, be it through contact with

> "The greatest operatic composer Italy had produced had at last become the man of the soil he had always wanted to be."

---

[*] Servadio gives no direct source for her assertion that Giuseppina was sterile, and I have found no reference to it elsewhere.

syphilis or – another theory – early menopause. Or it could be that Verdi had made it clear that marriage, for now, was out of the question. Either way, that would explain her use of the word 'legitimate' and the future tense.

What seems surprising is the pressure she is putting on Verdi not to have children by any other woman. It is quite possibly a decision he had already taken, but if he had, he had not confided in her. The fact that it would cause her 'sorrow' suggests she expects the relationship with Verdi to continue, something that is reinforced by the fact that they are already living together in the country, namely at Sant'Agata.

It is surely fair to assume that the two of them must have discussed the question of children, and their future life together. It is also quite possible that Verdi had already assured Giuseppina that he would marry her one day. She is unlikely to have used such language otherwise.

The move into Sant'Agata came on 1 May 1851. This was less than two weeks after his parents moved out – or, more accurately, were evicted by him. Just two days before the move, he had reached a financial agreement with his father, after months of wrangling and acrimony. Debts were settled in both directions.

Verdi's mother Luigia was still ill. It is not an exaggeration to say her health was broken by all the tension that had grown up between parents and son.

For Verdi, he had realised his dream. He was back living in the countryside he adored. Immediately he set to work to improve the house and the grounds. He brought in a team of carpenters, stonemasons, bricklayers and decorators.

He began to live the life he had for so long coveted. In a pattern that he would develop, but which then remained fundamentally unchanged for decades to come, he indulged in the physical effort of gardening, planting shrubs and trees; he took long walks across the fields and even longer drives in his carriage; he interested himself in the livestock, the delivery of calves and their sale at market; fruit trees and vines he nurtured, making sure the soil was well irrigated from the rivers that bordered the estate.

The greatest operatic composer Italy had produced, the most famous in Europe, had at last become the man of the soil he had always wanted to be. But it had come at a cost. Unequalled he might have been in the world of opera, but to the people of Busseto he was a man who had turned his back on them, lived inappropriately, disrespected his parents, flown in the face of tradition and morality.

Few visitors came to Sant'Agata. Those who did – and that included some of the workers he employed – became objects of scorn in Busseto. To say that Verdi was a pariah would be putting it a touch too strongly, but only a touch.

We know, of course, that Verdi's genius would supplant all this. He would be remembered long after the people of Busseto were forgotten. And, just as he had hoped, the joy of living in the countryside, on his own estate, stimulated his creativity.

Almost as soon as he moved into Sant'Agata, Verdi began work on a new opera.

16

'Without You, I Am a Body Without a Soul'

s soon as Verdi began living at Sant'Agata, his health improved. It could hardly fail to, given the fresh air and the physical exercise he was taking. He now had everything he wanted: surely he could not have been happier. But if he was, it did not last long.

Just weeks after he had moved in, thieves broke into the house. Verdi described in a letter to Piave how they had put a ladder against the wall, broken a window and ransacked his writing desk, stealing money he kept in a drawer. To make matters worse, it turned out the thieves were his own servants and he dismissed them. It was an inauspicious start.

Rather strangely, in the same letter he describes himself as living in 'this frightening solitude'.[66] If that was really how he felt about his new life at Sant'Agata, it was certainly not the impression he gave to anyone else, least of all the person who lived with him, Giuseppina. His new way of life was entirely of his own making.

A month later, in June 1851, Verdi's mother died. This caused him distress on an entirely different level. He descended into a spiral of grief. Muzio was with him and wrote to the publisher Ricordi that he was inconsolable:

> I cannot tell you his grief, it is so immensely great. Peppina suffers at seeing him weep . . . I had persuaded him to leave and come [to Milan], but then he changed his mind and now does not want to leave his house.[67]

For several weeks Verdi refused to see anybody. Alone with Giuseppina, his grief for his mother overwhelmed him. We can safely assume a large measure of that grief was caused by guilt. We do not know the last time he had seen his mother. Even if he had paid a visit to his parents before her death, and even if the dispute between him and them had been settled formally, the emotional rift between them had not healed. Now it was too late to make amends, even if he wanted to.

Slowly Verdi emerged from his grief, and his thoughts turned again to work. At least a year before, while still working on *Rigoletto*, he had decided that his next opera would be based on a Spanish drama entitled *El trovador*. Now he began in earnest.

As with the illegitimate child Santa Stroppelini, it is easy to attribute motive after the event. The new work, *Il trovatore* as it would become, is the only Verdi opera to focus on a mother rather than a father. Azucena, the Gypsy, is central to the action. Could his own mother's death have influenced him, consciously or subconsciously? It is possible, but we have to bear in mind that his decision to use the drama pre-dated his mother's death by some time.

Similarly, a particularly gruesome element of the plot is the discovery of the charred remains of a baby in the embers of the witch's funeral pyre. Guilt over Santa? All we can say is that Verdi's attraction to the drama pre-dated Santa's birth.

What we can certainly say about *Il trovatore* – and indeed about so many of Verdi's operas – is that the relationship between parent and child is seminal, and that surely can be no coincidence. Perhaps more significantly, considering Verdi's operatic career, this new opera was the first he was writing purely because he wanted to (the early *Oberto* excepted), as opposed to fulfilling a commission.

Not that that made the task any easier. The librettist he chose – the same Cammarano he had saved from prison by agreeing to set *Luisa Miller* – raised all sorts of objections to the plot, pointing out that the censors would refuse to allow several elements, not least the depiction of nuns on stage.

Verdi was now used to getting what he wanted. He sent Cammarano a stern injunction to write the libretto exactly as he wanted it, 'and I am all the happier if the pieces are new and bizarre'. Cammarano did as he was told, seemingly without questioning Verdi's meaning behind the slightly strange word 'bizarre'.

But progress was slow, and stopped altogether when, in early 1852, Verdi and Giuseppina left Sant'Agata for Paris.

"For several weeks Verdi refused to see anybody. His grief for his mother overwhelmed him."

Verdi had a few business matters to tie up in Paris, and Giuseppina was no doubt pleased to leave Sant'Agata, which she described in a letter to a friend as a 'hole'. While the couple were in Paris, they went to the Théâtre du Vaudeville to see a new play by Alexandre Dumas *fils* entitled *La Dame aux Camélias*. The moment he returned to the apartment they were renting, Verdi began to compose music based on the play. Already a new opera was forming in his mind.

He would go on to complete this new work in a remarkably quick time, and it would prove to be one of the most miraculous creations of his entire career. But that lies in the future.

On their return to Sant'Agata, Verdi settled once more into country life. In a revealing letter that Giuseppina wrote to a friend some time later, she affords us a remarkable insight into Verdi the countryman: in fact Verdi the reluctant countryman – contrary to everything he himself had given her to believe – and, indeed, Verdi the tyrannical countryman.

She writes that previously Verdi felt 'a kind of horror of staying in the country', but once he experienced it, took to loving it so much, and with such passion, that she found herself overwhelmed in this 'cult for the Sylvan Gods'. As for my use of the word 'tyrannical', well, just read her description of how he takes over. She does it with humour, but I imagine it's written in a tone of defiance.

> *We began, to our infinite pleasure, planting a garden which, at the beginning, was called* Peppina's garden. *Then it was extended and called* his *garden. And I can tell you that he acts as Czar over this garden of* his *so much that I am now confined to a few plots of terrain, where he, by established convention, must not stick his nose. In all conscience, I couldn't say he always respects this convention, but I have found a way of calling him to order, by threatening to plant cabbages instead of flowers.*[68]

It is easy to imagine the man, who was now so used to getting his way in professional matters, standing up defiantly to the censors, bullying compliant librettists such as Piave and Cammarano to make sure he got what he wanted, attempting to overrule Giuseppina with a dismissive wave of the hand, but not entirely succeeding.

It is also not difficult to understand how this woman, who had given up everything to come and live with Verdi, who had left the artistic milieu in Paris in which she thrived, abandoned her career as singing teacher, tolerated the scorn of Busseto so as not to upset him, struggled to adapt completely to their life in Sant'Agata.

At the end of the same letter in which she tells of losing her private little garden, and threatening the 'Czar' with cabbages instead of flowers, she writes:

> The sun, the trees, the flowers, the immense and various family of birds, who make the country so beautiful and animated for a good part of the year, leave it sad, mute and bare in winter. Then I do not love it. When the snow covers those immense plains, and the trees with their naked branches seem desolate skeletons, I cannot raise my eyes to look outside. I cover the windows with flowered curtains as high as a person, and I feel an infinite sadness, a desire to flee the country, and to feel that I live among the living and not among the ghosts and silence of a vast cemetery.[69]

They are telling words to write. Still under forty years of age, Verdi had found his little bit of paradise in Sant'Agata, even if he did not always admit it. Giuseppina, born and brought up in the bustling town of Lodi in Lombardy, who lived in sophisticated Milan in her teenage years (having been accepted by the Conservatory, unlike Verdi two years later), had given it all up to become a recluse in a house she loved in summer and hated in winter, living with a man who did not always make her life easy. It is a measure of her devotion to him.

Just a few months later, when Verdi was in Rome for the production of his latest opera, she would write:

> My dear Verdi,
>
> I confess my weakness to you, but this separation has been more painful for me than so many others. Without you, I am a body without a soul. I am (and I think you are the same) different from so many others who need frequent separations to keep their love alive. I would stay for years and years with you without being bored, or weary.[70]

He might not have been so explicit in his letters to her, but there is no doubting his dependence on her, his reliance on her to keep his life on an even keel, to help him juggle all the demands made on him. He sought her advice on professional matters, from contractual issues, as we have seen, to musical ones. She knew exactly what a professional soprano would expect from a composer, and what she would not want, and he was more than ready to listen to her advice and take it.

Does that equate to true love? Who can say, but it was certainly sufficient to sustain a long-lasting and mutually beneficial relationship.

Ultimately, whatever the reason, their companionship was essential to both of them. One quite simply could not live without the other, which is why they continued to live together for almost a further half-century, until death finally separated them.

Above

Giuseppe Verdi in the courtyard of Sant'Agata.

Progress on *Il trovatore* continued to be slow, not least because Verdi not only indulged his new lifestyle as a man of the soil, but he pursued it with a passion. It was not long before he could boast a farm containing several horses (which he adored), four oxen, sixteen cows, ten bulls, eleven calves and six rams. This was as well as an abundance of fruit trees, not to mention any number of ornamental shrubs and flowers.

New trees by the dozen were planted. The makings of a natural lake existed in the grounds, fed by the abundance of rivers nearby, and over the years Verdi would drain it and turn it into a beautiful lake with ornamental bridge.

As well as livestock, he and Giuseppina had two dogs, which Verdi, in line with his lifelong antipathy to the clergy, named Pretin (Little Priest) and Prevost (local dialect for Provost).

Had he so wished, he could have devoted all his energy to his farm, leaving precious little time for anything else, least of all the effort it took to write opera. Over the years to come, many was the time when Giuseppina would have to be as stern as she was able, and remind him of his musical obligations.

Now, though, there was work to be done on *Il trovatore*. Once again – it is not the first time I have said this, nor will it be the last – Verdi was creating something entirely new. The main protagonist is a woman, the Gypsy Azucena; she does not appear until the second act; and Verdi makes her a mezzo-soprano. Operatic convention differed from this in

---

Much of this can still be seen today (see Afterword).

every respect: the main character was usually a tenor, and he would make an early and dramatic appearance. It was what audiences expected.

Much of the opera takes place in the darkness of night. The singers frequently refer to the night, with its silence and stillness. Fire, too, in one form or other, permeates the opera, whether at the stake, or in the passion expressed by characters.

Verdi was working hard, but always there was tension in the air. It had been almost a year since his mother's death when suddenly his father fell dangerously ill, to such an extent that it was feared he too would die. We do not know if Verdi went to see him, but there must have been relief when the old man recovered.

Just a short time after this, Verdi, who was perplexed that he had not heard from Cammarano in a while, picked up a theatrical paper and read that the librettist had died. Verdi was shocked to the core. He wrote to a friend:

> [The news was] a bolt of lightning . . . It is impossible to describe to you my deep sorrow over this! I read of his death not in a friend's letter but in a stupid theatrical journal!!! . . . Poor Cammarano!!! What a loss!!!

Cammarano had died without completing the libretto. It was yet another hurdle in an already fraught state of affairs. The premiere of *Il trovatore* had been set for 19 January 1853 at the Teatro Apollo in Rome. It was now August. Five months to go, and the libretto had not even been finished!

Hardly surprising that Verdi's health played up once more, the familiar headaches, sore throat and stomach problems resurfacing. He complained, as always, about the stress he was under, but by this point it seems almost as if it were a necessary precondition of his creativity. A new, much younger, librettist was brought in by the name of Leone Emanuele Bardare. He was actually Cammarano's pupil, which allowed a certain continuity. Verdi worked on.

He finished the opera on 14 December, and rehearsals began just after Christmas, perilously close to the opening date of 19 January 1853.

Verdi must have known he had made himself a hostage to fortune by having two lead female roles, one a soprano and one a mezzo, even if the mezzo's was the larger role. The two prima donnas did not get on, making rehearsals difficult. At first they refused to rehearse in the same room. This added tension made Verdi's health even worse. He was confined to his hotel room in Rome and was unable to attend rehearsals.

In the true tradition of opera, and a familiar problem for Verdi, rehearsals did not go well, and the composer braced himself for failure. He could only hope the first night would not be a complete disaster.

The premiere of *Il trovatore* was not just successful, it was an unmitigated triumph. At the end of the performance, Verdi was called on stage and presented with a crown of laurel leaves intertwined with embroidered red ribbons.

On the night of the third performance, in an echo of the success of *Macbeth* in Florence, Verdi was escorted back to his hotel surrounded by an ecstatic crowd carrying torches. Underneath the balcony of his room, a band played a selection of music from his operas. On the fourth night, the theatre was decorated with white banners and flowers, as it would have been for royalty.

'*Il trovatore* did not go badly,' Verdi wrote to a friend, with classic and familiar understatement. He wrote to another that the cast could have been better, and in response to criticism from some that the opera was too sad and gloomy, he responded characteristically, 'But after all, in life isn't everything death? What else exists?' It is an understandable remark from a man who had had such experience of death in his lifetime.

For an opera so permeated with darkness, and indeed death, what sets *Il trovatore* apart from its predecessors is its sheer energy. The pace does not let up. The most famous numbers are 'The Anvil Chorus' sung by the Gypsies, and the tenor aria *'Di quella pira l'orrendo foco'*, sung by Manrico, an army officer – rhythms and propelling energy from first note to last, ending on a show-stopping high C. The tunes are instantly memorable on first hearing, and it is no wonder the audience reacted with such wild enthusiasm.

Verdi himself, some years later, with the opera firmly established in the repertory, remarked drily and with, I suspect, a cynical smile concealing deep inner pleasure, 'When you go to the Indies or the middle of Africa, you will hear *Il trovatore.*'

As always, success for Verdi came at a price. He left Rome after the fourth performance of *Il trovatore* and returned to Sant'Agata. He was still in poor health, the usual complaints now compounded by rheumatism in his right arm. For a composer who needed to sit at the piano, and write on manuscript paper, it was a debilitating condition.

And he most certainly needed to do both of those tasks. A full year before, with relations once again on a reasonably level footing, he had signed a contract with La Fenice in Venice for a new opera. It was

about the same time that he and Giuseppina had seen *La Dame aux Camélias* in Paris.

The two gelled in Verdi's mind. He had actually begun work on a new opera based on Dumas' drama while he was still in Paris. He had entrusted the libretto to Piave, and he had worked intermittently on the opera throughout 1852, as he was struggling to bring *Il trovatore* to the stage, but hardly surprisingly, with everything that had been going on, he had not completed much of the new work. Now he was in dire straits. The contract with La Fenice stipulated that he should be in Venice at the beginning of February, start rehearsing on the 8th, and have the opera ready for its premiere on the last Saturday of the month, 26 February.

Given that he only returned from Rome, and *Il trovatore*, on 15 January, he had before him an impossible task – five weeks to bring the new opera to completion and have it ready for opening night. He must have wondered why he had ever taken it on. Failure was inevitable. Perhaps to save face, he complained about all the principal singers hired by the theatre, saying it would be impossible to write for them. He rejected several other suggested singers, before a compromise was reached.

Above

Set design by Giuseppe and Pietro Bertoja for The Garden in the Palace, from Act One, Scene Two of *Il Trovatore*.

Verdi remained unhappy, even using the dreaded 'f' word in a letter: 'I have no faith whatsoever that it will succeed, and – on the contrary – it will be a complete fiasco.'

The opera, which was to be called *Amore e morte* ('Love and Death'), would indeed fail. But if that seems only to be expected given the time constraints, think again. Before its premiere the opera's name would be changed to *La traviata*, and it was to become not just the best loved of all Verdi operas, but one of the most popular operas any composer would ever write.

17

THE BEAR OF BUSSETO

The auguries were not good. Verdi summoned Piave to Sant'Agata and put him under huge pressure to complete the libretto. Working alongside each other, which we can imagine was not entirely the way Piave wanted it (he must have dreaded being confined to his room and the door locked, Verdi's tried and tested technique), composer and librettist completed a rough draft in just five days. Muzio was also there to tend to the two men's needs.

It was one of the wettest Octobers anyone could remember: 'When it rains here, I assure you that . . . [we] look in the mirror to see whether we still have human shape or whether we have been turned into toads or frogs!' wrote Muzio.

Verdi composed swiftly, but could see nothing but problems ahead. The biggest of these, as far as he was concerned, was the singers that La Fenice had engaged, and of these it was the lead soprano he was insistent on replacing – even though he had earlier agreed to her engagement.

Fanny Salvini-Donatelli was singing in her debut season at La Fenice, and word reached Verdi at Sant'Agata that in performances elsewhere her voice had left much to be desired. Potentially just as damaging, she was a large lady – 'stout' was the word used – and Verdi challenged the theatre on how she could possibly be expected to portray a frail woman dying of consumption.

He went further. He wrote to the management demanding that the entire cast of singers be replaced, otherwise there would be no opera. The strain of all this, he wrote, was severely damaging his health. The rheumatism in his right arm had worsened; he had no intention of damaging his health even further, and if his demands were not met, he would refuse to honour his contract and would produce medical letters to support his case.

The theatre reminded Verdi his date for demanding changes to the singers was past, and that he had previously agreed to them, including Salvini-Donatelli singing the role of Violetta. As to his health, they wished him well, and urged Piave to calm the man they now openly called 'The Bear of Busseto'.

It was on receipt of Piave's news that no singers would be changed that Verdi wrote that letter I quoted in the previous chapter predicting the opera would be a fiasco.

Piave also reported back that the censors had now seen the libretto for the new opera, and had demanded that the setting be altered from the modern day to the era of Louis XIV, a century and a half earlier.

Verdi exploded in disgust. He was adamant that the modern setting should remain, insisting that the drama had such force precisely because it was set in modern times. The audience could thus relate directly to the tragedy unfolding on stage.

In fact Verdi and Piave had gone to great lengths to disguise Violetta's profession, knowing the censor would forbid it. She is a prostitute, but there is no direct reference at any point in the libretto, or in the action on stage, to this fact.

It seems that in this, at least, they succeeded. Either that, or the censor was satisfied, provided the setting was put back 150 years, that the audience would not be corrupted by seeing a courtly courtesan receive due punishment for her reprehensible way of life by dying of consumption.

By now the opera had the title it would retain, *La traviata*. In English it translates as 'The Fallen Woman', which makes the censors' decision to allow it all the more surprising. That alone might have gone some of the way to mollifying the Bear of Busseto, since he accepted now that the opera would have its premiere at La Fenice on 6 March 1853, one week later than originally planned – another peace offering by the theatre.

To understand the extreme pressure Verdi was under, resulting in his outbursts of anger as well as his poor health, we need to remember that in the closing months of 1852 he was fully stretched trying to bring *Il trovatore* to the stage. With his natural pessimism, he was expecting to have two failures back to back.

He barely had time to digest the unexpected success of *Il trovatore* before all his worries and concerns were transferred to *La traviata*. As he undoubtedly saw it, he might have got away with the former but, as for the latter, he knew it was doomed.

It was thus a thoroughly dispirited and demoralised Giuseppe Verdi who arrived in Venice to rehearse the singers for *La traviata*. The atmosphere in the rehearsal room cannot have been good; the singers knew they did not have the confidence of the composer.

Verdi did nothing to ease their anxiety. He criticised them openly, and reported to the theatre management that all the principals were unable to sing their roles satisfactorily. The principals countered that he was impossible to work with. By now there was nothing anybody could do. Opening night was set; it was too late to replace any singers, and Verdi was still predicting a fiasco.

It did not begin that way. The Prelude to Act One brilliantly sets the scene for what follows, opening with high violins depicting the frailty of Violetta. In fact it presages the final scene in which she dies, followed by a yearning phrase she will sing when declaring her love for Alfredo. It lasts less than five minutes and it is a small masterpiece. The audience knew it. Even before the final notes sounded they were on their feet, calling for Verdi to take bows.

Act One was similarly well received. Verdi was called out after the drinking song – the *Brindisi* – in the party scene, and again after the great love duet between Violetta and Alfredo. Other passages were applauded. Things were looking good.

Then, in Act Two, it all started to go wrong. By now the voice of the tenor singing Alfredo was tiring, and the baritone playing his father was never up to the role. At one point – we do not know exactly when, though clearly it was inappropriate – there was laughter in the audience. There can be no greater humiliation for composer or singers.

Act Three of *La traviata* begins with great intensity – the high violins again with the consumption theme – and we know there can be no other ending than the death of Violetta. Verdi had not written anything as searingly emotional as this in any of his previous operas.

That was not how it played out on opening night. As the end nears for Violetta, the doctor announces that her consumption has worsened and she has only hours to live. What the audience saw was an overweight singer clearly in the rudest of health.

The audience is said to have burst out laughing at this point, with one voice shouting, 'I see no consumption, only dropsy!'

The curtain finally fell, no doubt with tears of frustration on stage contrasting with tears of laughter in the audience, but perhaps a sense of relief all round that the evening's entertainment had finally ended.

Verdi was, naturally, devastated, but at the same time vindicated. The following morning he dashed off a series of letters, liberally using that same 'f' word he had used in his dire predictions. But interestingly, there is more than a hint that he might somehow bear some of the responsibility himself. Could it be that he suspected, deep within himself, that there was still work to be done on the opera?

To Muzio: '*La traviata*, last night, fiasco. Is it my fault or the singers'? Time will tell.' To Ricordi: 'I am sorry to have to give you a piece of sad news, but I cannot hide the truth from you. *La traviata* was a fiasco. Let's not ask about the causes. This is the story.' To a friend in Rome: 'I did not write to you after the first performance of *La traviata*. I am writing after the second. It was a fiasco! An absolute fiasco! I don't know who is to blame: it's better not to talk about it.' To another friend: '*La traviata* was a fiasco. It is useless to ask why. It is a fiasco and that is that.'

Only to a colleague who was a conductor in Genoa did he give any suggestion that work might need to be done to ensure the opera's ultimate, and inevitable, success:

> La traviata *was an immense fiasco, and worse, people laughed. Still, what do you expect? I am not upset over it. Either I am wrong or they are wrong. As for myself, I believe that the last word on* La traviata *was not said last night. They will see it again, and we shall see! Anyway, dear Mariani, mark down the fact that it was a fiasco.*

Verdi's liberal use of the word 'fiasco' was an overstatement. *La traviata* ran for ten performances at La Fenice, bringing in an average evening profit of more than double that of his two previous operas in the same theatre.

However, Verdi did recognise that there was work to be done. The opera was staged a year later, again in Venice but at a different theatre.

Verdi had made several changes to the score, most importantly to the crucial Act Two duet between Violetta and Alfredo's father. This duet marks the turning point of the opera, the moment at which Violetta concedes to Alfredo's father that she will give up his son as her lover.

Another crucial difference was that the role of Violetta was now sung by the soprano Maria Spezia. At twenty-five she was thirteen years younger than Salvini-Donatelli, and considerably slimmer – far more credible as a consumptive, and despite her youthful age a fine actress as well as singer.

Piave reported to Verdi's publisher Ricordi that 'Spezia is made for this opera, and this opera seems made for Spezia . . . In her very pallor, her exhaustion, and her entire person, everything in her comes together to make her the true incarnation of [Violetta].'

Indeed, everything did appear to come together. A joyous Ricordi wrote to Verdi, who evidently was not at the performances, to tell him that

> there was never a success in Venice like that of La traviata . . . On the third night there was an uproar of indescribable applause, the [last] act was even more effective than on the other two nights, if that is possible . . . And this gives me all the more joy, because this means not only that your tears will be allayed, but the news of the immense success will be all the more welcome to you.

We can rely on Verdi to add a touch of cynicism to disguise what must have been deep joy: 'Then it was a *fiasco*, now it is creating an *uproar*!'

From Venice, *La traviata* travelled to Milan. It soon joined the ranks of *Rigoletto* and *Il trovatore* to become one of Verdi's best-known operas. And that was while it was still being performed in early eighteenth-century costume.

Remarkable though it seems to us today, given how familiar we are with contemporary productions placing the opera in a nineteenth-century milieu, the male singers continued to appear in long curled wigs, scarlet and blue silks, gold brocades, white lace collars, white silk stockings, knee-length balloon breeches and buckled and tasselled shoes.

Not until 1906, in Milan, was *La traviata* performed in the setting that Dumas *fils* had specified: mid-nineteenth-century Paris. Verdi never saw his most enduring and best-loved opera as he had imagined it.

His most enduring and best-loved opera – of that there is no doubt. But why has it achieved that status?

It is, of course, stating the obvious to say that it is packed with instantly memorable melodies, whether the rousing *Brindisi* of Act One, or the plangent love duets that run through the entire opera.

There are many other reasons. I find the following fact surprising, given what we know of the character of Giuseppe Verdi, of his love for women, of his intensely passionate and emotional nature, but *La traviata* is the only one of his twenty-seven operas in which the entire plot revolves around the love between a man and a woman. There are no political themes in it, no great and meaningful choruses, no longing for freedom from captivity.

Setting a love affair as the central element enabled Verdi to write a more intimate opera than he had ever written, or would ever write again. There are just three main characters: Violetta, her lover Alfredo Germont, and his father Giorgio Germont.*

Crucially, these characters are thoroughly believable (whatever century they are depicted as living in, and however they are dressed). They are characters to whom the audience can directly relate. Rarely for any opera, the audience is not required to suspend its disbelief for a single second. These are credible people experiencing credible events and exhibiting credible emotions.

Most importantly, the progress of Violetta from the opening of Act One to the close of Act Three is entirely plausible. Even in the party scene near the start of the opera, she collapses from the effort of carousing. The consumption that will kill her has already started its work.

At the heart of the opera, when Violetta agrees to give up Alfredo for the sake of his family, in mid-aria she holds a single sustained note. Verdi marks it in the score with a pause.

It is a moment even the most accomplished soprano approaches with a certain dread. It has to be sung quietly, the note held for as long as her breath will allow. The conductor in the pit will be studying the singer's face and head for an indication of how long she can sustain the note, conscious that he must move the unseeing orchestra on at the exact moment she needs to descend to the next note.

---

* My wife and I saw a performance of *La traviata* in a Venice *palazzo* with just three singers and four musicians. Stripping the opera back to its bare essentials demonstrates how the love affair carries the entire opera. It focuses your mind entirely on what is at the heart of the opera. There is no sense at all of anything missing. We both agreed that out of more than a dozen productions we had seen, from London to Verona to Sydney, it was the most memorable of all.

The party in Violetta's salon that begins *La traviata*.

One of the most emotional moments in the entire opera comes in Act Three, when Violetta is close to death. Alfredo knows it, as he holds her to him and sings that he will take her away from Paris, away from the city, where her health will come back and the future will smile on them.

Violetta joins him in duet, but Verdi marks her to sing with 'half-voice, as if in a dream' (*a mezza voce, come in un sogno*). While Alfredo sings lyrically of a shared future, Violetta responds in breathless staccato, anxious and painfully weak. Their voices come together at the end, before they, and the music, fade to nothing.

For both singers, this ultimate stillness has to be achieved after more than three hours on stage. The soprano has already performed one of the most demanding roles for any soprano, on stage and singing in practically every scene of the opera.

This is supreme Verdi, the composer at his very best, and he demands the same from his singers.

There is one nagging question that needs an answer, however, though ultimately we do not have one. If *La traviata* is so radically different from any other opera Verdi wrote, for all the reasons I have cited, why did he choose to do it?

Remember, he had the inspiration when he went to see *La Dame aux Camélias* with Giuseppina in Paris. He began writing down themes as soon as they returned to their apartment.

Could it be that Giuseppina, the woman he now lived with, encouraged him? By this time both intended to spend the rest of their lives together. They were, to all intents and purposes, a married couple, whether or not that was legally the case.

I suspect they returned to their apartment, deeply moved by what they had seen, both imagining how Verdi might use his genius to bring it to the opera stage. Did he suggest it first, or did she? Or did they, perhaps, open a bottle of wine, look at each other, and smile?

18

VERDI, GENTLEMAN FARMER

*I*n the space of a little over two years, Verdi had composed his three most enduring works. Especially given the short time in which he composed them, his trilogy ranks as one of the greatest achievements in all opera. Incredible, too, is the fact that he had composed eighteen operas in just eleven frenetic years. When *La traviata* had its premiere, Verdi was not yet forty years of age.

His achievement is all the more remarkable given that Verdi was in constant dispute with meddling censors, arguing with theatre managements, having to tolerate singers who were not up to the task forced on him, dealing with frequent bouts of ill-health, battling with his librettists to make them write and rewrite until he got exactly what he wanted, all at the same time as coping with domestic crises.

It really is little surprise, given the hurdles that lay between composition and production, that he held his own profession in such contempt, and that he had a constant yearning to devote himself to other, more relaxing pursuits. Now, after the strain of the last few years, was exactly the time to indulge them.

In October 1853, as he turned forty years of age, the most lauded opera composer in Europe owned forty-six animals and large stores of grain. Three tenants to whom he let smallholdings on the Sant'Agata estate farmed the land, but Verdi took control of every aspect of his estate.

He experimented with breeding cattle and horses; he worked on developing new strains of grapes, wheat and corn. He had his own slaughterhouse on the estate, and began selling pork products on the open market, where he had a reputation for driving a hard bargain. He demanded weekly reports from his farm managers, which he would sign off only when satisfied.

He became interested in ever more exotic strains of flowers and trees.[*] A tradition handed down within the family is that he planted a sycamore for *Rigoletto*, an oak for *Il trovatore* and a weeping willow for *La traviata*.

As he reached the milestone age of forty, Verdi was in better health than he had been for years. The fresh air, and the sheer physical effort of farming, had done wonders for his constitution – and, indeed, for that creative mind. Alone in the fields he had time to think, to plot, to create.

Verdi the farmer he might have become, but Verdi the operatic composer he remained at heart. There was no denying it; it was part of his very being. And so, as soon as he had decided to give up composing once and for all, he began . . . to compose.

To begin with, his long-held desire to set Shakespeare's *King Lear* revolved in his mind as he tended his plants and livestock. It was the one ambition that accompanied him, that weighed on him, for all his adult years. Cammarano had already provided large swathes of libretto, when Verdi had previously worked on the idea; following his untimely death in July 1852, Verdi brought in another librettist, Antonio Somma.

Somma completed what Cammarano had left unfinished. Verdi was satisfied, sending him payment for the work he had done. He told Somma he had to set it aside temporarily, but would get down to it as soon as he had finished another project he was working on. He kept saying that for the next two years, and for decades beyond that. *Lear* would remain his dream, with never a note being written.

So what was that 'other project' occupying his time? Hadn't he given up composing to concentrate on his farm? Yes, but he had a prior commitment with the Paris Opéra to compose a new work, and he was under pressure to honour it.

---

[*] See Afterword for the banana tree that still thrives today (page 260).

As had become his custom, he raised objections – the promised libretto had not arrived, the management had kept him in the dark about their plans, and as well as that he was angry that they had staged a production of one of his earlier operas, *Luisa Miller*, without his permission, and had made a mess of it.

The *real* reason he wanted to be released from his commitment, he hid from them. He wanted to get away from Sant'Agata during the winter of 1853–4, and he wanted to take Giuseppina with him.

Aware of the potential problems of being seen in public with his mistress, he tried to cloak the proposed trip in secrecy. Despite his past problems in Naples, it would at least be warm there, plus it was away from the opera 'powerhouse' cities of the north so it would be easier to hide themselves away.

He wrote to a friend in Naples, asking him to find a comfortable apartment by the sea, ideally with two servants or, failing that, just one, and asking him whether he thought he would be subjected to any bother from the police, and whether 'a lady companion with a regular passport would have to endure the same trouble'. And he added, 'I repeat: it must be a secret.'

His final stipulation was a rather endearing one, that despite his fame he wanted to be seen as just an ordinary man on holiday:

> If I do come, in Naples I shall be Signor Giuseppe Verdi and not Maestro Verdi, which is as much as to say I do not want to hear operas, nor propositions for operas, etc., addio *and silence!*[71]

Endearing, but at the same time rather unrealistic. Signor Verdi, the moment he was recognised, would be just as much an object of veneration as Maestro Verdi, and he must have known that.

In the event, the visit to Naples failed to materialise. Paris was calling, and he was in no position to resist. He was under contract; he had no choice. And so he and Giuseppina packed their bags and prepared to leave, once more, for the French capital.

⸺ ⌁ ⸺

The couple expected to be away for just as long as it took to complete the new opera and see it onto the stage. Given past experience, that should not have taken longer than six months. In fact they were in Paris for a full two years.

Given that they were away for such a long time, with no evidence that either returned to Sant'Agata for even the briefest of visits, it is

"Verdi the farmer he might have become, but Verdi the composer he remained at heart."

worth pausing for a moment to consider why they stayed away so long from home and whether, despite past words from both of them, they really were happy there.

Winters in the Po valley can be cold and very, very wet. I have already quoted Muzio moaning about the constant downpours. In letter after letter Verdi complained about conditions at Sant'Agata – cold, damp, overrun with workmen – yet he also wrote about how much he missed it and how he longed to be home.

For a man who had seemed obsessed with every aspect of farming activity, he showed not the slightest interest (as far as we can tell) during those two years in Paris. There is no evidence he was in touch with his farmworkers, or that they forwarded any information to him.

As for Giuseppina, I have already quoted from that letter in which she complains of how the trees stand like desolate skeletons in winter, and how she covers the windows with flowered curtains.

However, even if at times it could feel rather like a prison that kept them enclosed and away from the world, it also remained a refuge for the couple, and was to continue to do so until the end of both their lives.

In October 1853, with Verdi just past his fortieth birthday, and before autumn had had a chance to take hold in the Po valley, Verdi and Giuseppina took up residence in the rue de Richter near the Opéra.

This was a very different Paris from the one they had left behind only four years before. A new emperor was on the throne, Napoléon III, and he had brought in a *prefet* by the name of Georges-Eugène Haussmann to redesign the city of Paris, to construct wide boulevards, lay out parks, improve sanitation and the water supply; in effect to bring Paris into the modern era.

Thousands of workers were about to turn the capital city into a building site, which did nothing to improve Verdi's mood. He was in a city he did not especially want to be in, working on an opera he did not want to write. And sure enough, it told on his health. The usual symptoms returned – he had a sore throat, his digestion was playing up, and he had pain in his abdomen. At least he had his Peppina by his side; she spent a lot of time nursing him.

For Giuseppina herself, things were rather different. When she had lived in the city previously, she had been a single woman, with a small circle of friends, earning her living as a singing teacher. She was now accompanying the famous and revered Maestro Verdi, and neither she nor he made any attempt to hide it. This was not Italy, there were no family or friends to berate them, there was no tut-tutting in quiet corners. Here they could be as open as they liked.

According to Giuseppina's biographer, Verdi referred to her in public as 'my wife', and she began to sign herself 'Giuseppina' or 'Joséphine Verdi'. She had white handkerchiefs trimmed with lace with the initials 'G.V.' embroidered on them.

A measure, though, of how sensitive both of them were to the issue came when an old friend, Giuseppina Appiani, referred to her in a letter as Giuseppina Strepponi, causing Verdi to send a stinging reply, terminating the friendship.[*]

Giuseppina, in contrast to Verdi, was clearly enjoying being back in continental Europe's most sophisticated city. A new emperor and

---

[*] Servadio speculates that Verdi might have had an earlier affair with the woman, and that the tone of his rebuke suggests it was dictated by Giuseppina.

empress brought with them a return of style and elegance, the emperor retaining a certain cachet as the nephew of Napoléon Bonaparte, even if his image was somewhat tarnished for having chosen as his new bride a Spanish woman of noble, rather than royal, heritage.

Giuseppina considered herself now to be a lady, and she behaved like one. She enjoyed shopping expeditions, accompanied by her English maid. She wore a silk dress, with a cashmere shawl in blue to match her hat, and beige shoes just visible beneath her dress when she walked.[72]

Inevitably an invitation came to call on the royal couple at Les Tuileries. One can imagine Giuseppina brimming with excitement, going to great lengths to dress for the occasion, and Verdi being rather less keen.

Giuseppina reported that the empress shone with beauty, if not charm, and that Spanish was spoken more openly at court than French. Small of stature, the emperor wore elaborately waxed moustaches, was the height of elegance in tight white garters and epaulettes, and sported a magnificent array of medals and decorations.[73]

Verdi, however, was more interested in the several visits that he and Giuseppina paid on Italy's most famous composer of opera, until that accolade was taken from him by Verdi.

Gioachino Rossini, now in his early sixties, had inherited the crown from the recently deceased Donizetti, who in turn had lifted it from Bellini. Now it was the turn of the still relatively young man who had come to pay his respects to his forerunner in Paris.

It is unlikely Rossini minded too much about losing his crown. The composer of forty operas, including such masterful and popular works as *Il barbiere di Siviglia*, *La Cenerentola*, *La gazza ladra* and *Semiramide*, had not written an opera since *Guillaume Tell* nearly twenty-five years earlier, and would not write another in his remaining fifteen years.

Rossini had taken voluntary retirement to enjoy the good life, and it showed. A voracious appetite* had left him with a vast and rotund stomach, and that, together with a 'ridiculous' black wig on top of a bald head, made him an unprepossessing figure.

We know this because, on one of their visits, with Verdi in the next room playing billiards, Rossini seated himself on the sofa next to Giuseppina, when Verdi put his head round the door at just the right moment.

---

* Several dishes were named after him, including the best known, *Tournedos Rossini*, fillet steak topped with foie gras.

Rossini said to him, 'Your wife is scolding me!'[†]

'But why?' asked Verdi.

Rossini shrugged his shoulders. 'I was praising her beauty and her skill as an artist of our times.'

'And I really can't take that,' said Giuseppina.[74]

On several occasions, when recounting the episode, Giuseppina was heard commenting on Rossini's portliness and wig perched on his bald head.

On another visit, a baritone – actually King Louis of Portugal – offered to sing an aria from *Il trovatore*. Verdi got up to go to the piano, but Rossini – in an overt compliment to Verdi – said, 'Leave it to me, this is music I understand.'[75]

[†] Note Rossini's use of the word 'wife'.

The two men clearly got on, Rossini seemingly not jealous of the younger man who was taking his pre-eminent place in the world of Italian opera. On one occasion, Rossini flung his arms round Verdi, exclaiming, 'Look what a Carnival you've got yourself into!'

There is a wonderful and legendary quote, which I have been unable to source, where Rossini says, clearly with a twinkle in his eye, 'I am a rotten pianist, but Verdi is four times worse.'

Social visits apart, there was an opera to be written, and unsurprisingly Verdi was running into all kinds of problems. His contract was for a four- or even five-act opera, to a libretto written by the French dramatist Eugène Scribe.

Scribe was one of France's greatest living dramatists, but he was not good enough for Verdi. Verdi rejected Scribe's first suggestion, and then his second too. Scribe was not used to such criticism, especially from this foreign *parvenu* musician who was more than twenty years his junior.

Eventually a libretto was agreed on, with Scribe bringing in a colleague to help him mould it to Verdi's liking. Verdi began work, but was unhappy from the start. Weeks became months, and months became years.

Throughout the process of composition, Verdi tried again and again to have his contract annulled, threatening to break it if he did not get his way. His longing to return to Sant'Agata intensified. He wrote to a friend, 'I am insane to go home . . . I have a ferocious desire to return to my house.' Yet there is no evidence he returned to Italy at any point, for however short a time.

This was, yet again, to be an opera unlike any of his previous works – for the simple reason that opera in Paris made different demands on a composer. There, it was customary for an opera to be long – as many as four or five acts – with huge crowd scenes and an obligatory ballet.

Given that his previous opera was the most intimate he had ever composed, this new one would inevitably prove a radical departure. That in itself was not as daunting for Verdi as it might have been for another composer. It seemed almost as though every opera he undertook stretched him in new directions.

The usual problems reared their heads: dissatisfaction with the libretto, constant demands on Verdi's part for passages to be reworked and rewritten, problems with theatre management and frustration over the singers who were contracted to perform.

Only, in this case, it was frustration of a different kind. Rehearsals were well under way when the lead soprano, the German singer Sophie Cruvelli, suddenly disappeared. She simply vanished.

Verdi, surprisingly, found himself amused by this, and naturally used it as yet another reason to demand release from his contract. He wrote to Piave:

> *La Cruvelli has run off!! Where? The devil knows where. At first this news was like a kick in the crotch, but now I am laughing up my sleeve . . . This disappearance gives me the right to cancel my contract, and I did not let the occasion slip by. I formally demanded [my release].*[76]

Cruvelli's disappearance was a sensation. She was sought across Europe. Her apartment in Paris was put under lock and key, and her possessions confiscated. In London a new farce was staged, entitled *Where's Cruvelli?*

The Paris Opéra was in a difficult position. If Verdi took the matter of his contract to court, he might win a case against them. A government minister, no less, came to negotiate with Verdi, offering him all sorts of emoluments on behalf of the Opéra, when, just as suddenly as she had disappeared, a month later La Cruvelli reappeared. She had, apparently, been on the Côte d'Azur with a certain Baron Vigier, a Parisian of immense fortune whom she was to marry a few months later.

The date for the premiere of Verdi's new opera, now entitled *Les vêpres siciliennes*, was set for 13 June 1855. Problems pursued Verdi right up until opening night. No less a figure than the composer Hector Berlioz, a clear admirer of Verdi, wrote, 'Verdi is at odds with all the Opéra people. Yesterday there was a terrible scene with him at the dress rehearsal. I feel for the poor fellow, for I put myself in his place. Verdi is a noble and honourable artist.'[77]

The opera, despite the vicissitudes that had dogged its creation, was a success, both with audiences and critics – all the more remarkable given the subject matter concerned an uprising of the people of Sicily against their French oppressors in the Middle Ages.

It ran for more than its allotted number of performances, which encouraged Verdi's publisher Ricordi to have an Italian version prepared and put into production in Italy. Inevitably the Italian censors objected to the subject matter, and it was many years before *I vespri siciliani* was seen in Italy.

Given its reception in Paris, it is perhaps surprising that *Les vêpres siciliennes* never achieved the popularity of its famous predecessors, nor has it ever truly entered the repertory. Probably its sheer length and scale – a full five acts spanning several hours, as well as the complexity of the plot and demands made on the singers – was simply not what audiences expected from Verdi.[*]

As for the composer himself, he was at least relieved that the little-lamented contract with the Paris Opéra was finally laid to rest, and he could move on, both professionally and personally.

It was time, at last, to return home. On New Year's Eve 1855, Verdi and Giuseppina, and Muzio, saw in the New Year in the familiar surroundings of Sant'Agata.

---

[*] Not until as recently as October 2013 was the full version staged for the first time at the Royal Opera House, Covent Garden, and even then the ballet was dropped. Reception was mixed.

19

'VERDI IS MY TYRANT'

Back in Sant'Agata, Verdi's thoughts turned once again to the land, and in April 1856 he bought a huge estate adjacent to Sant'Agata. The purchase made him one of the major landowners in the Po valley.

While most people, never mind composers of opera, would be satisfied with such a large estate, what Verdi now owned was nothing to what he would acquire over the next few decades. By the end of his life, he could lay claim to being one of the largest landowners in the entire country.*

Verdi was over-stretching himself financially once more, which meant a necessary return to the work for which he now had a certain amount of dread, namely composing operas.

I say 'dread', because work on *Les vêpres siciliennes* had taken its toll. It had been long and arduous, and had left Verdi exhausted. The stomach pains brought on in Paris had not left him. He wrote to his friend Countess Maffei that he was not sure when he would ever compose again.

Embracing the nickname he knew he had acquired, he wrote almost in despair:

Excluding estates inherited by the aristocracy.

[This poor Bear of Busseto] is neither reading nor writing . . . I go around in the fields from morning till evening and try to cure – in vain, so far – the stomach trouble that Vespri *left me. Damned, damned operas!*[78]

It is close to a *cri de coeur*. It is hard to equate the most famous and successful opera composer of his day with the words 'Damned, damned operas!'

Coming to know Verdi as we have, though – and knowing the great works still to come – we would not be far wrong in assuming his mood was not quite that low, that there might have been a certain amount of exaggeration for effect. He was, after all, a dramatist by profession.

His public and professional face, though, was one of stern resistance to further work. When La Fenice of Venice wrote to him asking for a new opera, his answer was an unequivocal 'no', giving as his reason his determination never to subject himself to a deadline again.

That might have sounded unequivocal, but La Fenice sensed there was a chink of light. What if they were slightly more relaxed about the deadline than was usual? They wrote to him a second time, but received a similar reply: '[I have an] unshakeable determination never to tie myself up again to a set date, neither for composing nor staging.'

But La Fenice was not giving up. It needed a new opera for the new season, and there was no living composer who could match Verdi. A direct approach having failed, it decided to ask Piave to use a little persuasion.

It was a good move. Piave came to stay with Verdi at Sant'Agata at the end of March, and found he was pushing at a door that was ever so slightly open. A new opera was not out of the question, he told Piave, but no deadline! He would agree only to have it ready for the end of the Carnival season the following year.

That was good enough for La Fenice, who pencilled in 12 March 1857 for the premiere – as Verdi must surely have known they would. Verdi quickly decided on a play by the Spanish playwright Antonio García Gutiérrez, whose *El trovador* had served him so well three years earlier. It was entitled *Simon Boccanegra*, a political drama set in medieval Genoa, but with an emotional father–daughter relationship at its heart.

Verdi set to work with an intensity that surprised Piave. What did not surprise him was how totally Verdi took control of every aspect, first of all making specific demands of the theatre for singers he knew and trusted, as well as of the libretto.

This was Piave's territory of course, but his compliant character was not of the sort to complain – at least not to the Bear of Busseto himself. To a friend he wrote that he felt like 'a donkey tied up in his master's stall. Verdi is my tyrant and you cannot believe how many and how various are the demands he makes on me and my poor verses.'[79]

He had reason to complain. Verdi supplied Piave with a complete account of the action in prose, insisting he submit this to the censors rather than any future libretto. Just turn it into poetry, was his single instruction to Piave. To add insult to injury, he brought in another poet – a Tuscan politician and playwright by the name of Giuseppe Montanelli – to draft several scenes. One can understand Piave's frustration.

When Piave submitted his libretto to Verdi, the composer took it apart, rewrote whole sections, inserted new verses by the second poet without even telling Piave who that was, then returned it to Piave with the mercilessly abrupt note:

> Here is the libretto, shortened and altered more or less as it had to be. You can put your name to it or not, just as you please. If you're sorry about this I am sorry too, perhaps even more so than you. But I can only repeat, 'It had to be.'[80]

Simon Boccanegra was premiered at La Fenice on 12 March 1857. Again Verdi had composed a new style of opera. Gone were the set-piece arias, the moments of singing virtuosity calculated to bring on applause. In fact the main male character who gives his name to the opera does not have a single solo aria. In addition, he is a political character for whom it is difficult to feel much sympathy when he falls prey to intrigue from his own side.

The opera has a preponderance of low voices – two baritones and two basses – with only a single major part for the female voice. This might have been of interest to those deeply immersed in the musicology of opera, but it was not calculated to engender audience enthusiasm. Add to all this the fact that the whole plot, with its myriad intrigues, is almost impossible to follow, and you have a recipe for disaster.

'I have had a fiasco in Venice almost as great as that of *La traviata*.'[81] We are used to Verdi exaggerating how bad things are, of turning success into failure, of condemning his own work with faint praise, but in this case he was not too wide of the mark.

The premiere was judged a failure. The audience left thoroughly depressed – no tunes to hum, no hint of optimism at any point in the drama, overall just too dark and gloomy. Muzio predicted that in time the opera

"Verdi is my tyrant and you cannot believe how many and how various are the demands he makes on me!"

Francesco Maria Piave

Right

The cover of the libretto for the 1881 revised version of *Simon Boccanegra*.

G. VERDI

Simon Boccanegra

Melodramma in un Prologo
e tre Atti
di
F. M. Piave.

Edizioni Ricordi

would come to be recognised as one of Verdi's great creations. But it was not to be. An audience at a production in Florence the same year considered the plot so convoluted that at one point they produced the ultimate insult: laughter. At La Scala in Milan some time later it fared no better.

Verdi, inevitably, was hurt by the reaction. After the Florence performance, which he considered a disaster, he wrote revealingly to his publisher:

> *I don't intend to condemn the public. I allow its right to be severe. I accept its hisses on condition that I'm not asked to be grateful for its applause.*[82]

Nicely put, but the exact opposite of what any composer of opera, Verdi not excepted, would want.

As a further indication of just how much the failure affected him, when he heard rumours in the opera world that the libretto had been largely his own work – which in a sense it had – he reacted with fury, with a calculated insult to his long-suffering librettist. He wrote to a friend:

> *That story about the libretto being my composition was just about the last straw! A libretto with Piave's name on it is always judged thoroughly bad poetry in advance.*[83]

It was, in fact, a double insult: not only was Piave a bad librettist, but his name alone was enough to condemn his work. We do not know whether Piave was ever made aware of these words; we can only hope not.

In fact, Verdi was far from finished with *Simon Boccanegra*. At the behest of his publisher – actually several behests over many years – Verdi returned to it more than twenty years later.

With the clarity that comes from hindsight, and with the emotions of failure stripped away, Verdi could see clearly what was wrong with his opera.

> *The score is not possible as it stands . . . I shall have to redo all the second act . . . to give it more contrast and variety, more life.*[84]

He did all of that, and more, adding the famous Council Chamber scene at the end of Act I, to give us the acknowledged masterpiece we know today.

In a recurring pattern, the latest opera out of the way, it was time to return to the fields. In an echo of the earlier letter already quoted, he wrote to another friend:

> *From morning to evening, I am always out in the fields, the woods, surrounded by peasants, animals – the four-legged variety are the best. Getting home tired at night, I have not found the time and the courage until now to take my pen in hand.*

Three months later, in July 1857, he wrote to a sculptor friend asking for advice on buying two large horses from the province of Friuli in north-eastern Italy.

But it was not possible to keep his thoughts away from the world of opera for too long. He began mulling over his lifelong ambition to create *Re Lear*, though it was soon set aside once more as other matters occupied him.

One of these was a joyful reunion with the man to whom he owed so much, who had been the first to recognise his truly extraordinary gifts, and who had nurtured him when no one else was prepared to: his father-in-law Antonio Barezzi.

There had been a significant change in Barezzi's circumstances. His wife had died a few years earlier, and he had since married his young maid. For a prominent citizen of Busseto to do such a thing inevitably caused a scandal. In his new life, he could clearly no longer berate his son-in-law for his socially unpalatable domestic circumstances. When the two were reunited, their relationship once again resumed its natural ease and mutual affection.

If operatic matters were churning round in Verdi's mind, they were not entirely evident to the person who was likely to spot them most readily. As far as Giuseppina was concerned, the man she was living with was a full-time farmer.

She described in a letter how his 'love for the country has become a mania, madness, rage, fury, everything exaggerated. He gets up at dawn to go and look at the wheat, the corn, the grapevines, etc. He comes back dropping with fatigue.'

He must have worked really hard for it to have such an effect on him. At the time Giuseppina wrote that letter, Verdi was forty-three, which is by no means old even by mid-nineteenth-century standards. In contrast to purely physical exertion, the effort needed to create an opera and bring it to the stage, and then to have to consider reworking it should it not be successful, was taking more of a toll on him each time.

Still, it did not stop him. Discarding *Re Lear* yet again, he turned to a new opera he had promised the Teatro San Carlo in Naples (once again setting aside his previous antagonism towards the city) for the following Carnival season. Sticking with Somma as his librettist – with whom he had been in touch for the projected *Re Lear* – he asked him to adapt the libretto for an earlier opera by the French composer Daniel Auber about the assassination of King Gustavus III of Sweden in the closing years of the previous century.

It was not the wisest choice of subject, and it is hard to believe Verdi did not recognise this. The assassination of a monarch? It was almost as if he were trying to bait the censors, and unsurprisingly they rose to it. Impossible in its present form, they decreed.

E tu ricevi il mio! (Scena ultima)

Un Ballo in maschera Opera di Verdi

Verdi agreed to change the king into a duke (echoes of *Rigoletto*), and to set the action further back in time. There was also a title change, from *Gustavo III* to *Una vendetta in dominò*.

Verdi and Somma completed the opera, and Verdi moved to Naples to prepare the opera for the stage, taking Giuseppina and her dog with him, no doubt to make a return to the city he disliked more palatable. No sooner had they arrived than the censors had a rethink, and decided the opera was still unsuitable for the stage without major amendments, including having the assassination take place offstage.

Above

Illustration of the final scene of *Un ballo in maschera* on the piano/vocal score.

Verdi exploded. An attempt by the theatre to find a compromise, including a new title, failed, and Verdi decided he had had enough. After a tense and strained four months in the city, ignoring any contractual obligations he withdrew the opera and moved it instead to Rome, where the censors were known to be more lenient.

The journey to Rome was made by sea. Nineteen hours in a boat, which left Giuseppina very ill, and her little dog Loulou not much better. Verdi himself reported that he was not seasick, but he lay on his bunk for sixteen hours without moving.

He thus arrived in Rome in a thoroughly bad mood – which was felt by the soprano engaged to sing the lead role. When she asked Verdi to rehearse her at the piano, he told her angrily that he was not a *répétiteur*, and she should have come to Rome having already learned the part.

More lenient the censors in Rome might have been, but they still made similar demands to those in Naples, namely that the king should be demoted to duke and the locale should be changed.

Verdi realised that if he did not acquiesce, his opera would probably never be staged anywhere. And so the action was moved to the colonies of North America, to Boston, and the opera retitled yet again. It was now to be called *Un ballo in maschera*.

This time it was Somma's turn to explode. Stating that the finished opera bore little or no resemblance to what he had originally written, he demanded that his name be removed from the published libretto.

He might have had cause to regret that decision, because against all the odds the premiere of *Un ballo* at the Teatro Apollo in Rome on 17 February 1859 was a huge success. Verdi had learned the lessons of *Simon Boccanegra*. Now the action moved swiftly, scenes blending into one another in rapid succession. None of the arias was too long. The two lead roles were a soprano and a tenor, and despite reports that their singing was not of the highest quality, the evening was a triumph.

Vindicated, Verdi returned with Giuseppina to Sant'Agata, yet another opera launched after a thoroughly stressful period of composition and preparation. Back in familiar surroundings, able to focus his attention once more on agriculture, could he bring himself to continue in the profession he had come to hold in such low esteem?

For the time being, most certainly not. Other matters were intruding. Some he could not do anything about; one was entirely in his control. It was, he decided, about time he made a substantial change in his private life.

A Wedding At Last

Giuseppe Verdi was not an easy man to live with. His seemingly endless battles with censors and theatre managements were something Giuseppina grew accustomed to sharing with him. She was also used to adapting her own life around his need to compose.

Giuseppina told a friend how on one evening at Sant'Agata, when it was time for dinner – always at six o'clock sharp – the cook they employed had prepared everything, but there was no sign of Verdi. She could hear passages of music being played on the piano in his room. Finally, aware the dinner was being spoiled, she went to his room, but hesitated to knock on the door for fear of provoking a temper tantrum.

Finally, with tears in her eyes, as she summoned the courage to knock, the door itself opened. Verdi emerged. 'Ed ora andiamo a pranzo [And now, let's go to dinner],' he said in a matter-of-fact tone of voice.

Strepponi herself recounted this to a friend. She also told him that the piece of music that Verdi was composing became the heartbreaking aria in Act Three of *La traviata* where Violetta, knowing she will soon die of consumption, sings a farewell to her happiness and a future with Alfredo.

The friend, who passed this story on to a later biographer of Verdi, apparently did not specify whether Giuseppina's tears were of frustration at the spoiled dinner or of emotion at the beauty of the music she heard.[85]

Accepting the fact that nothing, not even mealtimes, should be allowed to disturb the act of composing, Giuseppina had little to complain about when it came to food and wine. Verdi was very fond of both.

A twentieth-century biographer recounts that Verdi's favourite dish was veal cutlet *alla milanese*, and that when ordering it in his favourite *trattoria* in Cremona, he would always say to the waiter, 'Remember, plenty of butter.'[86]

Verdi kept a well-stocked cellar at Sant'Agata, including French Bordeaux and champagnes, as well as copious supplies of his favourite Italian wine, Chianti. Another favourite was the local sparkling red wine, which Verdi would often order with a veal cutlet when dining out, ordering simply 'rough local red'.[87]

Perhaps we should not be surprised, given Verdi's love of local produce (especially ham produced in Parma and the Po valley, judged then as now to be the finest in Europe), that Verdi could himself cook. His showpiece dish, according to Giuseppina, was *risotto alla milanese* – presumably with extra butter.

On one occasion, commenting on Verdi being applauded as he took his seat in Parma's Teatro Regio, Giuseppina wrote to Antonio Barezzi, 'If only they knew how well he composes *risotto alla milanese*, God knows what ovations would have showered on his shoulders.'[88]

She was well aware of the effect this rich diet was having on her, even if not on Verdi himself. Photographs throughout his adult life show a slim man, whereas Strepponi bemoaned the loss of her figure in a letter to Countess Maffei, saying she had developed an embarrassing 'embonpoint'.[*]

When Verdi was in a particular city for a prolonged period of time, if his wine was unfinished he would write his name on a slip of paper, roll it up and put it in the neck of the bottle so he could finish it the following evening. He was popular with waiters, because he was in the habit of tipping generously.[89]

It appeared after *Un ballo in maschera* that Verdi was about to have much more time to enjoy his food and wine, and his exploits in the kitchen. After this latest round of battles with censors, managements, singers, librettists, he had once again made the decision to retire from composing – only this time he was determined that it really was final.

---

[*] Her word, taken from a letter quoted in Martin (1988).

At a dinner in Rome he announced several times that he would not compose again. At the end of the evening he repeated it, just in case anybody was in any doubt: he had stopped composing. One of the guests at the dinner was a journalist, and predictably – as Verdi must have known it would – his decision was reported in a newspaper.

Even Giuseppina was convinced that this time he meant it. She wrote to a friend in Naples, 'I am afraid he has unlearned [everything he knows] about music.' Verdi himself, to the same friend, wrote:

I have not done any more music, I have not seen any more music, I have not thought any more about music. I don't even know what colour my last opera is, and I almost don't remember it . . . [even if I wanted to] I would not know how to take my pen in hand to write down notes.

Given the finality of the decision, and Giuseppina's apparent acceptance of it, we can imagine she must have considered what life with the Bear of Busseto would now be like: no more composing, no more trips to Naples, Rome, Venice. Would it strengthen their relationship, or tear them apart?

There was, however, a complication, and it was something over which neither of them could exercise any control. When Verdi and Giuseppina arrived back at Sant'Agata in March 1859 from Rome, they found themselves in the middle of a war.

The city of Piacenza, just twenty miles from Sant'Agata, was occupied by six thousand Austrian troops, sent there to quell growing unrest in the region of Piedmont. The Austrians had suppressed moves towards Italian independence eleven years earlier, but now it appeared revolutionary fervour was bubbling up once again. The aim was a unified Italy under the rule of Vittorio Emanuele II, King of Sardinia.

The Austrian army moved swiftly, occupying the valleys west of Piacenza and moving into Piedmont. As they advanced, reinforcements took their place in Piacenza. This time, however, the Italians had the support of France. French soldiers were fighting alongside their Italian compatriots – a much more formidable force for the Austrians to deal with.

Giuseppina wrote to the same friend in Naples:

Our health is good, [we are] not afraid, but [we are] worried about the serious events that are taking place. This morning at eight the bridges were sealed up, and the gates of Piacenza, which is about 32 kilometres from us, were sealed . . . Tomorrow, or perhaps this

"I have not done any more music, I have not seen any more music, I have not thought any more about music."

Verdi

evening, we will hear the thunder of cannons. Everything is being prepared to make this a war of the giants. Verdi is serious, grave, but calm and trusting in the future. I am certainly more upset, more agitated; but I am a woman, with a more excitable temperament.

The conflict was on their very doorstep. A conductor friend of Verdi, Angelo Mariani, advised him to put jewellery, silverware, linen and other valuables into a strongbox and bury it somewhere on his land.

But just as it seemed Sant'Agata itself would fall prey to the Austrian army, the tide turned in favour of the Italians and their French allies. The Austrians evacuated Lombardy and its capital Milan. They then began to evacuate Piacenza, though not before effectively blowing the city apart with dynamite, leaving piles of rubble in their wake.

But there it ended. Noisy demonstrations in support of Vittorio Emanuele took place in Parma and Piacenza, but independence did not extend to Veneto and Venice. There the Austrians remained, to the utter disgust of Verdi:

> Peace has been made . . . Venice remains Austrian!! *And where, then, is the independence of Italy, so long hoped for and promised? . . . What? Venice is not Italian? After so many victories, what an outcome! How much blood shed for nothing! How many poor young people deluded! . . . I am writing under the influence of the deepest outrage.*

It was a time of uncertainty, a time of danger, and it was time for Verdi to make a decision.

It was not a sudden decision; we know it was one he had discussed over the previous months with Giuseppina, because she wrote to that friend in Naples, cautioning him not to tell anybody, and asking him to teach his children to say, 'Peppina Verdi this autumn'.

Once they were able to leave the Po valley safely, away from any wagging tongues, away from the hostility of Busseto, Verdi and Giuseppina travelled to the little village of Collange-sous-Salève, just outside Geneva. Why did they choose that location? Only they know.

There, in the local church, on 29 August 1859, Verdi married his Peppina. There were just two witnesses, the coachman who had brought them there, and the church bell-ringer. Verdi would probably not be pleased that we know even that much.

Signor and Signora Verdi, Maestro Verdi and his wife, returned to Sant'Agata man and wife, and no one knew it. They had kept it a secret from everyone. It is possible they had told Barezzi and Piave, possibly

Muzio, but if so they kept it quiet. The newlyweds made no effort to make their news known. Word filtered out only slowly.

It is possible that there was another factor behind Verdi's decision. Another career was beckoning. We are about to meet Giuseppe Verdi, politician.

The timing was propitious. No longer distracted by the arduous efforts of composing, Verdi was now able to devote his time to a cause that had always been dear to him, even if he had not hitherto been particularly active in promoting it: Italian unification.

In fact, the impetus for his involvement in political affairs came largely from others rather than as a result of his own volition. His name was now being used for overt political purposes.

Seen first in Naples some time in 1859, scrawled on the walls, were the letters V E R D I. Thoroughly seditious, the acronym expressed support for the king of a united Italy: Vittorio Emanuele Re D'Italia (Vittorio Emanuele King of Italy).

But of course the letters had a double meaning. The explanation, offered to the police by independence activists when they were arrested, was a thoroughly innocent declaration of support for their favourite composer.

It caught on. Soon, and more dangerously, the letters were seen on the walls in Milan and other cities across northern Italy. Verdi's name was becoming synonymous with the drive towards the expulsion of the Austrians, and the declaration of a united and independent Italy under a monarch, Vittorio Emanuele.

At about the same time, certain of Verdi's operas were held up by activists as shining symbols of a united Italy, the most notable example being *Nabucco* and 'The Chorus of the Hebrew Slaves'.

Verdi was powerless to stop it, even if he had wanted to. He had become a local, and indeed national, hero. He embodied the widespread desire for freedom and independence, and his operas were symbols that his supporters could point to. Even to hum 'The Chorus of the Hebrew Slaves' in Venice, where uniformed Austrian soldiers still patrolled the streets, was to risk arrest.

It was perhaps inevitable that a political life would beckon for Verdi. The intense pressure he had earlier felt in Busseto had inevitably softened over time, particularly given his continued – and ever increasing – fame.

The return of the composer and his wife to Sant'Agata after their marriage coincided with a local election for members to the new provincial council of Parma province. Verdi allowed his name to go forward; or, to put it more accurately, he did not resist it being proposed, protesting all the while that he had no desire for the role.

Because he was still officially a resident of Busseto, it was there that Verdi needed to cast his own vote. On election day, he must have had a certain amount of trepidation as his carriage approached the town that had in effect ostracised him, and that had been so cruel to the woman who was now his wife.

He need not have worried. The town band marched down the road to greet him, playing tunes from his operas. When the carriage entered the main street, a cheer went up from the crowd. The mayor delivered an official message of greeting, and an impromptu concert of his best-known music was held. Cries of 'Viva Verdi!' mingled with cries of 'Viva l'Italia!'

"Verdi had become a national hero. He embodied the widespread desire for freedom and independence."

His election was a foregone conclusion. Verdi was now an official representative of Busseto as deputy to the Assembly of Parma Provinces. In his formal letter of acceptance, he pledged himself to help bring about the annexation of Parma to Piedmont, as a step towards a fully independent and united Kingdom of Italy.

In annexation to the Piedmont rests the future greatness and regeneration of our native land. Anyone who feels Italian blood running in his own veins must desire this strongly and constantly. Thus the day will dawn for us when we can say that we belong to a great and noble Nation.

As an overt act in support of unity under a monarch, five members of the council were selected to present the results of the election to King Vittorio Emanuele in Turin. Naturally Verdi was one of them; more than that, it was he who was chosen to head the delegation and personally hand over the scroll to the king.

The whole time they were in Turin, noisy demonstrations of support were held outside the delegation's hotel and under their windows. Everywhere they went, they were met by city officials, bands and schoolchildren offering flowers.

After presenting the results to the king, all five Bussetans were called out again and again on to the balcony of their hotel, with Verdi given his own special ovation. At a banquet thrown for them in a *palazzo* Verdi was guest of honour.

It would be wrong to form the impression that Verdi was in any way impressed by any of this. If he was a politician at all, he was a very reluctant one. In fact we get a real insight into his character in the aftermath of the trip to Turin.

The delegation returned to Busseto by way of Milan, a city now free of the Austrians. As in Turin, they were greeted at the station by dignitaries, huge crowds and bands, which followed them to their hotel. That night they were guests at a gala in their honour at La Scala.

Verdi's friends and allies turned out in force, including Countess Maffei, who had been the first to introduce him to salon life in Milan as a young composer struggling to make his music heard, and with whom both he and Giuseppina had corresponded so often, and so intimately, from Sant'Agata.

This was the first time Verdi had been in the city of Milan for ten years. Anticipation at La Scala was high, but it was announced from the stage, to universal disappointment, that the composer would not

Above

Bedroom of Giuseppe
Verdi at Sant'Agata.

be present. In fact he had already left for home. He had no appetite for ostentatious celebration. This truly is Verdi, the man revealed.

But if Verdi was already tiring of politics, the feeling was not mutual. The following year he was elected to the provincial council of the province of Emilia. He refused to take it up.

Piave's reaction must have amused Verdi. 'So you didn't want to be a deputy? That's all right, we will make you a senator.' And that, ultimately, is what happened. On 3 February 1861, Verdi was elected to the Parliament of Piedmont-Sardinia in Turin, which a month later became the Parliament of the Kingdom of Italy. This time he accepted, but he later said he agreed only on the condition that after a few months he would resign (a pledge he would stick to).

Thirteen years later, he was appointed a member of the Italian Senate, but by that point his interest in politics, never overly strong, had disappeared. He never took part in any of the Senate's activities and finally carried out his threat to leave the political world.

Verdi was not born to be a politician, and he knew it full well. It seems he was content to be seen as a symbol of Italian independence, even allowing his music to be adapted to the cause, but beyond that he was not cut from a politician's cloth.

At this stage in his life – in his late forties – farming was all he wanted to do. Music was still far from his mind.

If anyone doubted that he had given up composing and was leading the complete rural life, he was very happy to disabuse them. This is what he wrote to his French publisher:

> *Now that I am not manufacturing any more notes, I am planting cabbages and beans, etc., etc., but [since] this work is no longer enough to keep me busy, I have begun to hunt!!!!!!! that means that when I see a bird,* Punf! *I shoot. If I hit it, fine. If I don't hit it, good night!* [*] *I have a supply of good St Etienne guns, but now I have the idea of getting a double-barrelled* Le Faucheux *with a double action; that is to say,* the old system *where you load powder and shot, together with* the system called Le Faucheux *with cartridges. Here they have these beautiful, fine Belgian guns at a reasonable price; but I have a craving to have a real one from the inventor, so long as the price is not too high . . . Tell the man-ufacturer that it has to be used not for a skilled hunter but for a* maestro di musica.

These are not the words of a man toying with the idea of hunting; he is passionate about it, even asking his publisher in Paris to look into acquiring French shotguns on his behalf. But look at that final sentence. He might have given up composing, but he still chooses to describe himself as a '*maestro di musica*'!

If there was plenty to occupy Verdi in the fields, the same was true inside the villa itself. Phase one of the remodelling work had now fin-ished, and he decided to embark on phase two. More workmen, more dust and disruption, but given that he was no longer composing, it was a minor inconvenience.

---

[*] And yet he sacked a farm worker for shooting a rabbit! See Afterword.

If he had known that this second phase would take the best part of twenty years, he might have had second thoughts. But his ideas were grandiose. He and Giuseppina were to have large separate but adjacent rooms. There were to be several living and dining rooms, as well as a library and pantries.

Unusually for houses in the Po valley, the entire house was raised just three shallow steps above the ground, with all the main rooms on the ground floor. There was the constant risk of flooding, given that the estate was virtually surrounded by water, but Verdi wanted to be able to step straight out on to the soil he loved so much.

His own room contained a bed, a desk that he could reach with just two steps, and a piano in the corner. This layout suited his habit of getting up in the night to compose, and the wall between his room and Giuseppina's meant he would not disturb her.

Why arrange his room like this, when he had no intention of ever composing again? For the same reason he called himself a '*maestro di musica*' in that letter. Verdi would remain a master operatic composer until he left this earth. Deep down he must have known that.

But what sort of offer could possibly tempt him back into the world he had despised for so long? It would have to be something truly different. In December 1860, he received a proposal for a new opera from the Imperial Theatre in St Petersburg.

See Afterword, page 260.

21

A SOPRANO
IMPRESSES VERDI

*I*t was actually Giuseppina who first received news of the offer from St Petersburg. She was alone at Sant'Agata. Verdi was away in Turin trying to persuade Count Cavour, the first prime minister of an independent Italy, to excuse him from running for Parliament.

The offer came in the form of a letter from the celebrated Italian tenor Enrico Tamberlick, who was currently on tour in Russia. On the authority of the director of the Imperial Theatre in St Petersburg he wanted to make an offer to Verdi for a new opera.

His language was suitably flattering, calculated to elicit a positive response. He knew that Verdi had stated his career as a composer of opera was over, but pleaded with him 'to add another jewel to the crown of your operas . . . and fan the spark of your genius . . . The audience that adores you without ever having seen you will be very pleased to have you.'

Giuseppina was more than happy to accept on her husband's behalf. She replied immediately that she would do all in her power to persuade him to accept, and would '*insist, annoy* him until we get what we want'.

Knowing her husband as she did, she could be confident that she was on reasonably safe ground in doing so. First of all, there was the financial consideration. Verdi was spending an enormous amount of

"Verdi was beginning to show signs of becoming bored with the life of a countryman."

money on improvement works to Sant'Agata. Now that he was a politician, he maintained a hotel suite in Turin where he entertained, kept a servant and had to dress in formal clothes every day, which involved purchasing a sizeable quantity of new suits. These were not costs he had expected or planned for.

Then there was the further consideration, of which she alone was aware, that Verdi was beginning to show signs of becoming bored with the life of a countryman. Activities at Sant'Agata had settled into a routine.

He would spend the morning dealing with correspondence, and the afternoon in the fields. There was a large coat-stand in the hallway, which bore the initials GV; Verdi kept his hats, cloaks and walking sticks there. If any item had been moved even slightly, he would fly into a rage. Dinner was prepared by the staff and served at six in the evening. Verdi expected it to be punctual. He and Giuseppina dressed each night for dinner, and Giuseppina made sure her dresses and hairstyle were up to date with French fashion, in order to please him.

The evenings were spent pursuing Verdi's two favourite pastimes, billiards and cards. He retained the habit, acquired as a young man in the salons of Milan, of playing with deadly earnest and not taking kindly to losing, which made him a not altogether pleasant opponent.

There was the added tension of his continued frosty relations with the townspeople of Busseto. Although he was no longer entirely shunned by them, neither was he entirely at ease in the vicinity. He was no longer living in sin of course, but he was aware that his anti-clericalism continued to attract opprobrium.

His early scepticism towards religion, formed in the small church in Le Roncole, had hardened into atheism following the deaths of his children and wife. When discussing religion, he was prone to quote a proverb: *Fidarsi è bene, ma non fidarsi è meglio* ('To have faith is good, but not to have faith is better').

In a letter to a friend he wrote: 'When I can, I avoid going into Busseto because . . . people point to me because I am an atheist, proud, etc., etc.'[90]

He refused point blank to attend any services or observe any Roman Catholic rites, something that undoubtedly exacerbated his already strained relationship with his father, who, until the very end of his life, and even when seriously ill, would leave his sick bed whenever he could to attend daily Mass.

Giuseppina wrote in graphic language to a friend:

[This] brigand *[Verdi] permits himself to be an atheist . . . I exhaust myself in speaking to him of the marvels of the heavens, the earth, the sea, etc., etc. Wasted breath! He laughs in my face and freezes me in the midst of my brightened speech and divine enthusiasm by saying, 'You're all mad', and unfortunately he says it in good faith.*[91]

It did not make for a happy atmosphere at Sant'Agata, and it is therefore understandable that Giuseppina was extremely pleased when the offer came in from St Petersburg. She had not misread her husband, who – possibly somewhat to everyone's surprise – swiftly accepted the job.

But almost from the start, familiar problems arose. Verdi's first choice of drama, Victor Hugo's *Ruy Blas*, was immediately vetoed by the censors in St Petersburg. After his usual complaints – refusing to sign a contract until he had suitable singers, stipulating that he would not be held to a deadline – Verdi settled on a play by a Spanish writer, giving it the Italian title *La forza del destino* ('The Force of Destiny'). He agreed to a projected premiere in late 1861. That gave him the best part of a year, ample time.

He chose the amenable and obliging Piave to write the libretto from the original play, and immediately set about tyrannising him, complaining about this or that verse, demanding rewrites, accusing him of using more words than was necessary, an unforgivable insult for a poet. His language was uncompromising:

For God's sake, my dear Piave, let's think about this carefully. We can't go on like this: it's absolutely impossible with this drama. The style must be tightened up. The poetry can and must say all that the prose says, and in half the words. So far you're not doing that.[92]

Piave, well used to Verdi's ill humour during the creative process, let it run off his back.

Satisfied at last with the libretto, Verdi began serious work in the summer of 1861, and by November he and Giuseppina were ready to make the journey to St Petersburg. Neither of them was in the best frame of mind. Giuseppina was mourning the death of her beloved Maltese terrier Loulou; Verdi was rather more concerned with the fact

---

* In her diary, Giuseppina describes her husband in this period as angry, restless and unable to control his temper. It is a credible assumption that around this time husband and wife stopped having sexual relations.

that his old ally and benefactor, Antonio Barezzi, had suffered a heart attack, though he appeared to have recovered.

The trip was projected to last for three months. In advance of their departure, Verdi had complained to his wife that they would have to put up with freezing temperatures, which he was not looking forward to. There would naturally be a problem with the language, since he had no knowledge of Russian. He also told her he was not looking forward to eating strange dishes, and as for wine he was dreading being without his favourites.

Giuseppina took the hint on all fronts. She decided that they should take two servants from Sant'Agata, as well as an interpreter. She ordered a hundred bottles of table wine from Bordeaux, twenty bottles of fine claret, and twenty bottles of champagne. She also made sure they took plentiful supplies of pasta, cured ham, rice and cheese.

The couple's reception in St Petersburg was extraordinary. The theatre had leased a magnificent apartment for them, which was warm and comfortable. Members of the orchestra gave them a formal welcome, and when Verdi went to the opera house for the first time, he found the cast waiting to accord him a welcome befitting Italy's greatest operatic composer.

But it was all to prove in vain. There was one singer missing from the reception given to him, and she was the most important of them all. The prima donna soprano, the Sicilian Emma La Grua (born Emmy Funk) was ill; not just ill, but thoroughly indisposed, with no sign of imminent recovery.

By general agreement, there was no other soprano who could assume the demanding role of Donna Leonora at short notice. Verdi – as he was accustomed to doing back home in Italy – demanded to be released from his contract. The Imperial Theatre refused. Finally a compromise was reached: the premiere would be delayed until the following autumn.

In late June 1862, after leaving Russia and then stopping in Berlin, Paris and London, Verdi and his wife returned to a house in disarray. Not only were several of the servants ill but, as Verdi wrote to Mariani, the young conductor who was making a serious name for himself, and who had asked Verdi if he could visit him at Sant'Agata:

My house is in utter disorder, with bricklayers, carpenters, blacksmiths, etc. etc. and not one room, not one single room is completely finished and ready to receive a gentleman.

Left

Verdi in Russia for
the premiere of *La
forza del destino*.

It was with some relief that Verdi and Giuseppina left again for St Petersburg at the beginning of September the following year. The premiere of *La forza* took place on 10 November 1862, according to the Russian old-style calendar.[*]

---

[*] 22 November 1862 on the standard calendar.

For once, Verdi allowed himself to enthuse, not only about the production, but also over the reception his new opera received:

> *Last night the first performance of* La forza del destino. *Result: good. Performance very, very good. Settings and costumes extremely opulent.*

And two nights later:

> *We have done three performances of* La forza del destino *with very full houses and excellent success.*

On the fourth night the tsar and tsarina were in the audience. After Verdi was called to the stage and showered with wreaths and flowers, he was invited into the royal box, where he chatted at length with the tsar and tsarina about the opera. Afterwards the tsar honoured Verdi with the Cross of the Imperial and Royal Order of St Stanislaus. This he was able to add to the Order of St Maurizio conferred on him back home in Italy a few months earlier.

However, just as in past years he had been pessimistic when he had every right to enthuse about the reception his work received, now the converse was true: Verdi was enthusing when in fact the reception for this new opera was less wholehearted than it appeared.

Several critics noted that while the reception was warm, it was not over-enthusiastic. The opera was long (four full-length acts) and the plot, set in Spain and Italy in an earlier century, difficult to follow. Verdi had blended a variety of forms: there was a classic love-triangle, as well as scenes of religious grandeur, along with several moments of comic opera. Verdi himself was later to call it an 'opera of ideas'. A less kind description is that it was a 'patchwork' drama.

But for the moment Verdi was well pleased with its reception. In fact, he had taken rather a liking to St Petersburg; his earlier misgivings had proven to be unfounded. He and Giuseppina stayed in the city for a month longer than they had intended, and happily accepted invitations to dinners and soirées. Verdi was even amenable to playing the piano, and did not object to his music being played in front of him.

This was a relaxed Verdi, away from the tensions of home, and the dust and disruption that marred life at Sant'Agata. It was not until December, when the seriously cold weather began to settle in, that the couple returned home.

Over the ensuing years, *La forza del destino* was staged around the world – Madrid, Rome, Reggio Emilia, Vienna, New York, and even as far afield as Buenos Aires. But the opera's reception was never rapturous; it became normal practice to pick holes in the plot, and even in the music. Verdi was routinely accused of trying to do too much, of attempting to blend too many disparate styles.

As had happened so often in the past, Verdi must have known deep down that the opera was not yet right. More than any other musical form, it is opera that has to be assessed in performance to understand what improvements need to be made. It is rare that an opera survives intact and unchanged after the first performance, or even after the first few weeks. Weak points are spotted, the action is tightened up, passages are cut, new arias are added, and very often the music is changed specifically to suit singers who are brought in for new productions.

Verdi was used to adapting and rewriting his operas after they had opened, sometimes many years later, and he was about to do so now

Above

Set design for Act Four, Scene Three of *La forza del destino.*

LA FORZA
DEL DESTINO

OPERA DI
G. VERDI

A. Lecocq

1° Don alvaro (en moine)   Mr Tamberlick   pr tenor
2° Dona Leonora   Mme L. Barbot   1er soprano
3° Don carlo   Mr Graziani   1er Baryton (b. seria)

Th de St Petersbourg (nov 1862) (Créateurs des Rôles)

with *La forza*. What is truly surprising, though, is his swift agreement to the terms put to him.

These were presented by his publisher, Ricordi, who had the nerve to utter the unmentionable name: La Scala. Verdi had not visited Italy's most prestigious opera house for close on a quarter of a century, after his terminal falling-out with the theatre manager Bartolomeo Merelli.

Ricordi used all his powers of persuasion. He assured Verdi he could take charge of the entire theatre for as long as he needed to produce one of his operas. He could choose his own singers, take charge of the sets and costumes, supervise the rehearsals, select the conductor and, possibly the clincher, if he were not satisfied, he could withdraw the whole production from the schedule.

The passage of time had mellowed Verdi's antipathy towards La Scala. Merelli had long since retired to the country; there was no one left in Milan's artistic circles towards whom he had any reason to feel antagonistic.

He accepted, and he decided that he would revise *La forza*. The changes he made were extensive and greatly enhanced the drama. He added a final scene to Act Three following a duel between two of the protagonists, making the ending of the act less abrupt. He also changed the ending to the whole opera. As Leonora dies, her suitor Don Alvaro now prays for her, rather than throwing himself to his death. It avoided an element of melodrama, which Verdi now considered to have detracted from the overall dramatic effect.

He also replaced the brief prelude to Act One with a full overture, containing an instantly memorable 'fate' theme, thus heightening the audience's anticipation before the curtain rose.[*]

The new version of *La forza* marked Verdi's triumphant return to La Scala, and replaced the old one in the repertory. There were two other new elements to this production, both of which affected Verdi deeply.

One was a source of great personal sadness. He had to work with a new librettist, one Antonio Ghislanzoni, who had been recommended by Ricordi. Why a new librettist? Because Francesco Piave, his loyal and long-suffering collaborator, librettist of nine full operas by Verdi, including *Rigoletto* and *La traviata*, was by this point paralysed and unable to speak, having suffered a severe stroke fourteen months earlier.

---

[*] The overture was memorably used in the 1986 French films, *Jean de Florette* and *Manon des Sources*.

He would be wheelchair-bound and unable to communicate for the rest of his life.

The second concerned the singer who took the role of Leonora. She was a thirty-five-year-old soprano by the name of Teresa Stolz, who had sung for the most part outside Italy. Her Italian debut had been in Turin five years earlier, though she had more recently sung at La Scala. Verdi had never heard her sing before.

She had been recommended to Verdi by Angelo Mariani, the conductor who had directed several of his operas and who had become his friend, visiting him often at Sant'Agata. Verdi agreed to give her the role on Mariani's recommendation. This decision would have a profound effect on both their lives.

Verdi was impressed by Teresa Stolz, seriously impressed, and by more than just her singing. She was about to enter Verdi's life, and she would never leave it. Deeply troubled times lay ahead.

22

'I AM AN ALMOST PERFECT WAGNERIAN'

The **Giuseppe Verdi** who left Sant'Agata to supervise rehearsals in Milan at the beginning of 1869 for the new production of *La forza del destino* was living up to his reputation as 'The Bear of Busseto'. Within the walls of Sant'Agata, Giuseppina was in despair over her husband's behaviour.

She wrote to a friend that he had flown into a rage over a window left open. Even worse, he had lapsed into a prolonged period of absolute silence. He would not talk to her. He did not respond to her questions, or if he did so, it was with a single unhelpful word.

Husband and wife were not communicating when Verdi left for Milan, though from there he wrote to her, inviting her to come and attend rehearsals. Clearly Giuseppina was unimpressed. The fact that he had not taken her in the first place had wounded her more deeply than it might otherwise have, had relations between them not deteriorated so badly.

She wrote him a lengthy reply, which is nothing less than a *cri de coeur*:

> *I have thought carefully and I shall not come to Milan. So I will save you from having to come secretly to the station at night to slip me out like a bundle of contraband goods. I have reflected on your profound silence . . . and my inner feelings advise me to turn down the offer you make me . . . I feel everything is forced in this invitation, and I think it is a wise decision to leave you in peace and stay where I am.*

While I am not enjoying myself, I am at least not exposing myself to further, useless, bitter remarks; and you, on the other hand, will have complete freedom . . . So please let my embittered heart find dignity in saying 'no'; and may God forgive you for the excruciating, humiliating wound that you have given me. [93]

They hardly sound like the words of a wife at ease with her husband. Giuseppina clearly felt herself deeply wronged. She must have known the effect her words would have on her husband, already prone to stress-related illness and hard at work supervising rehearsals of the new production of his opera. But she does not spare him.

What might have put Verdi into what seems to have been a deep depression, or at the very least the blackest of moods? It is not enough to point to an artistic temperament. The previous two years had brought much trauma into his life. The year 1867, two years before that letter was written, was an *annus horribilis* for him.

On 14 January 1867 Carlo Verdi died at the age of eighty-two. Verdi was in Paris. Relations between father and son had never been fully restored. The death of Verdi's mother sixteen years earlier had done nothing to bring them closer.

Carlo Verdi had suffered from kidney problems and heart disease for some time, and Verdi must have known the end could not be far away. Yet he was not there when his father died, in the same *palazzo* in the centre of Busseto where the composer had once lived with Giuseppina.

Carlo's death affected Verdi greatly. Giuseppina described him as being 'deeply grieved', as she was herself, although she adds that this was 'despite the fact that we had lived with him hardly at all and were at opposite poles in our way of thinking'. [94]

Verdi himself poured out his emotions in a letter to a friend:

Oh certainly certainly I would have wanted to close that old man's eyes, and it would have been a comfort for him and for me! Now I cannot wait to get home.

Verdi was not with either of his parents when they died, and he easily could have been. Did that result in a measure of guilt? We cannot know for certain, but he must have mulled over in his mind the years of estrangement, and whether they were really necessary. On the other hand, Carlo's death might have given him a certain sense of liberation;

there could be no further causes of tension, and resultant guilt, between them. At fifty-three, perhaps he was finally free of the past.

Certainly his reason for being in Paris was a strong enough one. Contracted by the Paris Opéra to produce a new opera, he had set Schiller's drama *Don Carlos*, which revolved around the sixteenth-century Spanish King Philip II and his son, for whom the play is named.

The compositional process – as always with Verdi – had been difficult, even tortuous. His librettist, Joseph Méry, died having completed roughly half of the text, and a new librettist Camille du Locle stepped in to complete it.

Paris, of all European opera houses, had a penchant for grand opera. Productions of four hours' duration were quite common. But Verdi exceeded even that. He produced a work so monumental that even during rehearsals he was cutting whole sections.

His father's death could not have come at a more inopportune time. The opening night of *Don Carlos*, set originally for 22 February, was put back to 11 March, less than two months after his father's death. He could not leave Paris and thus had to rely on others to make arrangements for the funeral and burial.

To universal consternation he stopped attending rehearsals for the new opera and refused to see anyone. The omens were not good. By the time he had recovered enough to resume work, his mood was difficult and unhelpful.

Don Carlos opened on schedule, and its reception was lukewarm at best. For once Verdi's innate pessimism was largely justified:

> *Last night* Don Carlos. *It was not a success! I don't know what will happen in the future, and I wouldn't be surprised if things changed . . . At the Opéra you do eight months of rehearsals and end up with an execution that is bloodless and cold.*[95]

That last sentence could have been written today. Verdi knew better than most that a truly completed opera was a rare thing. In fact the sentence before that was accurate too. Verdi began full-scale revisions almost immediately.

By the time the opera appeared in Italy under the title *Don Carlo* (which it retains today, rather than *Don Carlos*), it had undergone several changes. Verdi made more alterations five or so years later, and again nearly twenty years later. The version that finally entered the repertory was largely an amalgamation of different versions. As one musicologist put it, '*Don Carlo* seems destined to be an opera "in progress".'[96]

"Verdi was not with either of his parents when they died. Did that result in a measure of guilt?"

(Firea 1884) La Reine Elisabeth (M.me Bruschi-chiatti) Philippe II. (M.r Silvestri) Don Carlos (M.me Tamagno)

MILANO: TEATRO ALLA SCALA. — **DON CARLO**, opera in quattro atti, di *G. VERDI.* — (Atto IV, Scena III.)

Don Carlo would ultimately become a firm fixture in the repertory, and is regarded to this day as one of Verdi's finest works. In it he focuses on deep issues: the conflict between an individual's public duty and his human passions, and the need sometimes to sacrifice what is dearest to preserve honour. All the individual characters are somehow tied to each other, so that none is left unaffected by another's actions.

The music, too, is Verdi at his best. *Don Carlo* contains some of the greatest dramatic music he had written to date, with a magnificent series of confrontational duets. It was undoubtedly the music that led some critics to make comparisons with which Verdi was not best pleased.

> *I have read in Ricordi's* Gazetta *an account of what the leading French papers say of* Don Carlos. *In short, I am an almost perfect Wagnerian. But if the critics had only paid a little more attention they would have seen that there are the same aims in the trio in* Ernani, *in the sleep-walking scene in* Macbeth, *and in other pieces. But the question is not whether the music of* Don Carlos *belongs to a system, but whether it is good or bad. That question is clear and simple and, above all, legitimate.*[97]

It was not the last time a comparison with Wagner would be made, nor the last time Verdi would react angrily to it.

The depression that settled on Verdi after his father's death would not leave him. The relative failure of *Don Carlos* in Paris, or at least the re-alisation that much more work on it was needed, exacerbated matters.

The uncooperative behaviour, the moods and outbursts of anger, that were to affect Giuseppina to such an extent that she would refuse to join him in Milan for *La forza*, had their origins in this period.

But Verdi's troubles did not end there. The man who meant more to Verdi than anyone, more even than his own father, was in failing health and clearly had not long to live.

At the age of sixty-nine, Antonio Barezzi was on his deathbed. It sent Verdi into a spiral of misery and, it seems, a return of his habitual physical complaints. Giuseppina briefly kept a diary that summer, in which she wrote:

> *I try to raise Verdi's spirits because of his illness, which perhaps his nerves and his imagination make him think is more serious [than it is] . . . He is subject to intestinal inflammation, and his craziness,*

Left
Depiction of Act Four in the 1884 production of *Don Carlo* at La Scala, Milan.

his running back and forth . . . and his innate restlessness cause him some stomach upsets.

Inevitably it was Giuseppina, and those around her, who suffered most from Verdi's black moods:

Also he is angry against the servants and me, so that I don't know what words and what tone of voice to use if I have to speak to him, so as not to offend him! Alas! I don't know how things will end, because he is steadily becoming more restless and angry . . . I just have to be careful not to offend him and give him the idea that I am sticking my nose in where I shouldn't!

Giuseppina gives us there a perfect portrayal of an artist who is suffering setbacks professionally, and at the same time is grieving deeply at the loss of those closest to him.

Barezzi died at 11.30 a.m. on 21 July. Verdi and Giuseppina were at his side and, it seems, Barezzi died in Verdi's arms. Once again, it was in a letter that Verdi gave free rein to his emotions:

Sorrows follow upon sorrows with terrifying speed! Poor Signor Antonio, my second father, my benefactor, my friend, the man who loved me so very, very much, has died! . . . Poor Signor Antonio! If there is a life after death, he will see whether I loved him and whether I am grateful for all that he did for me. He died in my arms; and I have the consolation of never having made him unhappy.

Given the depth of his grief, we can perhaps forgive him that last sentence, which was so patently untrue. To another friend he wrote:

He recognised me almost until the last half-hour before his death! Poor Signor Antonio! You know what he was to me and what I was to him; and you can imagine my grief. The last tie that bound me to this place is broken! I wish I were thousands of miles from here. Addio!

Giuseppina's account of Barezzi's death largely accords with her husband's:

Signor Barezzi died in our arms and his last word, his last look were for Verdi, his poor wife, and for me.

Verdi, who had not been present at either his mother's or his father's deaths, was there for the man to whom he owed so much, whose daughter he had married. It is no wonder Verdi now compared this

"Sorrows follow upon sorrows with terrifying speed! Poor Signor Antonio!"

Verdi

year to that fateful year in which he had lost his young wife, following the deaths of his two small children: 'This [1867] is an accursed year, like 1840.'

In fact the year 1867 had not yet exhausted itself. It was on 5 December that his librettist Francesco Piave suffered the stroke from which he would never recover.

It was thus not the best time for the town officials of Busseto to raise an issue with Verdi, which they must have known would at best elicit a frosty response.

It had begun many years earlier, in fact long before he had upset them. When Verdi had first begun to make his mark in Milan, the townspeople of Busseto had the idea of replacing the small hall in the main square that was used for concerts and other gatherings with a brand new theatre, which they could dedicate to their greatest musical son.

Verdi was against the idea almost from the start – pretentious and foolish, he called it. The plan appeared to have been dropped (at least Verdi assumed it had) but in 1857 it was resurrected and the decision made to go ahead with it.

When Verdi found out he reacted with anger, which turned to fury when it was suggested to him that he had in fact been in favour of the idea when it had been proposed for the first time. Verdi's counter-argument that it was unfair to throw words at him that he had uttered so many years ago suggests they might have had a point.

Still, nothing happened for several years, and Verdi must have thought the whole idea had once again gone away. But no, construction work began on the building, and at this point a compromise was reached with Verdi. The town promised not to involve him in the theatre in any way, if he allowed them to name it after him, the Teatro Verdi.

He grudgingly agreed, but vowed he would never set foot inside it. The building was scheduled to open with much ceremony on 15 August 1868, with a special production of Verdi's opera *Rigoletto*.

Clearly hoping the *maestro* would mellow when the actual time came, the directors of the new theatre reserved a box for him and his wife, box number 10. The day of the opening was a holiday in Busseto, and there was much celebration.

Many of the townspeople wore green ribbons or carried green handkerchiefs, which they waved in honour of their famous son, a

Above

The Rocca Pallavicino in
Busseto, which houses
the Teatro Verdi.

demonstrative pun on his name: *verde* meaning green. A bust of Verdi
was unveiled before the performance.

As the hour approached, nervous eyes scanned the streets for the
arrival of Maestro Verdi and his wife. Finally the dignitaries had to take
their seats, after which all eyes were focused on Box 10.

It remained empty. Verdi had travelled with Giuseppina to the nearby spa town of Tabiano, about twenty miles south of Busseto, to take
the waters and have a massage.[*]

He kept his word. In his lifetime he never stepped inside the theatre
that was named after him, and remains so to this day.

The season of deaths had not passed. Only three months after deliberately shunning the opening of the Teatro Verdi, the composer learned

---

[*] To this day Box 10 is referred to as 'Maestro Verdi's box'. See Afterword.

that Gioachino Rossini had died in Paris. Verdi greatly admired his work and had come to know the man himself from his sojourns in Paris; it was yet another death he had to come to terms with.

But this was a fellow musician, not a family member or close friend. Verdi made the decision to honour Rossini in the only way appropriate: by proposing a Requiem Mass in which thirteen Italian composers would each compose a section. Verdi decided at the start he would write the 'Libera me, Domine'.

It was a bold initiative, and given the complexity of numbers involved, not to mention a planning committee, bound to run into bureaucratic difficulties. There was a delay before composers' names were announced, then delays before projected dates were settled.

Potentially most damaging of all, it was not until late in the planning process that a conductor was decided on, and the decision would lead to a raft of problems.

They could have decided on a conductor much earlier, because there was really only one name in the frame – the young conductor who had so impressed Verdi already, Angelo Mariani.

But Mariani had a raft of commitments, which he could not break. Added to this, he was suffering from health problems. When he made the planning committee aware of this, and Verdi was told, Verdi flew into a rage, writing an insulting letter to Mariani, accusing him of putting his own interests ahead of those which should come first, namely a collective honouring of one of Italy's greatest artists.

Mariani must have wondered what he had done to deserve such a broadside, and offered to do all in his power to make the performance of the Requiem Mass possible. But Verdi was in no mood for compromise. He accused Mariani of failing in his duty as a friend, and stated unequivocally that he should not be allowed to conduct the Mass under any circumstances.

It was almost as if this whole affair was the last straw for Verdi, after an intense period in which he had had to come to terms with personal loss and professional disappointment. Giuseppina had borne the brunt of his despair; now it was Mariani's turn to feel the full force of Verdian fury.

There was another factor that complicated Verdi's relationship with Mariani, which until now had been one of mutual admiration and friendship.

Mariani had been working with the soprano Teresa Stolz, and had fallen in love with her. It appeared the singer reciprocated his affections, and the couple were about to become engaged. We can be in no doubt, given what was to ensue, that Verdi was also attracted to Teresa, and deeply so.

Could that have accounted for his change in attitude to Mariani? At the very least it surely added to the already tumultuous emotions he was struggling to deal with.

But an extraordinary opportunity was about to present itself to Verdi, one he could not in any way have foreseen. It would also offer the chance to send Mariani on a very long journey, several thousand miles away.

23

An Opera for Cairo

'**H**orses are like women; they have to please the man who owns them.' So wrote a thoroughly disgruntled and depressed Giuseppina. For the best part of a decade, she had been confiding in a diary, or in letters to close friends, about how miserable her life had become with a man who was driven, restless, unpredictable, prone to outbursts of temper over trivial matters; and how, no matter how hard she tried, she was unable to satisfy his needs.

This appeared to be the case in all areas. In her writing she barely disguised the fact that she and Verdi no longer enjoyed a sexual relationship. She was acutely aware that she had put on a great deal of weight, describing herself as looking like a housewife. Her days as the most admired diva in Italy were long since past.

At the time she was lamenting her decline, as 1867 gave way to 1868, along came a tall young woman – twenty-one years younger than Verdi, nineteen years younger than Giuseppina – Germanic in appearance, her thick blonde hair often adorned with flowers or jewels, at the height of her career as a leading soprano of the operatic stage.

Giuseppina had seen Teresa Stolz (born Tereza Stolzova in Bohemia) both on the stage and socially with her husband. She had an allure about her, a certain mystery, an air of the exotic. It was common knowledge in operatic circles that Teresa's elder sisters, who were identical twins, lived in a *ménage à trois* with a conductor, who had fathered children with both of them.

Meanwhile, both Giuseppina and her husband did have something special, outside the world of opera, to distract them and provide them with much-needed pleasure: at about this time they decided to adopt a seven-year-old girl – the orphaned child of one of Verdi's cousins.

When Filomena Verdi's impoverished parents had died, Verdi took the rather unusual decision to place the young girl in the care of his father Carlo in the Palazzo Cavalli in Busseto. After his father died, Verdi decided to adopt her formally and bring her to live with him and Giuseppina in Sant'Agata.

'Fifao' became the daughter the couple never had. From Verdi's time to this, there has been speculation she was, in fact, their own child, that they had given her away, as Giuseppina was known to have done with her children, then brought her back. It seems unlikely. There is little or no reference to her in earlier correspondence, and no official papers that could relate her to them.

Did they take the action for the lesser, but more credible reason, that they felt a measure of guilt over the earlier children who were given away, who we know to have been Giuseppina's, and *might* have been Verdi's? We can only speculate, always remembering the lengths the couple went to in order to hide their actions from prying reporters.

That Fifao brought them much joy is undisputed. There is a delightful anecdote of Verdi walking proudly into a printer's store with Fifao, for all the world like father and daughter. The sales assistant, who of course knew the *maestro*, recorded that when he ordered visiting cards for himself and his wife, the little girl looked up at him and asked, 'And nothing for me?' 'Wait until you are a bit bigger,' replied the great man.[98]

Giuseppina doted on the girl, who provided her with much-needed distraction, and the chance, at last, to be a mother. There was genuine sadness in the house when Fifao became old enough to go to school.*

In the meantime Giuseppina had Teresa Stolz to contend with, a woman who she was in no doubt represented a genuine rival for her husband's affections. Teresa soon became a regular guest at Sant'Agata, invited by Verdi to stay for days at a time. Giuseppina was as welcoming as she could be, operating on the principle of 'keeping your enemy close'. But she had no hesitation in describing the situation in a letter as

---

* Fifao became Verdi's sole heir, and her descendants live in Sant'Agata to this day.

a *ménage à trois* – something to which, given her family circumstances, Teresa was no stranger.

It was not long before the rumour mill picked up on the apparent mutual attraction between composer and singer. Clandestine meetings, it seems, took place in Cremona – or maybe they were not so clandestine.

Some years after Verdi's death, a librettist by the name of Luigi Illica, writing to the composer Pietro Mascagni, described these meetings as if they were common knowledge, stating that they took place in a 'modest' hotel every Saturday. On one such occasion, Verdi apparently lost his wallet and it was found in Teresa's suite.

To Giuseppina's dismay, an opportunity for her husband to become even more closely involved with Teresa was about to arise, and it had its origins many thousands of miles away. Verdi had accepted a commission to compose an opera to mark the opening of the Cairo Opera House.[†]

[†] Not, as is often stated, for the opening of the Suez Canal, which had already taken place.

Above

Set design for Act Two,
Scene Two of *Aida*'s
premiere in Cairo.

Set in ancient Egypt, the plot revolved around conflict between Egypt and Ethiopia, and a love affair that straddled the divide. So far, so conventional, but Verdi set about composing a work unique in his output, in that he recreated the evocative colours of a lost world. He contrasted the rigidity and power of Egypt with the exotic and sensual world of Ethiopia, and he composed it seemingly effortlessly, completing the opera in just four months. The preparations for the production were somewhat less smooth.

France was at war with Prussia, and the sets and costumes, which were being made in Paris, were stuck there, and it was not possible to ship them out. The first performance was put back by eleven months, to 24 December 1871.

Verdi had been invited to conduct the premiere himself but had declined, it seems for no other reason than that he simply could not face the journey and the unwholesome living conditions in Cairo.

His choice of conductor, which was surprising since he had all but broken off relations with him, was Angelo Mariani. Mariani, though, was suffering from increasingly poor health, and on his doctor's advice declined Verdi's invitation. Verdi refused to accept Mariani's reasoning. A visitor to Sant'Agata reported that Mariani's name was not to be uttered within its walls.

Over the course of 1871, Verdi's mood darkened, as it so often did in the run-up to a first performance. Increasingly irritated by comparisons to Wagner, he took himself off to see a production of *Lohengrin* in Bologna. He had with him a vocal score, which he followed sitting at the back of a box. On the first page of the Prelude to Act Three, he scribbled his thoughts, which were that the music was nice, but too slow and rather boring.*

Verdi knew that his *Aida* was a remarkable piece of work, and as soon as he had completed it, he began making plans for it to be performed closer to home, namely at La Scala. In contrast to the Cairo premiere, in which he took little interest, he was meticulous over the planning for the La Scala premiere, making some small changes in the score, and personally handpicking the best possible company of principal singers.

He did not hesitate to choose Teresa Stolz to sing the lead role of Aida. In fact it is not too much of an exaggeration to say that he created the role with her in mind. Once again demonstrating that in his eyes professional matters overrode personal relationships, Verdi asked the luckless Mariani to conduct the La Scala premiere. Once again Mariani declined, citing ill-health.

There was quite possibly more on Mariani's mind than his physical well-being. At some point during this period, Teresa Stolz broke off their engagement. It would be logical, indeed convenient, to be able to say that Verdi put pressure on Teresa to take this step, given his closeness to her, but that would be pure speculation. Just as, decades earlier, he had left no trace of the course of his early relationship with Giuseppina, so there is no paper trail to illuminate his relationship with Teresa.

The La Scala premiere on 8 February 1872 echoed that in Cairo, where it had met with huge acclaim. In Milan it was an unequivocal triumph, the magnificent scenery and costumes matching the grandeur of the music. Verdi was called out on to the stage no fewer than thirty-two times, receiving a magnificent ovation at the final curtain.

---

* The page is preserved at Sant'Agata.

From the exquisite and challenging tenor solo as Radamès sings of his love for the Ethiopian slave, *'Celeste Aida'*, to the great 'Triumphal March' and the death scene at the end, with just Radamès and Aida entombed alone together, the music is of a quality never before reached by Verdi, in its sheer richness and diversity.

Within a matter of months *Aida* was being performed across Italy, and soon throughout the world. It crossed the Atlantic to Argentina and the United States only a year after opening at La Scala, and in the following three years was performed in Germany, Spain, Austria, Hungary, Poland, France, Sweden, Russia, Britain and Monaco. The following year it was staged in Australia.

As *Aida* swept the world, Mariani endeavoured to heal relations with Verdi. He was deeply upset that the man he admired so much had abjured him. He wrote letter after letter to Verdi, imploring him to forgive any wrong he might have committed.

Verdi was unmoved. The young conductor he had so admired, and who had been a frequent guest at Sant'Agata, was now entirely *persona non grata*. Mariani, alone now that Teresa had deserted him too, continued to suffer from declining health, and on 13 June 1873 died of bladder cancer at the age of fifty-one.

Another death occurred just three weeks before Mariani died: Italian writer Alessandro Manzoni, someone Verdi had met and admired all his adult life. His novel *I Promessi Sposi* ('The Betrothed'), with its patriotic message of a unified Italy, was regarded in its time as a symbol of the struggle for Italian independence – to literature what Verdi's *Nabucco* was to opera.[*]

Verdi was shocked and moved by Manzoni's death, although at the age of eighty-eight it was not entirely unexpected. He resolved to compose a *Messa da Requiem* in his honour. This time he would avoid the pitfalls that befell his previous attempt to create a Requiem, following Rossini's death, and keep the reins entirely in his own hands.

The decision to compose a religious work caused some surprise, given Verdi's detestation of clerics and his tendency towards atheism, or at least agnosticism. The answer comes in the work itself.

Verdi created what is essentially an operatic piece, albeit set to a sacred text. The conductor Hans von Bülow described the Requiem as

---

[*] To this day, it is by far the most popular novel in the Italian language.

'Verdi's latest opera, in ecclesiastical dress'. Brahms dismissed the comment, remarking, 'Bülow has made a fool of himself; this is a work of genius,' which is not exactly a refutation.[99]

Because of its fine acoustics, Verdi chose the Church of San Marco in Milan for the first performance on 22 May 1874, the first anniversary of Manzoni's death. Verdi conducted, and it was a triumph. The sound, particularly in the terrifying *Dies irae*, must have been overwhelming. There was a chorus of a hundred and twenty voices and an orchestra of a hundred. Three days later the Requiem was repeated in its more natural home, La Scala, with Verdi again conducting.

We can be sure that Giuseppina was pleased for her husband but no doubt dismayed that once again he chose Teresa Stolz as soprano soloist. When Teresa's engagements took her away from Milan, she wrote letters continuously to Verdi at Sant'Agata. On a packet of these letters, Giuseppina wrote, 'Sixteen letters!! In a short time!! What activity!!'

At around this time, Giuseppina's health began to fail. She suffered what today would be called severe depression. Meanwhile Teresa was

also struggling: she experienced the first real humiliation of her career. Performing Verdi's *La forza del destino* in Rome, her voice failed in the second act. She apologised to the audience and left the stage in tears.

Her voice recovered, and such was the demand for the Requiem that Verdi took it on a European tour, with himself conducting and Teresa singing the soprano part. He insisted that Giuseppina accompany him, even though she protested that it would be better for her health if she stayed at home in Sant'Agata.

In Naples, Paris and Vienna, Teresa Stolz stayed in an apartment with Verdi and Giuseppina. For himself and his wife, Verdi reserved two bedrooms and a salon; for Teresa one bedroom, with a salon and a smaller room for her maid. Verdi gave instructions that all meals should be served in his suite for three people. This was the *ménage à trois* Giuseppina had written about, and continued to do so.

It was inevitable that matters would come to a head. Some time in late 1876 there was a heated confrontation at Sant'Agata. It was certainly initiated by Giuseppina, releasing tension built up over three months of sharing her husband with Teresa in hotel suites across Europe, followed by Verdi's insistence on Teresa accompanying them to take the waters in Tabiano.

The following is speculation, but it is based on a story that was common currency in Busseto, and was told in the middle part of the last century to Verdi biographers Frank Walker and Mary Jane Phillips-Matz by elderly Bussetans who were alive when it happened.

Giuseppina ordered Verdi in direct and unequivocal language to send Teresa away once and for all. Verdi responded by threatening to kill himself. Giuseppina stormed out of Sant'Agata, leaving Verdi alone – with Teresa.

Knowing Verdi as we do, a suicide threat seems unlikely. But that was certainly the rumour in currency half a century later.

Events then took an unexpected turn. Shortly before the confrontation at Sant'Agata, Teresa had announced her decision to retire from the operatic stage. She now reversed this, and left to take up an engagement in Russia. Perhaps the gossip and upset had finally taken its toll on her relationship with Verdi.

Once in Russia, Teresa adopted a conciliatory tone in her correspondence home. She addressed letters to both Verdi and Giuseppina together. The words she used were those of a good friend and nothing more. She filled pages with gossip from the opera world, and complaints about her life as a 'Poor Gypsy' who could not wait to return to her house in Milan.

Giuseppina took a different tack in her letter of Christmas wishes. She told Teresa to stop complaining about a well-paid engagement she had chosen to accept. Her language was hardly that of a wronged woman. 'Dry your tears, have someone serve you a good dinner, and drink a glass of champagne to the health of your old friends.'

It was fully three months before Teresa replied, and not before Giuseppina had sent a follow-up letter and she herself had finally returned to Milan. She had been very ill in Russia, she wrote, suffering from a catalogue of ailments – insomnia, bronchitis, overwork and depression – causing her to lose a considerable amount of weight.

Most significantly, she referred to Strepponi's 'good-natured castigation' of her. Giuseppina was able to read as much or as little as she wished into this. In the following months, Teresa continued to write, either to Giuseppina alone or to her and her husband as a couple. Sometimes she would ask Giuseppina to pass on 'regards' to Verdi, sometimes she would not refer to him at all.

It was as if, in their correspondence, the relationship between the two women evolved into one that was almost sisterly. They discussed fashion, actually sending each other samples of lace and hats, coats and furs, and discussing various styles of furniture. Giuseppina, it appeared, had seen off her rival – for the time being.

The crisis in the Verdis' marriage was over, even if we have no indication of any reaction to this from Verdi himself. Maybe he was too busy being the gentleman farmer once again. *Aida* and the Requiem out of the way, he now pursued his earlier resolve to retreat from the world of opera.

This time his resolve lasted a little longer: it would be a full decade before he composed anything new.

24

'THE ALL-POWERFUL CORRUPTOR OF ITALIAN ARTISTIC TASTE'

As if to convince himself that he really was done with the world of music and all that goes with it, Verdi closed the piano in his room at Sant'Agata, and ordered the carpenter to seal it 'hermetically'.

He had more important, or at least more pressing, duties to attend to. Sant'Agata, now a huge estate with a multitude of outbuildings and tenant houses, was in need of serious work: not just upkeep or redecoration, but significant repairs.

Verdi already had a substantial estate, and he was shortly to take control of what amounted to a modest landowning empire. At the end of 1876 he bought two more farms and over the next decade acquired a further six, as well as several smaller parcels of land. In 1888 he bought railroad stock and bank bonds.

He also donated money for a hospital to be built in nearby Villanova sull'Arda,[*] and later bought a site in Milan for the building of a home for retired musicians.[†] In 1890, as I have previously mentioned,

---

[*] Verdi refused to have his name on the façade. To this day it bears the single word 'Ospedale'.

[†] Still in existence today.

he established a company to sell the Sant'Agata pork products, under the brand name 'GV'.

He was fully occupied managing his estates. A team of farm managers reported to him, and he had daily contact with labourers, carpenters, stonemasons, stablehands, marble cutters, gardeners, coachmen, butchers, bakers, tile-factory workers, dairymen, house servants and their families.

Music was far from his mind. To what extent Teresa Stolz was far from his mind is not entirely clear. She wrote regularly from her home in Milan – but always to Giuseppina, asking her to convey her regards to 'il Maestro'. She would not come to visit, she wrote, for fear she might be 'annoying'.

A rare letter to Verdi alone, dated 27 June 1878, explained that she had not written before, for fear of causing problems for him. She had, it seems, taken the hint. Giuseppina's tactics had worked.

Teresa was conspicuous by her absence from a rare moment of happiness in the otherwise sombre surroundings of Sant'Agata. On 11 October 1878 Filomena married Alberto Carrara, the son of a lawyer friend of Verdi.

The wedding took place at the villa itself. Verdi described it as a very simple affair. He walked his adopted daughter to the altar in the small chapel, with just a few close relatives and friends present. There was an abundance of tears, including from the priest.

It was not that Verdi and Teresa never met. In the spring of the following year the Po flooded, bringing disaster to many of the towns of the Po valley. Verdi organised a concert at La Scala to raise funds, and asked Teresa to take part.

The concert, which took place at the end of June, was a great success. The people of Milan and the valley itself knew how reluctant Verdi was to leave his estate and come to the city, and the gesture was appreciated even before the event.

Verdi conducted his Requiem with Teresa as soprano soloist. Several times the performance had to be halted for encores. Verdi was seen to be smiling – something rare enough to be commented on. Teresa's singing was described as faultless and perfectly pitched.

After the concert, Verdi returned to his hotel to find a huge floral arrangement in the lobby bearing the words 'Viva Verdi' at its centre. He was called out onto the balcony of his apartment, to see the orchestra of La Scala processing towards the hotel, playing music from his operas.

Music had, in a sense, returned to Verdi's head, and it was not about to leave it. While in Milan, Verdi met up with his publisher Giulio Ricordi.

There was a dinner, at which the conversation turned to Rossini's attempts to set Shakespeare's *Othello* to music, but how the libretto had been below standard, rendering the finished opera unpoetic and undramatic.

Ricordi had an ulterior motive. He wanted Verdi to compose again. He had the subject matter in mind; he also had a librettist lined up. But he knew he had to tread carefully. Verdi was officially in retirement, his composing days over. Any direct attempt to lure him back into the world of opera was bound to meet with a rebuff.

Ricordi himself later said that when he first raised the subject of *Othello* at the dinner table, Verdi's eyes fixed on him with 'interested suspicion'.[100] Verdi knew perfectly well what was afoot, but Ricordi had chosen his moment well. The concert at La Scala had reawakened all the familiar musical instincts in Verdi. The crowd's adulation had reminded him that there was a world outside the confines of Sant'Agata.

The librettist Ricordi had in mind was Arrigo Boito, a poet, novelist, librettist, and also a composer, then in his forties. Verdi had had dealings with Boito some years earlier, which had been unfruitful. But Boito was a man after Verdi's own heart. In an earlier time he had played an active role in Italy's struggle for independence from Austria, and had fought under Garibaldi in the brief war that had resulted in Venice being returned to the Kingdom of Italy.

Ricordi must have breathed a huge sigh of relief when Verdi agreed to meet Boito at the hotel three days later. Boito brought with him an outline of how he proposed to tackle *Othello*, and Verdi declared himself impressed. He told Boito to go away and work on a libretto.

Ricordi's plan was in fact more subtle and far-reaching than Verdi could possibly have realised. He was convinced that the way to get Verdi composing again was to persuade him first to have another look at some of his earlier operas, which had not been the success the composer had hoped for, and which, Ricordi believed, deserved better.

He was, Ricordi must have been truly surprised to find, pushing at something of an open door. Taking up his publisher's suggestion, Verdi began to revise *Don Carlos*, working intensely for five months to produce the Italian version, *Don Carlo*, which was to become definitive. Then it was time to turn to another of his earlier works, *Simon Boccanegra*.

In what would prove a masterstroke, Ricordi – no doubt wondering if he would bring down the wrath of the Bear of Busseto on his shoulders – suggested Verdi allow Boito to rework the libretto. He might well have pointed out (though we have no proof of this) that it would be a good way of deciding whether Verdi could trust Boito with *Othello*.

"Music had, in a sense, returned to Verdi's head, and it was not about to leave it."

Once again, the door was open. Verdi was satisfied with Boito's pro-posals and the two began work together on an extensive reworking of the opera. The new *Simon Boccanegra* had its first performance at La Scala on 24 March 1881, and was an unqualified success. Verdi could finally affirm, with customary understatement, twenty-four years after the premiere, 'The legs have been adjusted on the old *Boccanegra*.'[101]

It was time to turn his attention to *Otello* (the Italian title of the opera) and to an extent Verdi reverted to type. Boito soon learned that the composer could be a hard taskmaster. Backwards and forwards the libretto went, with Verdi demanding change after change.

But Boito had been well briefed by Ricordi. He was prepared for the process to be somewhat tortuous. He was also aware that *il Maestro*, the most revered composer in Italy, was preparing himself to produce his first completely new opera in well over a decade. Word had leaked out about the project; interest was already stirred. There was a lot at stake.

As was his custom, Verdi did not begin serious work on composition until he was entirely satisfied with the finished libretto, and that was clearly still a long way off. In the meantime, other factors distracted him.

On 13 February 1883 Richard Wagner died. Comparisons between Verdi and Wagner were not unusual, and opinion was largely divided by geography. North of the Alps, Wagner was seen as the superior talent. His was a new form of opera, a *Gesamtkunstwerk* ('complete work of art'). His operas were *durchkomponiert* ('through-composed'), in a single sweep, with no stopping for showpiece arias. Wagner's characters were identified by their own themes, their own *leitmotifs*.

South of the Alps, the preferred style was romantic. Arias were calculated to bring on applause. Love affairs were of this earth, not set in some world of Teutonic mythology where true love could be experienced only through death. Here Verdi ruled.

Verdi was unsettled by comparisons with Wagner, in which he had frequently come off worse. The great German conductor Hans von Bülow, unrivalled in his conducting of Wagner, had disparaged Verdi down the years. This culminated in a vitriolic attack, having heard the *Requiem*, in which he called Verdi 'the all-powerful corruptor of Italian artistic taste'. Later, on studying Verdi's music more carefully, he recanted. 'Now I admire you, I love you! Will you forgive me? Long live VERDI!'

Verdi, with characteristic humour, responded: 'There is no trace of sin in you. Besides, who knows? Perhaps you were right the first time!'[102] Verdi's forgiveness may have been influenced by the fact that von Bülow had recently lost his wife Cosima to Wagner.

Nevertheless he was aware that Wagner was doing something new with opera. He had even had his own opera house built, for goodness' sake!

Verdi knew he was the last in a traditional line: Cherubini, Bellini, Donizetti, Rossini. He might be better than all of them, his operas might have proved more popular, the melodies more instantly memorable, but no one could claim he had transformed opera in the way Wagner had. Take the Tristan chord, for example, which appears in the opening phrase of *Tristan und Isolde*, and is part of Tristan's *leitmotif*. This was a new sound, a new form of music.

It would be an exaggeration to say Verdi felt inferior to Wagner, but there is an element of truth in it. The words he wrote to Ricordi on learning of Wagner's death are revealing. Were they a wholehearted expression of grief? Were they an unequivocal endorsement of Wagner's unique greatness as an operatic composer?

> *Sad! Sad! Sad!*
> *Wagner is dead!!*
> *Reading the dispatch yesterday, I was, I can say, terrified by it!*
> *Let's not talk about it! A great individualist has disappeared! A name that leaves a very powerful mark on the history of Art!!! Ad-d[io] add[io].* [103]

'Individualist' is an interesting word to use. Not explicitly complimentary; not necessarily disparaging.

Verdi the farmer, the man of the land, had returned to his natural habitat of music after a long break. He was working very hard indeed, and it was taking a toll. In April, only two months after Wagner's death, Verdi suffered a slight stroke or heart attack. He and Giuseppina were staying at the Grand Hotel in Milan. One morning she found him unconscious on his bed. He had felt dizzy and then fainted.

He recovered swiftly and said later it had been a spot of heart trouble. The news was not publicly released. Muzio was one of the few who knew, and helped Giuseppina get Verdi back to the safety and seclusion of Sant'Agata.

It was not long before Verdi was well enough to get out into the fields again and resume agricultural duties. He was approaching his seventieth birthday, and still showed no signs of slowing down. He was also hard at work on the new opera, which was a lengthy process. Boito reported on a number of occasions that things were proceeding well, and – like Piave before him – was happy to accommodate any requests and amendments *il maestro* might make.

A date for the premiere of *Otello* was finally set for 5 February 1887 at La Scala. Anticipation had been steadily growing over the years. This was to be the first new work by the master of opera since *Aida* sixteen years earlier. Even before it had been seen, *Otello* was being called the most important event in the history of Italian opera.

On the day itself, the mayor of Milan ordered all the streets and squares around La Scala to be closed to traffic from early in the morning.

It was a bitterly cold day, but that did not stop the crowds from lining
the appropriately named Via Manzoni between the Grand Hotel and
the opera house, along which they knew Verdi would walk.[*]

---

[*] Verdi revered the great poet of Italian independence Alessandro Manzoni, as
we have seen.

Rumours swirled all day long, mostly concerning the tenor Francesco Tamagno, who had the lead role of Otello. He was ill, so it was said. A doctor was sent for; nothing was wrong. Late in the afternoon someone said his wig would not fit, and that another was needed.

By early evening every window and balcony on the Via Manzoni was filled with eager spectators. Bright tapestries and cloths of gold and scarlet damask hung from balcony railings. A continuous refrain of 'Viva Verdi!' echoed off the buildings. [104]

Failure was simply inconceivable. *Otello*, the Milanese had decided, was a triumph even before a note had been heard on the stage. We can only imagine what was going through Verdi's head, given his natural pessimism. There are no reports of physical ailments, but we can assume these debilitated him as they did before any premiere.

Giuseppina and Boito sat together in a box. Verdi was backstage. Teresa Stolz, her voice now past its best, was not involved in the production and was not present.

If there was even a shred of pessimism in Verdi's head, it was soon to be dispelled. From the very first note, the crowd roared their approval. There were continual cries for encores, and at the end of the evening dozens of curtain-calls.

In a rare act of generosity, Verdi called Boito onto the stage, took his hand, and drew him down to the footlights. It was something the younger man would never forget. [105]

When it was all over, it proved almost impossible to leave the theatre. At the stage door Verdi was mobbed so intensely that it was reported his clothes were nearly torn off. His carriage had barely moved when the cry 'Unhitch the horses!' went up. More than a dozen men tried to lift the carriage onto their shoulders, but it was too heavy. Eventually they pulled it along the Via Manzoni to the Grand Hotel.

At the hotel Verdi struggled to dismount from the carriage, such was the ardour of the crowd. Finally he managed to get inside, soon emerging on the balcony, where the shouting and applause continued. A band played his music in the street until five o'clock in the morning.

The verdict of the crowd on that first night is one that has endured. *Otello* is without doubt one of Verdi's greatest works. Boito had delivered a masterful libretto, tight and concise. He omitted Act I of Shakespeare's play entirely, beginning the action in Cyprus.

Verdi focused his attention on the three main characters. Otello's descent into manic jealousy is reflected in the gradual collapse of his melodic language. Iago, as the incarnation of evil, veers between quiet

'half-voice' passages in which he becomes even more dangerous, to moments of high drama. Desdemona throughout has the feminine qualities of a woman in love, trusting and loyal, and an almost unbearable dignity as she prepares herself for death. Her plangent 'Willow Song' is one of the most sublime passages Verdi ever wrote; all the more beautiful when contrasted with Iago's celebration of evil in his soliloquy, *'Credo in un Dio crudel!'* ('I believe in a cruel God').

In a later letter, Verdi gave an extraordinary insight into what he had set out to achieve:

> *Desdemona is a part in which the thread, the melodic line, never ceases from the first note to the last. Just as Iago has only to declaim and laugh mockingly, and just as Otello, now the warrior, now the passionate lover, now crushed to the point of baseness, now ferocious like a savage, must sing and shout, so Desdemona must always, always sing.*[106]

The master of opera had returned, and he had done it on home soil. Milan had welcomed back one of their own, a composer who had proved time and again, and surely now once and for all, that he had no equal.

On the back of such an unequivocal triumph, was it now time to retire gracefully from the world he had conquered, which after all he had never truly loved, and return to managing the land that meant so much to him? At the age of seventy-three, no one would begrudge him that.

He acknowledged it himself in a letter he wrote the following January, though he at least admitted it filled him with a sense of his own mortality. Even more significantly, he could see that the musicians he had worked with knew it, even if they did not say so.

> *That first night, when I was leaving the theatre in the midst of the affectionate good wishes onstage, I met – on the staircase – the orchestra players, who, affected, without saying a word, grasped my hands and on their faces were engraved these words: 'Maestro, we will never see each other again here, never again!!' Never again is a phrase that tolls like a bell for the dead.*

At last, surely, he had reached the end of his career. It had ended in a triumph. What more could he ask for? He had nothing left to say, or prove.

Not for the first time in his career, he was wrong.

25

SCANDAL AND COMEDY

There is a certain oppressiveness about the atmosphere at Sant'Agata, now as then. Verdi planted hundreds of tall trees, creating a small forest. This gave undoubted beauty to the estate, but it also created darkness and heaviness, still a feature of Sant'Agata to this day. We have already seen how Giuseppina complained about this in earlier years. In the winter the trees stood like skeletons, and in the summer the natural wetness of the Po valley brought rain, which clung to leaves and branches, meaning they were still dripping as the sun struggled to pierce the thick foliage.

Both Verdi and Giuseppina were prone to dark moods – in Giuseppina's case deep depression – and the ambience at Sant'Agata did nothing to improve this.

On one occasion, she and her husband were in a small rowing boat on the large artificial lake Verdi had had dug, which was surrounded by a wall of tall trees.* One of them must have moved carelessly, because the boat tipped and Giuseppina was thrown into the water. Verdi struggled to pull her to safety, while her heavy clothes threatened to drag her under. If she had fallen in while alone, no one would have seen her through the trees.

---

* It remains a very attractive feature of the estate today.

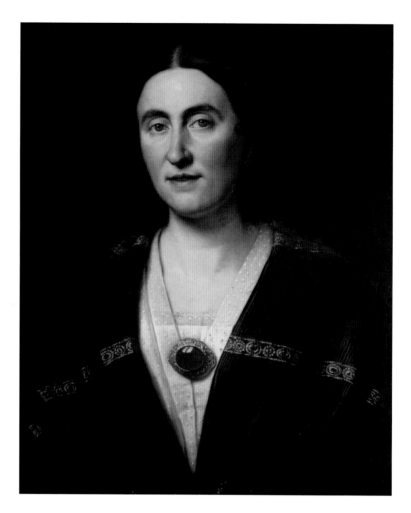

The lake was home to a flock of black swans, which had been a gift to Verdi from Teresa Stolz. Giuseppina woke up one morning to find they had been poisoned. The mystery of how it happened, whether it was deliberate, and if so who might have done it, was never solved.

At times Giuseppina felt almost as though there was a curse over the estate, a sensation that can only have been reinforced by events that occurred some years later.

Filomena's eldest son Angiolino, then seventeen years of age, spent three days out hunting. On his return to Sant'Agata, he laid his gun on the table and asked a maid at the house, twenty-six-year-old Giuseppina Belli, to clean it for him. When she did not immediately pick it up, he began to clean it himself. The gun was loaded and somehow during the cleaning he pulled the trigger and the young woman was fatally shot in the head.

Angiolino was arrested, charged with murder and brought before a panel of three judges. His defence was that he had forgotten to unload the gun, and that it went off accidentally. It was pointed out to him that he had ridden 14 kilometres on his bicycle over dirt roads with the gun on his shoulder, presumably loaded. Did he seriously expect his explanation to be believed?

He was found guilty but given an extraordinarily lenient sentence, just thirty-eight days in prison and a paltry fine. He appealed nonetheless, but the appeal was rejected. It is probable, though no evidence exists, that Verdi himself then intervened at the highest possible level, because no less a figure than the King of Italy reversed the sentence with a royal decree.

Verdi wrote a letter to the king, thanking him for his 'lofty act of clemency' on behalf of his 'unfortunate nephew'. One untidy detail, the existence of the dead woman's brother, who was also on the payroll at Sant'Agata, was 'dealt with' – the young man was given sufficient funds to emigrate.

A scandal threatened. There were rumours in Busseto that the boy was being made a scapegoat for his father, Fifao's husband. But as swiftly as the matter exploded, it faded away. No more investigation, no further newspaper reports.

The matter was never satisfactorily cleared up; all that can be said with certainty is that somehow a major crisis was avoided. This can be attributed to the fame of the man in whose house it occurred, a multi-decorated musician who could count the King of Italy among his friends. Nevertheless the whole grim affair took its toll. Verdi wrote to Ricordi that life was like that: a rare moment of joy, then misery, sorrow, disenchantment. He said the whole family had been plunged into utter despair.

To add to that misery and sorrow, there were the deaths of close friends to cope with. Francesco Piave, responsible for ten librettos for Verdi, including his two best loved, *La traviata* and *Rigoletto*, and who had taken his share of bullying from Verdi with good grace, had died at the age of sixty-five, his last nine years spent in a wheelchair, incapacitated and unable to communicate.

An even greater shock to Verdi was the sudden and unexpected death of his oldest friend. Verdi and Emanuele Muzio had known each other for more than sixty years. They had grown up together, and over the years, as Verdi had become more and more occupied, his fame spreading across Europe and then the world, Muzio had always been at his side, ready to ease the strain. His death at just sixty-nine shocked Verdi – almost eight years his senior – to the core.

Verdi and Giuseppina were now in old age. Verdi was approaching eighty, his wife just two years younger. Both were suffering from various ailments, Verdi complaining about his joints, aggravated by the damp of the Po valley, and his increasing difficulty in walking. His sight and hearing were also beginning to deteriorate.

Giuseppina was in much poorer health than her husband. Her lungs began to function abnormally, and she had trouble breathing. She was often unable to speak for days on end. It was in stark contrast to the days when voices were continually raised, often in anger, within the walls of Sant'Agata. She spent most of her time cloistered within the house, dressed in black and moving from room to room, it was remarked, like a phantom. Husband and wife barely communicated.

In a long life full of paradox and the unexpected, Giuseppe Verdi had one final surprise for an unsuspecting world. Having finally, once and for all, decided to give up writing opera, he decided . . . to write an opera.

Even more surprising, it was to be a comedy. From remarks he had been making over the last couple of years to Ricordi, it was clear that the idea of composing a comedy had been revolving in his mind. Ricordi did not know how much seriousness to attach to this, but he was certainly not going to discourage Verdi. Any new composition would be welcome.

Why did Verdi settle on a comedy? We cannot be entirely sure, because Verdi never explained himself. But informed speculation can bring us close to an understanding.

Verdi had written just one comic opera in his entire career, and it flopped disastrously.

Un giorno di regno had been written nearly a half century earlier, in the aftermath of the deaths of his young children and his wife. Such a disaster had it been that it was abandoned after its opening night, after just a single performance, never to be rewritten or reworked or adapted. Had the failure rankled with Verdi ever since, simmered deep within him? It is quite possible.

There is another factor. We know it with hindsight, but Verdi knew it too: this really would be his final opera, his last offering to the world. He did not have the strength, the inclination, or the health, to compose into his eighties.

As the matter revolved in his mind, he invited Boito, who had made such a good job of the libretto for *Otello*, to visit him at Sant'Agata. Significantly, he warned Boito not to expect elaborate hospitality. Giuseppina was seriously unwell; there would be no convivial dinners with plentiful wine. Boito would stay just as long as was necessary for the work at hand to be accomplished.

It was Boito, it seems, who came up with the subject. Given that the two of them had had such a success with *Otello*, why did they not turn again to Shakespeare for a comic subject? Boito's suggestion was that Verdi should allow him to adapt *The Merry Wives of Windsor*, and that the adaptation should make Falstaff the central character in the opera. The comic potential of the 'fat man' was boundless, he assured Verdi.

Verdi, predictably, had his doubts, but he gave Boito the go-ahead to see what he could come up with.

In July 1889 Boito produced a synopsis based largely on *The Merry Wives* with elements from both parts of *Henry IV*, with the title of *Falstaff*. Verdi, unpredictably, was absolutely delighted with it. There were one or two points he took issue with, but in general he was very pleased.

Doubts soon surfaced, though, and they were mainly to do with his advanced years. He pointed out to Boito that he was likely to be eighty, or more, by the time the opera reached the stage. He was not even sure he would ever be able to complete it.

By this point Boito was not to be dissuaded. He wrote to Verdi:

You have longed for a good subject for a comic opera all your life, which proves you have a natural aptitude for the noble art of comedy. Instinct is a good guide. There is only one way to end your career more splendidly than with Otello, *and that is to end it with* Falstaff. [107]

Boito's flattering words were perfectly calculated; they were exactly what Verdi needed to hear. Comedy was the one area – the sole area in all opera – in which he had failed. If he could pull off a successful comedy, then he would have proved himself the master of all operatic forms.

Verdi responded in a way none of his previous librettists had ever enjoyed:

What a joy to be able to say to the public, HERE WE ARE AGAIN!! COME AND SEE US! . . . Amen, and so be it! Let us then do Falstaff. *Let us not think now of the obstacles, my age and illness! But I want to keep it the deepest* secret, *a word I underline three times to tell you that no one must know anything of it.* [108]

And a secret it was kept. Not even Giuseppina knew, at least at the start. Gone were the days when Verdi confided in his wife, asked for her advice, discussed projects with her.

He made several trips to Milan. Did he go to see Teresa, herself now in her late fifties and not in the best of health? Did he discuss the possibility of a comic opera with her? We can only speculate. He was a lifelong master at covering his tracks.

Unusually for Verdi, he began composing almost immediately. It seemed his mood matched the subject matter. It is easy to imagine him writing his comic opera with a smile on his face. He wrote to Boito:

> I'm amusing myself by writing fugues! Yes, sir, a fugue: and a comic fugue which would be suitable for Falstaff. [109]

He did not know it yet, but that fugue, once completed, would provide a glorious finale to the entire opera, indeed to his own operatic life.

Perhaps Verdi needed to believe that this was not a serious attempt to write opera; after all, he had given all that up, hadn't he? When finally he decided to tell Ricordi what he was doing, he described it in such a way that he could at any moment decide to abandon the whole thing, without repercussions:

> I am engaged in writing Falstaff to pass the time, without any preconceived ideas or plans. I repeat, 'to pass the time'. Nothing else. All this talk, these proposals, however vague, and this splitting of words, will end by involving me in obligations that I absolutely refuse to assume. [110]

Unlike poor Piave – and he was not the only one! – Boito found Verdi thoroughly accommodating. The composer accepted the libretto almost without alteration.

Again unusually for Verdi, he worked at the opera over some considerable time, devoting several weeks to it, then breaking off, before resuming again. It was as though he needed periodic stimulation away from the keyboard and manuscript paper.

It was a full two years before Verdi produced a workable version of the opera, and even then the orchestration was not complete. But the bulk of the work was done. In yet another departure from his usual process, he seemed to have maintained his sense of humour throughout the process, not falling prey to his usual psychosomatic illnesses. This, despite articulating the fear to Boito that he might die before completing the opera.

He dispatched the (almost) finished object to Ricordi with a humorous note addressed to the eponymous hero of the opera:

Tutto è finito,	All is finished.
Va, va vecchio John.	Go, go, old John.
Cammina per la tua via	Go on your way
Fin che tu puoi.	As long as you can.
Va, va	Go, go,
Cammina, cammina,	On your way.
Addio	Addio.[111]

Verdi had been done proud by his librettist. Boito had transformed Shakespeare's play once again, telescoping the action, amalgamating certain characters, developing the characterisation – all in all, presenting Verdi with exactly what was needed for him to set it to music.

It really does seem as though Verdi, for once, was relishing the challenge. When he arrived at La Scala to supervise rehearsals, it was remarked on how energised and lively he was, how he was in control of every aspect of the production, and – most remarkably, perhaps – how easy he was to work with. This was a new Giuseppe Verdi; the Bear had remained in Busseto.

The opening night for *Falstaff* was set for 9 February 1893 at La Scala. For the occasion, he brought his Peppina from her sick bed. He knew there would be no more premieres; he wanted her to be at this one. Teresa Stolz, we can be sure, was not there.

As with *Otello*, the anticipation was enormous, overwhelming even. Music critics and opera lovers came to Milan from all over the world. Verdi had installed Giuseppina in their usual suite in the Grand Hotel. From there she wrote to her sister, somewhat caustically:

> *Admirers, bores, friends, enemies, genuine and non-genuine musicians, critics good and bad are swarming in from all over the world. The way people are clamouring for seats, the opera house would need to be as big as a public square.*[112]

Again, as with *Otello*, a *succès fou* was guaranteed. By now Verdi could do no wrong in the eyes not just of his countrymen but of the world. Here was Italy's greatest operatic composer, at the end of his glorious career, offering one final jewel.

During the performance, Verdi was called on to the stage time and time again. Once more he brought Boito on to share the applause with him; once more he was mobbed as he left by a side door; once more he was called out on to the balcony repeatedly.

Falstaff, only the composer's second comic opera, was a triumph. He had proved there was nothing he could not do, nothing he could not turn his hand to.

There are so many tunes in *Falstaff*, so many melodies, that I have seen it described as having none. Verdi rarely repeats a melody, and is in fact more inclined to discard it without even developing it. A lesser composer would milk each melody for all it is worth. This was Verdi truly at the top of his powers.

The single passage in *Falstaff* that stands out, both musically and as a commentary on Verdi and his philosophy on life, comes, fittingly, right at the end of the opera. Falstaff leads the ensemble in a scintillating comic fugue: *'Tutto nel mondo è burla'* ('All the world's a joke').

As Verdi's final composition (though, as we have seen, it might well have been the first part of the opera that he wrote), it is matchless. This is Verdi looking back on a long career, which had its failures as well as successes, as though he is saying, 'So what? What does any of it matter anyway?'

In the audience at La Scala that night was another Italian composer of opera, a younger man aged thirty-five by the name of Giacomo Puccini, whose latest opera *Manon Lescaut* had received its first performance to huge acclaim in Turin just one week earlier.

Verdi was aware of the younger man making waves, and had been somewhat critical after seeing his early work *Le Villi*:

> *[Puccini] follows modern trends, which is natural, but he keeps to melody which is neither ancient nor modern. However the symphonic vein appears to predominate in him. No harm in that, but one needs to tread carefully here. Opera is opera and symphony symphony and I don't think it's a good thing to put a symphonic piece into the opera merely to put the orchestra through its paces.*[113]

In one sense, damning with faint praise; in another, perhaps, the understandable envy of an older composer for a much younger one with, clearly, a fine career ahead of him.

There is no other comment in any of Verdi's correspondence on the man regarded from the start as his successor; nor am I aware of any opinion on Verdi expressed by Puccini. But we can be in no doubt as to Puccini's admiration for the older man. Four years after Verdi's death, Puccini would compose a Requiem to be performed in his memory.

As for composers admired by Verdi, one name stands out. When a festival was being planned in Bonn to honour its most famous son, it was proposed to Verdi that his name should be added to the honours list of musicians at the birthplace of the great man.

Verdi replied:

> *I cannot refuse the honour that is offered to me. We are talking about Beethoven! Before such a name, we all prostrate ourselves reverently.*

26

'ONE BUTTON MORE, ONE BUTTON LESS'

Throughout the summer of 1897 Giuseppina's health worsened. She refused to eat, complaining of a severe pain in her side and saying that the sight of food made her feel ill. For all but a few hours a day, she remained in bed in her room at Sant'Agata.

She spoke little, but when she said she was suffering from the cold, Verdi ordered a new coal stove to be sent from Milan and had it installed in her room. She was weak and listless, and the dark depression that had so often plagued her in the past lay over her like an impenetrable blanket.

The doctor diagnosed acute pneumonia and was as surprised as anyone when, towards the second week of November, she unexpectedly rallied. Verdi even helped her plan a visit to her sister in Cremona. But the improvement did not last, just as Violetta's did not in the final moments of *La traviata*. In a further echo of that opera, Verdi picked the last violets of the season and gave them to his wife. He urged her to smell their scent. 'Thank you, but I cannot smell them because I have a slight cold,' she replied.[114]

Verdi made the decision, as Giuseppina lay dying, to send a new composition, *Quattro pezzi sacri* (Four Sacred Pieces), to Ricordi. He had actually begun them several years before, and they had lain on his desk largely untouched. Occasionally he would add a passage here, or adjust another one there.

Verdi stayed by his wife's side throughout her final illness. Boito visited and reported that Verdi himself was suffering from fatigue, and his memory was failing. At half past four in the afternoon on Sunday, 14 November, Giuseppina died at the age of eighty-two. After more than fifty years together, Verdi had lost his Peppina.

At times it had been an uneasy relationship. Verdi had not always afforded Peppina the unconditional love she so wanted, particularly once Teresa Stolz had come into his life. But that he needed her, that he relied on her, that she was always there to ease his passage through difficult times, was in no doubt. She had guided him along many paths, not all of them successful. She had shared his successes and his failures. Though he was not always overtly grateful, she knew he could not have managed without her calming and encouraging presence.

In return Verdi had been her rock, her anchor, to whose fate she had irrevocably tied her own. Her career over, she had devoted the remainder of her life to him. By marrying her, he had given her status. Whatever his profligacies, no one could take away from her the fact that she was the wife of *il maestro*, Italy's most feted composer.

Final proof that Giuseppina was as much opposed to the ostentatious side of musical life as her husband came in her funeral instructions. She asked that it be conducted at dawn, and that there should be no flowers, no speeches, and no one present outside her family.

'I came into this world poor and without pomp, and without pomp I want to go down into the grave.'[115] Her body was dressed in black by the women of the household and a rosary placed in her hands, and she was laid on her bed under the dark, emerald velvet canopy.

Giuseppina had left instructions that a small envelope she had sealed fifty-one years earlier, and whose contents were a secret, should be buried unopened with her. According to Verdi's biographer Mary Jane Phillips-Matz, who spoke to descendants of the household staff, the envelope was searched for in every corner of Sant'Agata, but was not found. Giuseppina's coffin was closed. Later, the envelope was discovered among her papers. It is not known if the envelope was ever added to the coffin.[*]

Giuseppina achieved her wish that her funeral should take place at dawn, but not that there should be no dignitaries present. Verdi walked

---

[*] Gaia Servadio's account differs. She states in her biography of Giuseppina that the envelope was never found. Whichever version is true, the contents of the envelope have never been disclosed.

behind his wife's coffin when it left Sant'Agata at six thirty on the morning of 16 November.

At the parish church in Busseto – the town that had in the past treated her with such disdain – were local officials, mayors of nearby towns along with council members, heads of the local hospital, schools and care centres, all of which she had helped with financial contributions. All the families that lived on the huge Sant'Agata estate were also present.

The funeral service took place without music. There was a Mass, an absolution and a blessing of the coffin. There were no wreaths on the carriage as the coffin was transported by train to Milan. At every stop it was honoured by mayors, council members and local senators.

Among those at the main cemetery as Giuseppina's coffin was lowered into a temporary grave were Boito and his wife, and a young conductor by the name of Arturo Toscanini, who had played cello in the orchestra at the premiere of *Otello* at La Scala, and was making a name for himself interpreting Verdi's music.

The grave was temporary because both Verdi and his wife had expressed in their wills their desire to be buried alongside each other in the Casa di Riposo, the rest home for retired musicians endowed by Verdi that was in the process of being constructed.

Giuseppina named her husband as her sole heir, leaving him almost her entire estate. She left small amounts to family members, and also asked that gifts of money from her estate should be given every year to the poor of the village of Villanova, just a short distance from Sant'Agata.

Verdi must have been heartened that Giuseppina left three pieces of jewellery to Teresa, including a bracelet with the word 'souvenir' picked out in small diamonds. To Verdi himself she bequeathed a gold bracelet that he had given her twenty-five years earlier in Naples, which bore the inscription: 'To my dear Peppina 1872'. In her will she begged him to keep it as a 'sacred memory' until his death.

The final words of Giuseppina's will read: 'And now goodbye, my Verdi. As we have been together in life, so may God Almighty reunite our souls.'[116]

Verdi placed an announcement in the newspapers:

Deeply grieving, Maestro Verdi is unable to reply individually to the innumerable, compassionate condolences sent to him upon the loss of his dear companion Giuseppina. Deeply moved and in gratitude to all.[117]

One month later, in December 1897, Verdi wrote to Boito that his hands trembled so much he could hardly write; he was also, he said, half deaf, half blind and unable to focus on anything.

But he had Teresa. In that same month, just a few weeks after Giuseppina's death, Verdi gave Teresa his manuscript score of the *Requiem*, with the inscription on the first page:

> *To Teresa Stolz, the first interpreter of this composition. G. Verdi. Sant'Agata. December 1897.*

Teresa was now sixty-three years of age, and still close to the man she had admired so much for a quarter of a century. From then on she and Arrigo Boito, his closest male colleague, made sure Verdi was looked after. It is possible they made a pact that one or the other would be with him at all times, whether he was in Sant'Agata or Milan.

Their concern proved premature. Verdi regained his strength quickly after Giuseppina's death. He had a house overflowing with guests for Christmas, which Boito described as the time of year the great man liked best. He even suggested that Verdi regretted his loss of faith as a young man: 'Alas, like all of us, he had lost his credulity in miracles early; but, perhaps more than us, he kept a poignant regret for it all his life,' he wrote to a friend.

In the new year, Verdi moved to Milan and took up residence in the Grand Hotel, in the apartment in which he and Giuseppina had stayed so many times. Teresa was in a new apartment, just a single block away. Did they see each other regularly – or even occasionally? We have no reports of meetings between them, which does not come as a surprise.

Even at this age Verdi was still stopped whenever he stepped out onto the street. He was certainly the most recognisable individual in Italy, and one of the most recognised in Europe.

There is a wonderfully revealing photograph taken around this time, which shows him standing in the street outside La Scala, reading a newspaper. We see a bearded man in a black top hat and black overcoat, the rim of his hat almost hiding his eyes, both hands holding the large broadsheet.

Why is it so revealing? Because it is a rare – if not the only – photograph taken of Giuseppe Verdi that he did not know was being taken, and for which he did not pose. What we have, therefore, is the real man. He shows his age with a much lined face, and no hint of a smile disturbs his features. He could be anyone, which is not something that could otherwise be said about him at practically any stage of his adult life. There is no touching up here, no embellishments, as

there were in all the thousands of drawings and portraits of him made
during his lifetime.

Given his celebrity, it is tempting to suggest he could not possibly
have gone to see Teresa, or she come to see him, without someone
recognising one or the other, and reporting it. But as I have said many
times, all his life he was the master of evasion. Had he wanted a meeting to take place, he was quite capable of ensuring that it would do
so clandestinely.

Outside Milan, there was not the same need for secrecy. Together
Verdi and Teresa stayed several times in the spa town of Montecatini
in Tuscany. While she remained in their hotel, Verdi would take walks

and visit cafés. He seemed perfectly happy to be seen out there, though when the attention became too invasive, he would return to his rooms. Conversation did not interest him.

A young journalist wrote a vivid description of the famous composer in Montecatini:

> *Not at all expansive, severe in appearance, stingy with words, [he] stayed very much to himself. He wore black [suits] and his soft, wide-brimmed hat, and went in the morning to drink the waters . . . When he became aware that he was the target of stares of the too-curious, he moved or left. He spent almost all day in his apart-ment. He took lunch there, but for dinner he came down to the round table of the Locanda, sharing the meal, sitting at the head of the table, a place that everyone respectfully kept for him. In the evening he went upstairs early, and before going to bed he enjoyed himself for an hour or so playing card games . . . He prided himself on being very skilful at these games.*

It seems that card games were the limit of his sociability.

Verdi and Teresa also took the waters at the spa town of Tabiano, where he had previously spent many a sojourn with Giuseppina, Teresa often joining them. Strong evidence of the intimacy between the pair, and the extent to which he now relied on her to keep his spirits up, comes in a series of letters Verdi wrote to Teresa, while she was in Tabi-ano and he was at Sant'Agata.

> *Dearest*
>
> *Delightful hours but [they were] too short! And who knows when even ones as short as those will come again! Oh an old man's life is truly unhappy! Even without real illness, life is a burden, and I feel that vitality and strength are diminishing, each day more than the one before. I feel this within myself, and I don't have the courage or power to keep busy with anything . . . Love me well always, and believe in my [love], great, very, very great, and very true . . .*
>
> *We will write to each other again and see what we shall be able to do. I am feeling a moment of good humour, and I give you not one kiss but two. Addio, addio, addio . . .*
>
> *So everything is set for Saturday morning at nine. I will send a carriage to bring you to Sant'Agata . . . Oh! Joy! Joy! I am truly happy, even though my health is a bit off . . .*

Left

Verdi in the garden of Sant'Agata.

At the time Verdi wrote these notes, he was eighty-seven years of age, Teresa sixty-six. As his biographer Phillips-Matz observes, few could doubt, reading his words, that this man and woman were in love.

When he was not in Milan or Sant'Agata, Verdi stayed in Genoa, in an apartment he had bought some years previously and where he and Giuseppina had spent many summers. It was in Genoa that Verdi kept his business affairs. On 1 October 1900 he transferred his entire business operations from Genoa to Milan, against the protestations of his bankers.

A conservative estimate of his fortune put it at around 6 million lire.* This was augmented considerably by the annual income from his estates. In his will he had named his daughter Filomena, Fifao, as his sole heir.

During his stay in Genoa, his health worsened considerably. For the first time he needed to be carried up the stairs to his apartment. Back in Sant'Agata he said he felt so weak that he could not move easily, and found it difficult to concentrate on anything.

A visitor to the villa described him as 'melancholy and sad'. He quoted Verdi as saying:

I don't talk any more, I don't read any more, I don't write any more, I don't play any more! What a season! It is the seasons that depress me! . . . My legs won't carry me any longer!

When the visitor told him that, according to his doctor, he was blessed with a strong, healthy constitution, Verdi replied, with characteristic pessimism:

I know, I know, and if I were not, I would never have got to eighty-seven years of age. But it is the eighty-seven years that are a burden to me!

Verdi had lived into the new century, but he knew the end was near. Over his life he had filled two wooden crates with his early compositions. He instructed Fifao to ensure that they were destroyed. A giant magnolia that stood in front of the villa and obstructed the path, he ordered to be cut down. 'I planted that with my own hands when I first came to Sant'Agata,' he said as he watched it being felled.

Late in October 1900 he was described as 'serene and solemn with his white hair, his white beard . . . extraordinarily cordial and open, and with a very, very lucid mind'. That was not how he saw himself.

---

* Approximately £21 million today.

In January 1901 he stayed inside the villa for two full weeks, and in a letter to a friend he said he was vegetating, rather than living, and did not understand why he was still on the earth.

A day after writing this, he decided he needed to be in Milan. There were business affairs to attend to. He installed himself in his familiar apartment in the Grand Hotel. On 20 January, the conductor Arturo Toscanini came to see him. Verdi wanted to know how Mascagni's new opera had been received.

Toscanini reported that he had a good conversation with Verdi, who had asked him what a pavane was, before hurriedly stating that of course he knew. Toscanini said Verdi was in good spirits but sadly somewhat confused.

On the morning of 21 January his doctor came to see him. Shortly after he left, Verdi began to dress himself. He had trouble doing up the buttons on his waistcoat, so he called the chambermaid for assistance. He sat on the edge of the bed. His hands were trembling.

When the maid offered to do the buttons up for him, he insisted on doing it himself. 'One button more, or one button less,' he said, then fell back on the bed unconscious.[†]

The maid hurried out to fetch the hotel doctor, while Verdi's own doctor was also called. The hotel doctor was the first to examine him. His right side was paralysed; his eyes showed no reaction to light, though there was some movement in his arms and hands.

He remained unconscious, but breathing regularly, for several days. Boito was one of the first to reach his bedside. He reported that 'the silence of death' was upon him, and that he perfectly resembled a bust that a young sculptor Vincenzo Gemito had made of him thirty years before in Naples, in return for financial help Verdi had given him to avoid military service. 'Poor Maestro,' reported Boito, 'how courageous and handsome he was, right up to the last moment.'[118]

The hotel and the city of Milan took unprecedented measures. Noise and traffic around the hotel was controlled. Carriages were ordered to travel at the slowest speed possible; tram conductors were told not to ring their bells. Straw was laid down outside on the street that Verdi had walked along so many times.

"*Verdi had lived into the new century, but he knew the end was near.*"

[†] It is a poignant coincidence that both Verdi's final words and those of King Lear, about whom he never achieved his lifelong ambition of writing an opera, were about buttons.

Bulletins on Verdi's condition were regularly posted on a board to the right of the hotel's main entrance. His health was briefly overshadowed by the death of Queen Victoria on 22 January, but then the focus of attention returned once more to Italy's most famous son.

On 26 January, bulletins were issued twice in the morning and twice in the afternoon. Doctors then announced that no further bulletins would be issued. On the evening of the 26th, he stopped breathing, but then resumed again.

At 11 p.m. that night, with Boito and Teresa by his bedside, his breathing slowed, the pause between breaths growing longer. In the early hours of the night, Teresa fainted and was taken to lie down on a bed in another room of the suite.

Giuseppe Verdi took his last breath at 2.50 a.m. on 27 January 1901. He was eighty-seven years and three months.

As the news spread, crowds gathered in the street outside. By dawn, flags on government buildings and churches had been draped with ribbons of mourning. For the next three days most shops in the city were shut. Newspapers bore black mourning borders.

Later on the day of his death, despite it being a Sunday, the Italian Senate met and mourned the passing of 'that shining star who filled the whole civilised world with glory'.[119]

Giuseppe Verdi had outlived his wife Giuseppina by three years and three months. Teresa Stolz never recovered her health. She died a year after the man she so admired and loved. She was sixty-eight.

On the morning of 30 January, two hundred thousand people crowded into the centre of Milan, more than had ever gathered on the streets of that city before or since. They had come to bid farewell to one of their own.

He was a country lad, a farmer at heart, who all his life loved the soil on which he was raised, and the country for whose independence he strove.

Dressed in his best evening clothes, he was laid in his coffin with only palm fronds beside his body and an ebony cross on his chest. His instructions for 'two priests, two candles, one cross, and no flowers', together with an 'extremely modest' service, were respected.

A second-class hearse bore his coffin to the church of San Francesco di Paola, more than an hour away. Fellow composers Puccini, Mascagni, Leoncavallo and Giordano joined family members.

After the service, Verdi was laid alongside Giuseppina in the Cimitero Monumentale di Milano, the city's main cemetery, while

preparations were made to carry out their final wish, to be buried alongside each other in the Casa di Riposo.

Almost one month later, on 27 February, more than three hundred thousand people lined the route, as a funeral car, towering more than four metres above the street, looking like 'a black and gold boat sailing on a sea of humanity', was drawn by six horses, draped in black.

Before the cortège left the cemetery, Arturo Toscanini conducted a chorus of more than eight hundred voices in 'Va, pensiero', 'The Chorus of the Hebrew Slaves', from *Nabucco*. At the Casa di Riposo, the *Miserere* from *Il trovatore* was sung.

The procession included a royal prince, the Count of Turin, representing the King and Queen of Italy; consuls from several European governments; representatives of the Italian Senate and Chamber of Deputies, and the Mayor of Milan, as well as delegates from every other major city in Italy.

Above

Verdi and Giuseppina's
graves at the Casa di Riposo
per Musicisti, Milan.

All along the route tapestries, flags with mourning ribbons and coloured silk hangings were hung from balconies and windows. People leaned from rooftops and clung to the branches of trees.

At the Casa, at the end of a garden path and down circular steps, Verdi and Giuseppina were buried alongside each other. At some point thereafter, a plaque was set into the low wall at their feet, at a point midway between their two coffins, commemorating the soprano Teresa Stolz.

As for the elaborate ceremony of farewell, it would not have pleased Verdi at all. It was precisely the kind of scene he enjoyed depicting in his operas, and pricking for its pomposity.

He would, though, have been quietly pleased that the farewell from his fellow Italians was conducted on a scale, and with a depth of mourning, that the country had never seen before.

AFTERWORD

In this book, as in my earlier biographies of great composers – Beethoven, Mozart, Johann Strauss the Younger – I have attempted to reveal the man behind the music, to draw as accurate a picture as possible of each figure when he was away from his music. In other words, I have striven to present a fully rounded individual, rather than solely a genius involved in the creative process.

Have I succeeded in the case of Giuseppe Verdi? Probably not. He was, as I have pointed out throughout the course of this book, enormously protective of his private life and notoriously unhelpful to biographers, interviewers and journalists. He knew he had no choice but to allow himself to be presented to the public, if for no other reason than to interest them in his work. But he would go no further in enlightening them than was absolutely necessary, and if that meant hiding certain facts and embellishing others, he was perfectly capable of doing so.

Those who have previously attempted to chronicle his life have acknowledged the difficulties they face. Consider these *apologias* from three twentieth-century biographers. Frank Walker writes: 'Verdi has a way of escaping his biographers. The known facts of his long and busy career have been told and retold, but the man himself remains a distant figure, still protected by his habitual reserve and mistrust.'[120]

Claudio Sartori, with more than a hint of frustration, goes further: 'Verdi does not and probably never will allow us a direct, intimate, human understanding of him. It can almost be said that Verdi, the man Verdi, does not exist.'[121]

Equally strongly, and using modern analogy, Massimo Mila says this: 'Whosoever attempts to penetrate the mind of the man quickly

Above

The Casa di Riposo per Musicisti, Milan, Verdi's statue in the foreground.

finds himself in trouble. It is far easier to infiltrate the military secrets of the Pentagon or the Kremlin, than it is to reveal the soul of Verdi.'[122]

Indeed, as this book goes to press (May 2017), there is news that the Verdi-Carrara family, Verdi's heirs, have handed over to the Italian state archives 5,300 pages of his notes which were packed in a trunk at Sant'Agata, most of which have never been seen before.

They will be examined by leading Verdi musicologists, then digitised and published online, and are certain to throw light on hitherto unknown aspects of his artistic process. I suspect, if he could know, Verdi would scowl, then shrug his shoulders and permit himself a small smile with twinkling eyes.

It has been said that no other great artist was quite so averse to publicity as Verdi. Even when he read inaccuracies about himself, he refused to correct them. As he himself might have said, his philosophy on life and art was simple. The artist creates; the public applauds or boos; the critics criticise. All that was perfectly fine. But his private life had nothing to do with any of it.

'The bear would brook no intrusion in his den.' He was reserved and aloof, which was inevitably interpreted as 'boorishness, moroseness, or downright arrogance'.[123]

None of which, of course, has in any way impinged on the universal desire to learn more about this great artist, revered and honoured in his homeland more than any other composer.

Take the Milan Metro on the red line from the Duomo in the centre of the city to Buonarroti, six stops west, and you emerge onto one of the city's most spacious squares. Not its most beautiful, but certainly one of the most noteworthy in Milan.

Although named the Piazza Buonarotti, it is actually more a roundabout than a square, the centre of which is dominated by a larger-than-lifesize statue of Giuseppe Verdi. He stands with his hands behind his back, head turned to his left, gazing off into the distance, oblivious to the discordant sounds of traffic below.

It is a little strange that his head is not turned to the right. If it had been, he would be gazing at what he called his greatest creation. Not a piece of music, but a broad and imposing three-storey building. The double windows have high decorative arches, and above the top floor a panel stands proud of the roof, proclaiming:

CASA DI RIPOSO
PER
MUSICISTI
FONDAZIONE VERDI

This was Verdi's final gift to his profession, a home for retired musicians. But that is too general a description. He intended it specifically for musicians less talented than himself, whose careers had achieved little success or none at all, musicians who had fallen on hard times.

He was himself in old age, in his eighties, when the deed was drawn up. When he saw the words 'Alms-House for Musicians', he demanded they be struck out and replaced with 'Rest Home'. The musicians there, 'my less fortunate companions', were to be called 'guests' and treated with dignity and respect.

Today the Casa Verdi, as it is known by everyone in Milan, houses as many as a hundred men and women, musicians all. Funded initially by Verdi himself, who left instructions that his royalties should continue to support the home for many years to come, other illustrious names have since given financial support, including Arturo Toscanini, and Vladimir Horowitz, who was married to Toscanini's daughter.

A modern addition is young music students, who come to the Casa to take lessons from the residents, to talk about music and learn about the past. Thus, more than a century after his death, Verdi is providing more support for young musicians than he ever did in life.

He came to dislike his profession so intensely that far from encouraging young musicians he actively discouraged them. In his lifetime he never offered support of any kind – artistic or financial – to young musicians. His spirit, though, would surely approve of the Casa's beneficence.

In one room of Casa Verdi is the face of the maestro himself. It is the bust made by the young sculptor Vincenzo Gemito – the same bust that Boito said thirty years later exactly captured Verdi's mien as 'the silence of death fell upon him'. A replica of the bust stands in the Villa Sant'Agata.

With characteristic irony, Italy's greatest operatic composer said that of all his works, the one that pleased him most was the Casa he built to shelter those who had not been favoured by fortune, or had been unable to save their money. 'Poor and dear companions of my life!' as he wrote to his friend Giulio Monteverde, not a view he was otherwise often heard to express.

The building consists of four sides, enclosing a 'garden of honour', with a central path leading to a crypt where Verdi and his wife Giuseppina are buried side by side. They have simple tombs bearing only their names in a broad cross.

Set in a low wall at their feet and between their two tombs, perhaps rather surprisingly, is a small stone dedicated to Teresa Stolz. The inscription states:

TERESA STOLZ
CELEBRATA NEL CANTO
N. 1834 – M. 1902
SVE SPESE DECORO DI BRONZI DI MVSAICI
QVESIA TOMBA
RICORDO DI AMICIZIA DI VENERAZIONE

(Teresa Stolz/celebrated in song/born 1834 – died 1902/
At her own expense she decorated with bronzes and mosaics/
this tomb/in memory of friendship and of veneration)

The wording on the stone suggests that the plaque might have been put there on Teresa's instructions, given that she had taken it on herself to

beautify the crypt. I can find no reference to it in any of the literature, including the booklet published by the Casa di Riposo itself.

Teresa was herself buried in Milan's main cemetery, where Verdi's and Giuseppina's coffins were first taken. She remains there to this day.

On the day my wife Nula and I went to the Casa Verdi, we were the only visitors. Inside the crypt the small gate was unlocked. We descended a few steps. It was extraordinarily emotional to stand alone by Verdi's tomb, and contemplate this great artist and the profound gifts that he gave us. Not universally loved as a man in his lifetime – something that certainly did not trouble him – I am sure he would not be in the least surprised to learn of the esteem in which his works are held today.

The Po valley in northern Italy, where Verdi was born, which was in his blood, and where he lived all his life, is today a mixture of the agricultural, which Verdi knew, and the light industrial. Many an idyllic view is marred by factories and chimneys.

Turn off the main road between Milan and Parma, though, and you get some idea of the tranquillity and beauty that Verdi loved so much. But the modern is very close indeed. Stand in the front garden of the Villa Sant'Agata and you can clearly hear the roar of motorway traffic.

The villa itself, which Verdi cherished for more than half a century, which was his refuge and sanctuary, is now both a home and a memorial to its creator. It has been beautifully preserved, looking inside and out much as it did when Verdi and his wife lived there.

The gardens are as lush and exotic as they were in Verdi's day. He spent at least as much time learning about flora and fauna as he did composing. He learned which plants would flourish, and imported them from around the world. A banana tree that he imported from the West Indies and planted himself still flourishes today. In his lifetime he stressed to biographers and interviewers that he was an agriculturalist and a botanist, rather than a musician.

The paths through the foliage are laid with sand brought in from the banks of the River Po. This was on Verdi's instructions. He wanted no pebbles or stones that would make a noise and disturb his concentration while he walked.

The villa is today owned by direct descendants of the little cousin, Filomena, 'Fifao', whom Verdi and his wife adopted and brought up as their own daughter. By special decree Filomena was allowed to retain the name Verdi, so the occupants today are the Carrara-Verdi family.

They occupy part of the villa all year round, but five rooms on the ground floor have been preserved as Verdi and Giuseppina knew them, and are open to visitors. These include the couple's bedrooms, both containing many original items of furniture. The bed in Giuseppina's room is the bed she died in.

As I have written in the body of this book, Verdi's bedroom was much more than merely the room where he slept. He kept his desk just two paces from his bed so he could get up in the middle of the night and compose. It also housed the piano at which he composed, as well as furniture he personally bought, and items particularly close to him, such as a small portrait of Giuseppina's beloved toy Maltese dog Loulou. Loulou is buried in the garden of the villa. The inscription on the gravestone reads: '*Alla Memoria d'un Vero Amico*' ('To the memory of a true friend'). Loulou was undoubtedly one of the few beings on whom Verdi willingly lavished such praise.

A favourite item of mine is a note Verdi wrote, found after his death and enclosed now in a small glass case. Given what was to come in the succeeding century, we might compliment Verdi on his prescience. He wrote: *Un tedesco che sa, sa troppo. Un russo che sa è un pericolo.* ('A German who knows, knows too much. A Russian who knows is a danger.') We do not know what caused him to write it, but it surely accords perfectly with the character of this patriotic Italian.

Off the bedroom is an office where Verdi kept his accounts. It contains many piano scores, as well as the manuscript of Wagner's *Lohengrin* on the side of which Verdi wrote his withering assessment of Wagner's music.

There is a cabinet containing hunting rifles. Although Verdi was known to hunt occasionally, it was not something he particularly enjoyed, despite on one occasion asking a friend to source French rifles for him. When he found out that one of his employees had shot a rabbit for no reason, he sacked him.

Recreated in the villa is the small room of the Grand Hotel, Milan, in which Verdi died. The actual bed is there, covered in a white counterpane embroidered with an elaborate letter 'V'. A glass case holds the shirt he was wearing at his death.

To enter these rooms, you actually step directly from the garden path into Verdi's bedroom. When we visited, our guide explained as she unlocked the door that every time she entered she felt almost as if she was intruding.

This was Verdi's room, where he slept and worked, and which remained as he knew it. She told us that before stepping across the threshold she always asked his permission. 'Permesso, Verdi,' she said quietly as we entered.

Our guide, Cristina Micconi, gave us a personal tour in English. Her commentary brought Verdi and Giuseppina alive for us. She, in turn, expressed pleasure that our enthusiasm for the great man matched hers. At one wonderfully spontaneous moment, she turned to us smiling and said, 'I love him! I love him!' A sentiment shared by Nula.

Since that visit, I have contacted Cristina many times with questions and queries that arose during the writing of this book. Unfailingly she responded swiftly, patiently providing me with all the information I needed. I am profoundly grateful to her. My understanding of the years at Sant'Agata was able to reach a degree of intimacy and knowledge that would have been impossible without Cristina's help.

For anyone with the slightest interest in Verdi, the Villa Sant'Agata is a treasure trove, providing a unique insight into the man and his creative process, his interests away from music, and the manner in which he lived. We owe the Carrara-Verdi family an enormous debt for preserving it and allowing visitors to share it with them.

Verdi did not stray far from his roots. Just a few miles from Sant'Agata is the small town that was once called Le Roncole. There the simple house in which Verdi was (probably) born has been preserved and restored. Even in Verdi's lifetime it was revered as the house in which he was born, and was declared a national monument shortly after his death, which it remains to this day.

The house is open to the public. Rather incongruously the visitor is provided with a modern iPad, which describes the rooms and their contents. The furnishings are simple, and give a useful idea of living conditions two centuries ago, even if the front entrance is now on a different side of the building, the walls inside and out have been newly plastered, and the staircase is situated differently.

What is missing, of course, is the bustle, conversation and laughter of a grocery store during the day and a tavern at night. The iPad remedies this with a short film of drinkers sitting round the plain table, joshing with Verdi's father as he replenishes their glasses.

Upstairs is the room in which Verdi was born, furnished simply with a bed and a wooden crib at its feet. From the window the bell tower of the Church of San Michele Arcangelo is plainly visible across a courtyard. Here Verdi was baptised, here he played the organ, and, as he recalled later in life, it was in the tower that his mother hid with him in her arms as soldiers passed underneath. A plaque set into the wall of the church commemorates the event. The organ that Verdi played as a boy, dating from 1797 and much restored, sits in the loft high on the left side of the presbytery, as it did in his day.

Verdi's father would no doubt be proud to see a larger-than-lifesize bust of his son's head and shoulders atop a solid rectangular pillar in the small courtyard outside his grocery store and tavern. Only a certain amount of pride, perhaps, since father and son never truly got on.

Le Roncole is just one of many small towns – villages in Verdi's day – scattered across the Po valley, but it makes sure that its connection to the great composer is not forgotten. After all, Verdi never forgot Le Roncole. 'I was, I am, and I will always be, a native of Roncole,' he once said.

For that reason the town has adapted its name to honour its most famous citizen. It is today Roncole Verdi.

⊷

Five miles or so from Roncole Verdi is the town that Verdi was most associated with in the area: Busseto. Much larger than Roncole Verdi, Busseto is today a bustling market town, just as it was two centuries ago.

Here Antonio Barezzi, a wholesale grocer and distiller, lived in an opulent house in the centre of the town, as befitted its leading citizen. The history of music owes a debt to the fact that Barezzi was a dedicated music enthusiast, and that he spotted the potential in the young Verdi and nurtured him.

I have recounted in detail how Verdi came to despise the town and its people for the way they treated Giuseppina. The feeling is entirely unreciprocated. Verdi's image is everywhere. To call him a local hero is a significant understatement.

A massive statue of him seated in an armchair on a monumental plinth was erected in 1913, to mark the centenary of his birth, in the Piazza Verdi in front of the Teatro Giuseppe Verdi, the theatre whose construction he fiercely opposed, and where he refused to attend the first performance of *Rigoletto*, preferring to take the waters at a near-by spa.

Unintentionally, though perhaps appropriately, his back is turned towards the theatre. I suspect, though, he would probably be quietly satisfied that the town he came to dislike so intensely is now dominated by his name and likeness.

His name in large capital letters is embossed in gold on the plinth, and his gaze is directed across an open square – where outdoor concerts of his music are held – towards the Casa Barezzi, the house where he lived with his great benefactor. The house is today open to the public and holds a huge collection of memorabilia.

The large salon where Verdi gave his first public performance is frequently used for recitals, a portrait of his first wife Margherita gazing down at the musicians.

Opposite the Casa Barezzi, and a little further down Busseto's main street, Via Roma, is a building of great significance in Verdi's life. But you would not know it today. There is nothing to show any connection between Verdi and the Palazzo Cavalli, the substantial townhouse that he bought in 1845. We walked past it several times before we realised we had found it.

The building in which Verdi lived with his mistress, and whose first-floor windows were stoned by angry local people, is today the Palazzo Orlandi, 'Palazzo' being something of an exaggeration. A row of terraced buildings contains shops and cafés on the ground floor, apartments on the first floor. On the tourist map of Busseto it does not feature.

On the outskirts of the town stands the grand fifteenth-century Villa Pallavicino. Verdi knew its aristocratic occupants, and their opulent home, well. It was from this family that Verdi's father rented the house that is now designated the composer's birthplace. Today the palace is devoted to Verdi, one room dedicated to each of his twenty-seven operas.

Although Verdi is the only composer of note ever to have been associated with the town, Busseto has used its famous son to enhance and embellish its musical credentials. Streets in the town are named after Mozart, Bellini, Monteverdi, Donizetti, Berlioz, Schubert, Brahms, Ponchielli, Wagner, Chopin, Leoncavallo, Bizet, Tchaikovsky, Bartók, Sibelius, Ravel, Gershwin, and more.

Verdi souvenir shops abound in the town, and no visit is complete without a visit to the Salsamenteria, a small bustling restaurant devoted to the composer. Pictures of him are everywhere, and posters of performances; even in the front window a small upright piano is adorned with sheet music and more pictures.

An album of favourite Verdi arias plays on a loop, so you hear the great man's music as you dine on a plate of cold meats from the region. No menu, just a plate of Parma ham, salami and sausage. No knife and fork, just fingers. All washed down with chilled local sparkling red wine (yes, sparkling red wine), a drink Verdi knew well.

Verdi territory – Roncole Verdi, Sant'Agata, Busseto, all so close together – lies roughly midway between Milan to the north-west and Parma to the south-east. Just as Busseto conveniently forgets how it upset the maestro, so the two opera houses – La Scala in Milan and the Teatro Regio di Parma – prefer to remember the agreements rather than the disagreements.

La Scala has a whole room devoted to Verdi and performances of his operas there. A bust of Verdi stands in the foyer of the Teatro Regio, and each October (the month of Verdi's birth) the Parma opera house stages a month-long Verdi Festival.

There is not an opera house in the world that has not at some point staged a Verdi opera. It is said that every hour of the twenty-four, somewhere in the world the curtain is rising on one of the twenty-seven.

Then there is the other, bucolic, side to Verdi. All his life, while unleashing verbal onslaughts on opera houses and big cities in Italy and across Europe, he retained a love for his home territory, that small stretch of land in the Po valley of northern Italy.

Thus we have Verdi, composer of opera and man of the land. I suspect he would rather have it the other way round. He has hidden a lot, misled us over many an important juncture in his life. Of one fact, though, we – and musical history – can be certain. Verdi, for all his protestations, is the greatest operatic composer Italy, the home of opera, has ever produced.

I have no hesitation in going further: he is creator of the best-loved operas ever written.

NOTES

Unless otherwise noted, translated extracts are taken from Mary Jane Phillips-Matz, *Verdi: A Biography* (Oxford University Press, 1993).

1. Carlo Gatti, *Verdi: The Man and His Music*, trans. Elisabeth Abbott (Gollancz, 1955)
2. A. von Winterfeld, *Unterhalten in Verdis Tuskulum* (1887), quoted in Marcello Conati (ed.), *Interviste incontri con Verdi* (Milan, 1980)
3. Giuseppe Demaldè, *Cenni biografici del maestro di musica Giuseppe Verdi*, trans. Mary Jane Phillips-Matz and Gino Macchidani, *AIVS Newsletter*, 1976
4. Casati, Marisa di Gregorio, and Marco Marica, *Per amore di Verdi: vita, immagini, ritratti* (Grafiche Step, n.d.), trans. Julian Budden as *For Love of Verdi 1813–1901: Life, Images, Portraits* (Grafiche Step, 1905)
5. Conati, *Interviste*
6. *Il Fuggilozio*, III, 2 January 1857, quoted in Conati, *Interviste*
7. ibid.
8. ibid.
9. Demaldè, *Cenni biografici*
10. Pougin, Arthur, *Verdi: An Anecdotic History of His Life and Works.* (H. Grevel & Co., 1887), trans. James E. Matthew
11. ibid.
12. Gaia Servadio, *The Real Traviata* (Hodder and Stoughton, 1994)
13. Pougin, *Verdi*
14. ibid.
15. ibid.
16. Frank Walker, *The Man Verdi* (J. M. Dent, 1962)
17. Annibale Alberti (ed.), *Verdi intimo (1861–1886)* (Arnoldo Mondadori, 1931)
18. Julian Budden, *Verdi* (Oxford University Press, 2008)
19. Demaldè, *Cenni biografici*
20. Pougin, *Verdi*
21. Giuseppe Verdi, *I copialettere di Giuseppe Verdi* (Tip. Sticchi Ceretti, 1913)
22. ibid.
23. ibid.
24. Account by Verdi, quoted in Pougin, *Verdi*
25. Pougin, *Verdi*
26. ibid.
27. ibid.
28. Michele Lessona, *Volere è potere* (Barbèra, 1872)
29. Pougin, *Verdi*
30. ibid.
31. ibid.
32. ibid.
33. Lessona, *Volere*

34. Pougin, *Verdi*

35. Lessona, *Volere*

36. Pougin, *Verdi*

37. ibid.

38. Giovanni Bragagnolo and Enrico Bettazzi, *La vita di Giuseppe Verdi* (Ricordi, 1905), quoted in Phillips-Matz, *Verdi*

39. Budden, *Verdi*

40. Franco Abbiati, *Giuseppe Verdi* (Ricordi, 1959), quoted in Budden, *Verdi*

41. Charles Osborne (ed. and trans.), *Letters of Giuseppe Verdi* (Victor Gollancz, 1971)

42. John Black, *Francesco Maria Piave*, in Stanley Sadie (ed.), *The New Grove Dictionary of Opera* (Macmillan, 2004)

43. Osborne, *Letters*

44. George Martin, *Verdi: His Music, Life and Times* (Macmillan, 1965)

45. William Weaver (ed.), *Verdi: A Documentary Study* (Thames and Hudson, 1977)

46. Abbiati, *Giuseppe Verdi*

47. Barbieri-Nini quoted in Giorgio Bagnoli (ed.), *Verdi's Operas* (Amadeus Press, 2001)

48. Professor David Rosen and Andrew Porter (eds), *Verdi's Macbeth: A Sourcebook* (Cambridge University Press, 1984)

49. ibid.

50. Osborne, *Letters*

51. Francis Toye, *Giuseppe Verdi, His Life and Works* (Alfred A. Knopf, 1931)

52. Andrew Porter, 'Life, 1843–1880', in *The New Grove Masters of Italian Opera* (Macmillan, 1983)

53. Servadio, *Real Traviata*

54. ibid.

55. Weaver, *Verdi*

56. ibid.

57. Servadio, *Real Traviata*

58. Budden, *Verdi*

59. ibid.

60. Weaver, *Verdi*

61. Duilio Courir, *Guida all'Opera*, quoted in Bagnoli, *Verdi's Operas*

62. Osborne, *Letters*

63. Pougin, *Verdi*

64. *Financial Times*, 21 December 1990

65. Weaver, *Verdi*

66. ibid.

67. ibid.

68. ibid.

69. ibid.

70. ibid.

71. Servadio, *Real Traviata*

72. ibid.

73. ibid.

74. ibid.

75. ibid.

76. ibid.

77. Bagnoli, *Verdi's Operas*

78. Weaver, *Verdi*

79. Abbiati, quoted in Budden, *Verdi*

80. Marcello Conati, *La bottega della musica: Verdi e La Fenice* (Il Saggiatore, 1983), quoted in Budden, *Verdi*

81. Budden, *Verdi*

82. ibid.

83. ibid.

84. Franz Werfel and Paul Stefan (eds), *Verdi, The Man and His Letters* (Vienna House, 1973)

85. George Martin, *Aspects of Verdi* (Dodd Mead, 1988)

86. T. R. Ybarra, *Verdi, Miracle Man of the Opera* (Harcourt, 1955), quoted in Martin, *Aspects*, where it is stated that Ybarra gives no source for the anecdote

87. ibid. See also Afterword

88. Frank Walker, 'Introduction to a Biographical Study', *Verdi, Bolletino* (Parma: Istituto di Studi Verdiani, 1961), quoted in Martin, *Aspects*

89. ibid.

90. John Rosselli, *The Life of Verdi* (Cambridge University Press, 2000)

91. Martin, *Aspects*

92. Charles Osborne, *The Complete Operas of Verdi* (Victor Gollancz, 1969)

93. Weaver, *Verdi*

94. Budden, *Verdi*

95. Bagnoli, *Verdi's Operas*

96. ibid.

97. Osborne, *Letters*

98. Servadio, *Real Traviata*

99. Osborne, *Complete Operas*

100. Osborne, *Complete Operas*

101. Bagnoli, *Verdi's Operas*

102. 'The Verdi Requiem' by Troy L. Marsh at http://www.npr.org/programs/specials/verdi/verdiarticle.html

103. Osborne, *Letters*

104. Phillips-Matz, *Verdi*

105. ibid.

106. Roger Parker, *The New Grove Guide to Verdi and His Operas* (Oxford University Press, 2007)

107. Osborne, *Letters*

108. ibid.

109. ibid.

110. ibid.

111. Osborne, *Complete Operas*

112. ibid.

113. Budden, *Verdi*

114. Servadio, *Real Traviata*

115. ibid.

116. ibid.

117. ibid.

118. Walker, *The Man Verdi*

119. ibid.

120. ibid.

121. Claudio Sartori, 'Giuseppe Verdi', in Guido M. Gatti (ed.), *La musica: Enciclopedia storica*, vol. IV (Unione Tipografico-Editrice Torinese,1966), trans. Richard Stokes

122. Massimo Mila, *La giovinezza di Verdi* ('Verdi's Youth') (Edizioni Rai Radiotelevisione Italiana, 1974), trans. Richard Stokes

123. Conati, *Interviste*

BIBLIOGRAPHY

Abbiati, Franco, *Giuseppe Verdi* (Ricordi, 1959)

Alberti, Annibale (ed.), *Verdi intimo (1861–1886)* (Arnoldo Mondadori, 1931)

Bagnoli, Giorgio (ed.), *Verdi's Operas* (Amadeus Press, 2001)

Black, John, *Francesco Maria Piave*, in Stanley Sadie (ed.), *The New Grove Dictionary of Opera* (Macmillan, 2004)

Bragagnolo, Giovanni, and Enrico Bettazzi, *La vita di Giuseppe Verdi* (Ricordi, 1905)

Budden, Julian, *Verdi* (Master Musician series) (Oxford University Press, 2008)

Casati, Marisa di Gregorio, and Marco Marica, *Per amore di Verdi: vita, immagini, ritratti* (Grafiche Step, n.d.), trans. Julian Budden as *For Love of Verdi 1813–1901: Life, Images, Portraits* (Grafiche Step, 1905)

Conati, Marcello, (ed.), *Interviste incontri con Verdi* (Milan, 1980), trans. Richard Stokes as *Encounters with Verdi* (Victor Gollancz, 1984)

Conati, Marcello, *La bottega della musica: Verdi e La Fenice* (Il Saggiatore, 1983)

Demaldè, Giuseppe, *Cenni biografici del maestro di musica Giuseppe Verdi*, trans. Mary Jane Phillips-Matz and Gino Macchidani, *AIVS Newsletter*, 1976

Gatti, Carlo, *Verdi: The Man and His Music*, trans. Elisabeth Abbott (Gollancz, 1955)

Lessona, Michele, *Volere è potere* (Barbèra, 1872)

Martin, George, *Aspects of Verdi* (Dodd Mead, 1988)

Martin, George, *Verdi: His Music, Life and Times* (Macmillan, 1965)

Mila, Massimo, *La giovinezza di Verdi* ('Verdi's Youth') (Edizioni Rai Radiotelevisione Italiana, 1974)

Osborne, Charles (ed. and trans.), *Letters of Giuseppe Verdi* (Victor Gollancz, 1971)

Osborne, Charles, *The Complete Operas of Verdi: A Critical Guide* (Victor Gollancz, 1969)

Parker, Roger, *The New Grove Guide to Verdi and His Operas* (Oxford University Press, 2007)

Phillips-Matz, Mary Jane, *Verdi: A Biography* (Oxford University Press, 1993)

Porter, Andrew, 'Life, 1843–1880', in *The New Grove Masters of Italian Opera* (Macmillan, 1983)

Pougin, Arthur, *Verdi: An Anecdotic History of His Life and Works* (H. Grevel & Co., 1887), trans. James E. Matthew

Rosen, David, and Andrew Porter (eds), *Verdi's Macbeth: A Sourcebook* (Cambridge University Press, 1984)

Rosselli, John, *The Life of Verdi* (Cambridge University Press, 2000)

Sartori, Claudio, 'Giuseppe Verdi', in Guido M. Gatti (ed.), *La musica: Enciclopedia storica*, vol. IV (Unione Tipografico-Editrice Torinese,1966)

Servadio, Gaia, *The Real Traviata* (Hodder and Stoughton, 1994)

Toye, Francis, *Giuseppe Verdi: His Life and Works* (Alfred A. Knopf, 1931)

Walker, Frank, *The Man Verdi: Introduction to a Biographical Study* (J. M. Dent, 1962)

Weaver, William (ed.), *Verdi: A Documentary Study* (Thames and Hudson, 1977)

Werfel, Franz, and Paul Stefan (eds), *Verdi, The Man and His Letters* (Vienna House, 1973)

Winterfeld, A. von, *Unterhalten in Verdis Tuskulum, Deutsche Revue*, 1887

Ybarra, T. R., *Verdi, Miracle Man of the Opera* (Harcourt, 1955)

INDEX

136–7, 139, 140, 141, 142, 144, 221, 244, 249

Piacenza, Italy 185–6

Piacenza province, Italy 112

Piave, Francesco Maria 74–7, 79–80, 85, 86–7, 104–7, 116, 120, 121, 122, 123, 124–5, 136, 137–8, 141–2, 147, 155, 158–9, 161, 173, 176–7, 179, 195, 201–2, 209, 235

Piedmont, Italy 185, 189

Porter, Andrew 144

Pougin, Arthur 38, 44, 48–9, 51, 53, 69, 134

property investments 83–4, 111–12, 175, 223–4

see also Palazzo Cavilli; Sant'Agata, Villa

Provesi, Ferdinando 16, 17, 26

Prussia 4, 5, 216

Public Order Office 122–3

see also censors

Puccini, Giacomo 71, 242, 252

R

Radetz, General Radetzky von 102

Requiem Mass

for Alessandro Manzoni 218–19, 220, 246

for Rossini 211

revolutions (1848), European 100, 101–2, 104

see also Italian independence

Ricordi, Giulio 224–6, 227, 228, 235, 236, 239, 243

Ricordi, Tito 57, 60, 82, 108, 124–5, 147, 160, 161, 201

riots in Milan (1848) 102, 104

Rocester libretto 21

Rome, Italy 108–10, 153–4, 182, 185

Roncole Verdi

see Le Roncole, Po Valley

Rossini, Gioachino Antonio 8, 17, 63, 65, 170–2, 211, 225

Russian Army 2, 4, 5

Ruy Blas (V. Hugo) 195

S

salon culture, Milanese 63–4

Salvini-Donatelli, Fanny 157–8, 160, 161

Salzburg, Austria 7

Santa Streppini 139–41, 142, 144–5

Sant'Agata, Villa 11, 112, 133–4, 135, 136, 140, 145–6, 147, 149–50, 165–6, 167–8, 175, 184, 191–2, 194, 196, 203, 223–4, 233–5, 250–1, 260–2

Sartori, Claudio 255

Scarlatti, Alessandro 7

Schiller, Friedrich 91, 117, 205

Scribe, Eugéne 172

Seletti, Don Pietro 16

Seletti, Dorina 25

Seletti, Giuseppe 22–3, 25

Servadio, Gaia 38–9, 144–5

Shakespeare, William 86

see also individual plays by name

Solera, Temistocle 38, 52, 53, 56, 66–7, 69, 74

Somma, Antonio 166, 180–1, 182

Spezia, Maria 161

spinet, Verdi's first 9–10

St Petersburg, Russia 195–6, 197–8

Stolz, Teresa 202, 211–12, 213–15, 217, 219–22, 224, 230, 234, 239, 245, 246–7, 249, 252, 254, 258–9

Strepponi, Giuseppina 33–5, 37–9, 41, 55–7, 58, 60, 64–5, 66, 80, 96–100, 107, 113–16, 131–4, 137–8, 139–42, 144–5, 148–51, 164, 167–71, 180, 182, 183–4, 185–6, 192, 194–5, 203–4, 207–8, 214, 219–20, 228, 230, 233, 234, 236, 241, 243–4, 244–5, 254, 258–9, 260–1

rivalry with Teresa Stolz 213, 214–15, 219, 220–2, 224

ACKNOWLEDGEMENTS

This book, my fourth composer biography for Classic FM, is published once again by Elliott & Thompson, and I am indebted to the same wonderful team who produced the first three. Lorne Forsyth, Chairman, was encouraging from the first moment I mentioned Verdi to him. Olivia Bays, Director, was my editor, assisted by Pippa Crane and Jill Burrows. Pippa again sourced the illustrations, James Collins designed the layout and Tash Webber created the jacket. I am grateful to them all.

With Beethoven, Mozart, the Strauss dynasty and Verdi now published, a fifth is underway, *Tchaikovsky: The Man Revealed*, and I look forward to working with Elliott & Thompson once again.

PICTURE CREDITS

Page 7: MARKA / Alamy Stock Photo

Page 11: Bettmann / Getty Images

Page 14: Renaud Camus via Wikimedia Commons (https://creativecommons.org/licenses/by/2.0/legalcode)

Page 29: DEA / A. DAGLI ORTI / Getty Images

Page 31: DEA / A. DAGLI ORTI / Getty Images

Page 35: INTERFOTO / Alamy Stock Photo

Page 36: DEA / A. DAGLI ORTI / Getty Images

Page 45: DEA / A. DAGLI ORTI / Getty Images

Page 47: De Agostini Picture Library / Getty Images

Page 54: De Agostini Picture Library / Getty Images

Page 59: Lebrecht Music and Arts Photo Library / Alamy Stock Photo

Page 65: DEA / A. DAGLI ORTI / Getty Images

Page 68: DEA / A. DAGLI ORTI / Getty Images

Page 72: Paul Fearn / Alamy Stock Photo

Page 75: Granger Historical Picture Archive / Alamy Stock Photo

Page 87: De Agostini Picture Library / Getty Images

Page 92: Heritage Image Partnership Ltd / Alamy Stock Photo

Page 106: Zapping via Wikimedia Commons (https://creativecommons.org/licenses/by-sa/2.5/legalcode)

Page 109: Lebrecht Music and Arts Photo Library / Alamy Stock Photo

Page 115: Toni Budallaro / Alamy Stock Photo

Page 126: akg-images

Page 133: DEA / G. CIGOLINI / Getty Images

Page 137: NordNordWest via Wikimedia Commons (https://creativecommons.org/licenses/by-sa/3.0/legalcode)

Page 143: Hulton Archive / Stringer / Getty Images

Page 151: De Agostini Picture Library / Getty Images

Page 152: De Agostini Picture Library / Getty Images

Page 155: Granger Historical Picture Archive / Alamy Stock Photo

Page 158: ART Collection / Alamy Stock Photo

Page 187: DEA / A. DAGLI ORTI / Getty Images

Page 190: DEA / G. CIGOLINI / Getty Images

Page 199: DEA / A. DAGLI ORTI / Getty Images

Page 210: foundfootage_ / iStockphotos.com

Page 215: DEA / G. CIGOLINI / Getty Images

Page 220: DEA / A. DAGLI ORTI / Getty Images

Page 231: DEA / A. DAGLI ORTI / Getty Images

Page 234: DEA / G. CIGOLINI / Getty Images

Page 237: DEA / A. DAGLI ORTI / Getty Images

Page 240: David Lees / Getty Images

Page 247: akg-images / Fototeca Gilardi

Page 248: De Agostini Picture Library / Getty Images

Page 253: INTERFOTO / Alamy Stock Photo

Page 254: ASK Images / Alamy Stock Photo

Page 259: Sailko via Wikimedia Commons (https://creativecommons.org/licenses/by-sa/3.0/legalcode)

Page 264: Viva-Verdi via Wikimedia Commons (https://creativecommons.org/licenses/by-sa/3.0/legalcode)